(data) ·originating ✓ **W9-APF-692**
on experience/observation
— without system/
theory

· capable of being
verified by observation
or expiriment

Quá · in the capacity or
character of

reductio ad absurdum:
disproof by its absurdity
in its derivation to its
"logical conclusion"
"carrying to an absurd
extreme"

OTHER TITLES BY WILLIAM JAMES
AVAILABLE IN BISON BOOKS EDITIONS

Essays in Radical Empiricism

Some Problems of Philosophy
A Beginning of an Introduction to Philosophy

A PLURALISTIC UNIVERSE

Hibbert Lectures at Manchester College
on the Present Situation in Philosophy

BY

WILLIAM JAMES

Introduction to the Bison Books Edition
by Henry Samuel Levinson

UNIVERSITY OF NEBRASKA PRESS
LINCOLN AND LONDON

⊛ The paper in this book meets the minimum require-
ments of American National Standard for Information
Sciences—Permanence of Paper for Printed Library
Materials, ANSI Z39.48-1984.

First Bison Books printing: 1996

Library of Congress Cataloging-in-Publication Data
James, William, 1842–1910.
A pluralistic universe: Hibbert lectures at Manchester
College on the present situation in philosophy / William
James; introduction to the Bison books edition by
Henry Samuel Levinson.
p. cm.
Originally published: New York: Longmans, Green,
1909.
Includes bibliographical references and index.
ISBN 0-8032-7591-9 (pbk.: alk. paper)
1. Philosophy, Modern. I. Title.
B945.J23P58 1997
191—dc20
96-28484 CIP

Reprinted from the original 1909 edition by Longmans,
Green, and Co., New York.

INTRODUCTION

Henry Samuel Levinson

First delivered as lectures almost ninety years ago, and published in 1909, *A Pluralistic Universe* still presents William James's most representative ideas in ways that are startlingly fresh, radical enough to call for overhauling the Western philosophical tradition, and sufficiently winning to continue playing a significant role in contemporary philosophy and cultural criticism. What are these ideas?

1. *The best philosophers are public intellectuals.* Recalling the words of Lincoln and, before him, the prophet Jeremiah, James urges his readers to heed this warning: "Where there is no vision the people perish" (165). The people seek well-being and need a conception—not only *of* things—but *for* how they should conduct themselves. In a criticism that still resonates at the end of the twentieth century, James declares that "the over-technicality and consequent dreariness of the younger disciples (of philosophy) at our american universities is appalling" (16–17). Of course philosophers must be reasonable, giving arguments for their views. But the genuinely memorable things about philosophers are the *visions* they argue for, the messages they give that make a difference in human lives. Philosophies, James urges us, should spill out of the lecture hall or seminar room into private and public lives by summing up lifeways that have been "forced on one by one's total character and experience, and on the whole *preferred*—there is no other truthful word—as one's best working attitude." (21)

2. *Philosophy needs to catch up with a revolution-*

*ary cultural sea-change that has occurred, due to
two momentous developments:* "the vaster vistas
which scientific evolutionism has opened, and the
rising tide of social democratic ideals." Indeed, James
claims that these two advances have actually
"changed the type of our imagination" (30).

Were James offering critical advice today, he'd note
that intellectual changes effected by Darwin's revolution in science are still going on. As Daniel Dennett
or Stephen Jay Gould or Thomas Kuhn or Richard
Rorty or Stephen Toulmin would insist, we are still
coming to grips with Charles Darwin's revolution in
thinking. Like James before them, these contemporary philosophers and critics argue that Darwin
turned the sciences and arts on their heads by abandoning the quest for *eternal or fixed conditions* and
by showing, as George Santayana put it, how even
evolution evolves. Before Darwin, for example, philosophers had asked how fixed mind knows fixed
nature according to fixed principles, and humanists
as well as natural scientists had followed suit. After
Darwin, some philosophers, humanists, and scientists—James perhaps foremost—had realized that
the important question in this regard was this: How
do changing and variable minds understand changing and variable things according to changing and
variable principles?

But if this was the key issue, James asserted, "philosophy had been on a false scent ever since the days
of Socrates and Plato" (291). Ever since then, philosophers had searched for solutions to "the problem of the one and the many." Attempting to break
through time in their search for eternity, they had
asked: How do things stay one and the same despite
the appearance of variety and change? But Darwin

dissolved that problem, by asking rather how things *maintain continuity and coherence in light of all the real changes they undergo.* How, then, are things *both one and many?* This question goes a long way toward establishing James's agenda in *A Pluralistic Universe.*

But so, too, do James's social democratic ideals. Darwin's thinking rendered the universe and inquiry about it historical or temporal all the way along. James's political preferences, moreover, suggested root-metaphors for understanding how these historical things are ordered. They are constituted, he claimed, *e pluribus unum,* one out of many, from the bottom up, not from the top down. This is the thrust of the vision that James gives us in *A Pluralistic Universe:* Our temporal universe, which is the only universe we have, maintains whatever continuity and coherence it has through ordering itself one out of many. That makes the universe, as he puts it, "more like a federal republic than like an empire or a kingdom" (321–22).

3. *Within this context, philosophy becomes pragmatic and radically empirical.* Put positively, *pragmatist* philosophers conceive of their calling as recommending effective ways to cope with problems of human finitude. In their view, we people stand in need of philosophical visions because we contend with changing and variable environments or situations or contingencies that sometimes overwhelm our physical, intellectual, moral, and spiritual capacities to achieve or receive the well-being—the sorts of continuity and coherence—we demand. How do we take, and what do we make of, a world subject to natural disasters? What do we make of our own bodies, which can become diseased and will succumb to

death? What do we make of our own minds, which time and again fall short of fully understanding our situation? How do we deal with our moral and spiritual weaknesses? When things challenge our physical capacities, we suffer. When they disrupt our intellectual comprehension, we experience absurdity. When they undercut our ability to render life morally or spiritually harmonious, we encounter evil. Philosophers, according to the pragmatist view, argue for visions that help us deal with these difficulties. But because they consider what it is like to live propitiously in a universe that is historical in every respect, they are no longer interested in breaking through time to some purported eternity, as philosophers traditionally have been. In a world that is inevitably subject to change and variation, the pragmatists abandon the philosophers' quest for some fixed reality or essence or truth or power purportedly standing behind, below, above, or apart from the world we experience. In Darwin's universe, natural history goes on of its own accord, that is, without "providential" direction from transcendent or transcendental principles or powers that lie outside our ken.

Many philosophers before Darwin had pictured the universe as though it came in two editions, one "trade" and one "deluxe". The more common or "apparent" edition left things subject to chance variations and changes. The classy or "real" edition, to the contrary, presented the necessary and eternal structure of things. Coming after Darwin, James embraced the view that the universe only comes in one edition, the one we actually experience. What we see (or more broadly, what we may experience) is what we get. Nothing transcends our experience, at

least in principle. Indeed, this rejection of philosophical transcendence and transcendentalism brings us
to a negative characterization of James's *radical
empiricism*. Put more affirmatively, James, as a radical empiricist, contends that whatever is experiencable is real and whatever is real is experiencable.
There simply is no real, but unexperiencable, edition.

But here, we must distinguish between traditional
empiricism and James's *radical* empiricism. Traditional empiricists also tended to claim that whatever is experiencable is real and vice versa. But they
went on to assert that every experience we have is
disjunctive or discontinuous: They claimed, as a matter of "simple logic," that every experience, every
real thing, is discrete and distinguishable from every other experience or real thing. Traditional empiricists claimed *either* that things remain disjoint
and never conjoint *or* that whatever joins our disjointed experiences must transcend experience altogether. James rejects this limitation on empiricism
and this transcendental turn. He contends, rather,
that we experience both discrete and overlapping
experiences, both disjunctive and conjunctive experiences, both experiences of discontinuity and experiences of continuity, and sometimes both at once.
In James's view, for example, people *experience* some
continuous and coherent personality in light of, not
just despite, their own changing and variable lives:
Hence his famous notion of our *stream of consciousness*, which readers of existential phenomenologists
like Maurice Merleau-Ponty (indebted to James)
should find compelling. Indeed, on James's account,
people *experience* sharing intentions with others not
themselves and they also *experience* actively coop-

erating with others to realize those intentions. You and I can share goals. We can work together to bring them about. So, to take perhaps the most crucial example for James's vision of a pluralistic universe, a democratic federal republican "we, the people" can actually govern the life they live together. Contemporary political philosophers like John Rawls and Benjamin Barber would agree.

4. *Among philosophical visions a basic choice exists between sympathetic and friendly or cynical and alien ones.* James had always characterized philosophy as laden by temperament. Thus, for example, in *Pragmatism* (1907), he had pictured some philosophers as tender-hearted and others as tough-minded; even earlier and more generally, he had argued in his magisterial *Principles of Psychology* (1890) that normal intelligence or thought is emotional, interested, motivated: Only truncated intelligence is unemotional. In *A Pluralistic Universe* James suggested, more specifically, that perhaps the most telling split among philosophers in his time was largely a matter of mood, dividing those whose work was motivated by a basic *wariness* about the possibility of human well-being, an aspiration their work tended to belittle; and those *trusting* figures who sought to make or find conditions that gave people a chance to experience the well-being they sought. James pictures nineteenth-century "reductive materialists" as cynical because he thinks their vision leaves no room for things that let people care: "ideal" things like minds, meanings, intentions, and purposes. On the other hand, James views the variety of "spiritual" philosophies as sympathetic because spiritualists do make space for the realization of these things. Some contemporary readers see a philo-

sophical dispute between materialists and spiritualists the way James does in *A Pluralistic Universe*.
Many do not. Nonetheless, anyone who has followed
disputes in our own time, between, say, the follow-
ers of Foucault's anti-humanism and those of
Habermas's humanism, will still find James's divide
between "the cynical" and "the sympathetic" both
provocative and vexing. James, like Habermas now,
construed the conditions of human life as conducive
to beneficial human (and in James's case,
extrahuman) control. He opposed those, like Foucault on the contemporary scene, who pictured hu-
mankind as more or less *out of control* and swept
along by physical, cultural, social, and economic
forces (for example, the very languages we speak)
randomly related to distinctively human wish or will.

5. *Among sympathetic philosophical visions, we
may choose between more closed and totalistic ones
or more open and infinite ones.* Among philosophers
searching sympathetically for the conditions of human well-being, James discerned yet another great
divide. On the one hand, some "absolutists" (e.g.,
Josiah Royce) assumed that managing the difficulties of human finitude depended on discovering a
way to know "the whole," or the principle(s) inform-
ing *all* of being. Such philosophers tried to demon-
strate that there must be a place for everything and
everything must be in its place; that the point or
significance or meaning of any one thing depends
on its relationship to the "whole"; and that we are
able to understand this only by establishing that
there is one right *total* view of *all* being. Others,
including James himself, maintained that the universe is basically *excessive:* There is always going to
be *more* of it. James was "willing to believe that there

may ultimately never be an *all*-form (of reality) at all, that the substance of reality may never get totally collected, that some of it may remain outside of the largest combination of it ever made, and that a distributive form of reality, the *each*-form, is logically as acceptable and empirically as probable . . ." (34). James asserted, in other words, that "nothing includes everything, or dominates over everything. The word 'and' trails along after every sentence. Something always escapes" (321). Managing the difficulties incumbent on finite creatures requires dealing effectively with one thing after another *in(de)finitely*. We may need, first, to make this bit of suffering in our lives sufferable; and then second, to contend with those forces of social conflict; and then third, to try intellectually to comprehend this or that anomaly we experience, and so on. Our lives will demand that we deal with *each* such problem or situation as it comes along. But dealing with this pain or that conundrum or those vicious people never depends on taking up some "god's eye view" of the situation. On the contrary, it depends on an ability to formulate the specific problems or difficulties we are undergoing, along with strategies to solve or manage them adequately. Thus James makes way for an account of ethical and spiritual life that prefigures contemporary works like Emmanuel Levinas's *Totality and Infinity*.

6. *The most promising option among open sympathetic visions is a pluralistic, panpsychic pantheism which lets people assume a faith, or a "working attitude," that makes life a vital moral and religious drama.* James had argued since the middle 1880s that he was a practical religious pluralist. He had

maintained that the universe could be ordered by a plurality of agents, only some of which were human. His religious stance, he often asserted, was neither optimistic nor pessimistic but rather melioristic. James believed that things could get better and better if the requisite powers, such as you and I and our distinctive subliminal selves, each played their parts. But "shipwreck" was among the real possibilities. This was the case for two reasons: because we humans, at least, often failed to play our parts; and no matter what people *did* to achieve the well-being they demanded, they could never escape their own creatureliness. All our achievements lay constantly shadowed by an eventual physical decline and death. The question, then, was whether there was "something there" that guaranteed, at least, the *chance* of well-being and, at best, its realization.

James had attempted to answer that question in *The Varieties of Religious Experience* (1901–1902), where he had explicated a wealth of testimony supporting the view that people experienced supernatural powers at work in the world. They experienced powers, in other words, that enabled them to reach well-being, even as they found that they were unable to do so on their own.

But James made it plain in *Varieties* that the relevant testimony concerning religious experience did not stand on its own; it had to be transformed into evidence. To some extent, indeed, James thought he had done this, by offering a theory to account for various ways that desperate people, by *letting go* their own conscious efforts, had felt *help* from some other "self" who was *more capable* and so *superior* to their own. Relying on Frederic Myers's hypothesis of a subliminal or subconscious self, James concluded in *Varieties* that "the conscious person is continuous with a wider self through which saving experiences come."[1]

James knew, however, that this theory didn't go far enough to settle the question whether "the wider self" which brought about transformations in well-being was *anthropological*—a structure of the human psyche—or *theological*—a power or process that lay as much beyond the boundaries of human being as it could cross or overlap with them. If a theological option were to be useful hypothesis, James warned in *Varieties*, it would have to offer more than psychology alone could muster. It would have to predict other "remote objective consequences." If the "wider self" were some god or gods, it would need "to enter into wider cosmic relations in order to justify the subject's absolute confidence and peace." To make this claim intellectually responsible, James thought he had to show how wider selves could actually accomplish relevant *cosmic* work.[2]

To pursue this cosmic possibility is the final large task James takes up in *A Pluralistic Universe*. It motivates his attempt to vindicate the idea of the continuity of consciousness, along with his partial alignment with Henri Bergson's views. It leads him to champion the now long-forgotten Gustav Fechner's efforts to show empirically how both non-human things like plants and planets lead conscious lives with which we humans are "co-conscious" (155ff). It informs his panpsychic view that each el-

1. William James, *The Varieties of Religious Experience* (Cambridge MA: 1984), Harvard University Press, 510.
   2. Ibid., 517–18.

ement in the universe may not just be both distinct as well as linked with others. Each may be in some way *living consciously for itself*. It inspires his pluralistic pantheism, his belief in a finite "higher consciousness enveloping ours" (315), that may carry consequences for well-being on a cosmic scale. These are the pivotal psychic and theological adventures James invites readers to consider in *A Pluralistic Universe*. Trust me: They are well worth your careful consideration.

CONTENTS

LECTURE I

LECTURE II

CONTENTS

LECTURE III

LECTURE IV

LECTURE V

CONTENTS

CONTENTS

I

THE TYPES OF PHILOSOPHIC THINKING

LECTURE I

THE TYPES OF PHILOSOPHIC THINKING

As these lectures are meant to be public, and so few, I have assumed all very special problems to be excluded, and some topic of general interest required. Fortunately, our age seems to be growing philosophical again — still in the ashes live the wonted fires. Oxford, long the seed-bed, for the english world, of the idealism inspired by Kant and Hegel, has recently become the nursery of a very different way of thinking. Even non-philosophers have begun to take an interest in a controversy over what is known as pluralism or humanism. It looks a little as if the ancient english empiricism, so long put out of fashion here by nobler sounding germanic formulas, might be re-pluming itself and getting ready for a stronger flight than ever. It looks as if foundations were being sounded and examined afresh.

Individuality outruns all classification, yet we insist on classifying every one we meet

under some general head. As these heads usually suggest prejudicial associations to some
hearer or other, the life of philosophy largely
consists of resentments at the classing, and
complaints of being misunderstood. But there
are signs of clearing up, and, on the whole, less
acrimony in discussion, for which both Oxford
and Harvard are partly to be thanked. As
I look back into the sixties, Mill, Bain, and
Hamilton were the only official philosophers
in Britain. Spencer, Martineau, and Hodgson
were just beginning. In France, the pupils of
Cousin were delving into history only, and
Renouvier alone had an original system. In
Germany, the hegelian impetus had spent itself, and, apart from historical scholarship,
nothing but the materialistic controversy remained, with such men as Büchner and Ulrici
as its champions. Lotze and Fechner were the
sole original thinkers, and Fechner was not a
professional philosopher at all.

The general impression made was of crude
issues and oppositions, of small subtlety and
of a widely spread ignorance. Amateurishness

4

was rampant. Samuel Bailey's ' letters on the philosophy of the human mind,' published in 1855, are one of the ablest expressions of english associationism, and a book of real power. Yet hear how he writes of Kant: 'No one, after reading the extracts, etc., can be surprised to hear of a declaration by men of eminent abilities, that, after years of study, they had not succeeded in gathering one clear idea from the speculations of Kant. I should have been almost surprised if they had. In or about 1818, Lord Grenville, when ·visiting the Lakes of England, observed to Professor Wilson that, after five years' study of Kant's philosophy, he had not gathered from it one clear idea. Wilberforce, about the same time, made the same confession to another friend of my own. " I am endeavoring," exclaims Sir James Mackintosh, in the irritation, evidently, of baffled efforts, " to understand this accursed german philosophy." ' [1]

What Oxford thinker would dare to print such *naïf* and provincial-sounding citations of authority to-day?

The torch of learning passes from land to land as the spirit bloweth the flame. The deepening of philosophic consciousness came to us english folk from Germany, as it will probably pass back ere long. Ferrier, J. H. Stirling, and, most of all, T. H. Green are to be thanked. If asked to tell in broad strokes what the main doctrinal change has been, I should call it a change from the crudity of the older english thinking, its ultra-simplicity of mind, both when it was religious and when it was antireligious, toward a rationalism derived in the first instance from Germany, but relieved from german technicality and shrillness, and content to suggest, and to remain vague, and to be, in the english fashion, devout.

By the time T. H. Green began at Oxford, the generation seemed to feel as if it had fed on the chopped straw of psychology and of associationism long enough, and as if a little vastness, even though it went with vagueness, as of some moist wind from far away, reminding us of our pre-natal sublimity, would be welcome.

Green's great point of attack was the dis-

6

associationism

I. THE TYPES OF THINKING

green↓

connectedness of the reigning english sensationalism. *Relating* was the great intellectual activity for him, and the key to this relating was believed by him to lodge itself at last in what most of you know as Kant's unity of apperception, transformed into a living spirit of the world.) ?

Hence a monism of a devout kind. In some way we must be fallen angels, one with intelligence as such; and a great disdain for empiricism of the sensationalist sort has always characterized this school of thought, which, on the whole, has reigned supreme at Oxford and in the scottish universities until the present day.

But now there are signs of its giving way to a wave of revised empiricism. I confess that I should be glad to see this latest wave prevail; so — the sooner I am frank about it the better — I hope to have my voice counted in its favor as one of the results of this lecture-course.

What do the terms empiricism and rationalism mean? Reduced to their most pregnant difference, *empiricism means the habit of explaining wholes by parts, and rationalism*

apperception,
monism
empiricism
empiricism v rationalism

7

means the habit of explaining parts by wholes.
Rationalism thus preserves affinities with monism, since wholeness goes with union, while empiricism inclines to pluralistic views. No philosophy can ever be anything but a summary sketch, a picture of the world in abridgment, a foreshortened bird's-eye view of the perspective of events. And the first thing to notice is this, that the only material we have at our disposal for making a picture of the whole world is supplied by the various portions of that world of which we have already had experience. We can invent no new forms of conception, applicable to the whole exclusively, and not suggested originally by the parts. All philosophers, accordingly, have conceived of the whole world after the analogy of some particular feature of it which has particularly captivated their attention. Thus, the theists take their cue from manufacture, the pantheists from growth. For one man, the world is like a thought or a grammatical sentence in which a thought is expressed. For such a philosopher, the whole must logically be prior to

8

the parts; for letters would never have been invented without syllables to spell, or syllables without words to utter.

natural order leads to single idea of world

Another man, struck by the disconnectedness and mutual accidentality of so many of the world's details, takes the universe as a whole to have been such a disconnectedness originally, and supposes order to have been superinduced upon it in the second instance, possibly by attrition and the gradual wearing away by internal friction of portions that originally interfered.

chaos, dis connection, forced lead to order, man made concept made for man's sanity / @ of mind

Another will conceive the order as only a statistical appearance, and the universe will be for him like a vast grab-bag with black and white balls in it, of which we guess the quantities only probably, by the frequency with which we experience their egress.

mathamatic reasonable yet un-knowing order zable

For another, again, there is no really inherent order, but it is we who project order into the world by selecting objects and tracing relations so as to gratify our intellectual interests. We *carve out* order by leaving the disorderly parts out; and the world is conceived thus after the

order is a perception we make conclusions draw. relations with no natural basis analogy of a forest or a block of marble from which parks or statues may be produced by eliminating irrelevant trees or chips of stone. Some thinkers follow suggestions from human life, and treat the universe as if it were essentially a place in which ideals are realized. Others are more struck by its lower features, and for them, brute necessities express its character better.

All follow one analogy or another; and all the analogies are with some one or other of the universe's subdivisions. Every one is nevertheless prone to claim that his conclusions are the only logical ones, that they are necessities of universal reason, they being all the while, at bottom, accidents more or less of personal vision which had far better be avowed as such; for one man's vision may be much more valuable than another's, and our visions are usually not only our most interesting but our most respectable contributions to the world in which we play our part. What was reason given to men for, said some eighteenth century writer, except to enable them to find reasons for what

10

[handwritten margin notes:]
see universe in relation to human existence: our influence achieves good, beauty etc OR universe is harsh place and it can be explained through our harshness

contribution not the same:. ♂ have different worth in relation to the universe

men claim their importence (through) the importence of ideas some people contribute more. (judgements allowable they want to think and do? — and I think the history of philosophy largely bears him out. 'The aim of knowledge,' says Hegel,[2] 'is to divest the objective world of its strangeness, and to make us more at home in it.' Different men find their minds more at home in very different fragments of the world.

Let me make a few comments, here, on the curious antipathies which these partialities arouse. They are sovereignly unjust, for all the parties are human beings with the same essential interests, and no one of them is the wholly perverse demon which another often imagines him to be. Both are loyal to the world that bears them; neither wishes to spoil it; neither wishes to regard it as an insane incoherence; both want to keep it as a universe of some kind; and their differences are all secondary to this deep agreement. They may be only propensities to emphasize differently. Or one man may care for finality and security more than the other. Or their tastes in language may be different. One may like a universe that lends itself to lofty and exalted characterization. To another this may seem sentimental or rhetorical. One may wish for the right to use a clerical vocabulary, another a technical or professorial one. A certain old farmer of my acquaintance in America was called a rascal by one of his neighbors. He immediately smote the man, saying, 'I won't stand none of your diminutive epithets.' Empiricist minds, putting the parts before the whole, appear to rationalists, who start from the whole, and consequently enjoy magniloquent privileges, to use epithets offensively diminutive. But all such differences are minor matters which ought to be subordinated in view of the fact that, whether we be empiricists or rationalists, we are, ourselves, parts of the universe and share the same one deep concern in its destinies. We crave alike to feel more truly at home with it, and to contribute our mite to its amelioration. It would be pitiful if small æsthetic discords were to keep honest men asunder.

I shall myself have use for the diminutive epithets of empiricism. But if you look behind the words at the spirit, I am sure you will not

12

worth comes from desire to do good; have a final goal

I. THE TYPES OF THINKING

find it matricidal. I am as good a son as any rationalist among you to our common mother.

philosophy doesn't change worth.

What troubles me more than this misapprehension is the genuine abstruseness of many of the matters I shall be obliged to talk about, and the difficulty of making them intelligible at one hearing. But there are two pieces, 'zwei stücke,' as Kant would have said, in every philosophy — the final outlook, belief, or attitude to which it brings us, and the reasonings by which that attitude is reached and mediated. A philosophy, as James Ferrier used to tell us, must indeed be true, but that is the least of its requirements. One may be true without being a philosopher, true by guesswork or by revelation. What distinguishes a philosopher's truth is that it *is reasoned.* Argument, not supposition, must have put it in his possession. Common men find themselves inheriting their beliefs, they know not how. They jump into them with both feet, and stand there. Philosophers must do more; they must first get reason's license for them; and to the professional philosophic mind the operation of procuring the

because BASICALLY we want the same thing

inhereted beliefs. will?

13

matricidal

license is usually a thing of much more pith and moment than any particular beliefs to which the license may give the rights of access. Suppose, for example, that a philosopher believes in what is called free-will. That a common man alongside of him should also share that belief, possessing it by a sort of inborn intuition, does not endear the man to the philosopher at all — he may even be ashamed to be associated with such a man. What interests the philosopher is the particular premises on which the free-will he believes in is established, the sense in which it is taken, the objections it eludes, the difficulties it takes account of, in short the whole form and temper and manner and technical apparatus that goes with the belief in question. A philosopher across the way who should use the same technical apparatus, making the same distinctions, etc., but drawing opposite conclusions and denying free-will entirely, would fascinate the first philosopher far more than would the *naïf* co-believer. Their common technical interests would unite them more than their opposite conclusions separate them.

philosophers [14] who hold opposite beliefs are more alike than a "common man" who agrees because of their reflection / examination

as opposed to custom.

I. THE TYPES OF THINKING

Each would feel an essential consanguinity in the other, would think of him, write *at* him, care for his good opinion. The simple-minded believer in free-will would be disregarded by either. Neither as ally nor as opponent would his vote be counted.

In a measure this is doubtless as it should be, but like all professionalism it can go to abusive extremes. The end is after all more than the way, in most things human, and forms and methods may easily frustrate their own purpose. The abuse of technicality is seen in the infrequency with which, in philosophical literature, metaphysical questions are discussed directly and on their own merits. Almost always they are handled as if through a heavy woolen curtain, the veil of previous philosophers' opinions. Alternatives are wrapped in proper names, as if it were indecent for a truth to go naked. The late Professor John Grote of Cambridge has some good remarks about this. 'Thought,' he says, 'is not a professional matter, not something for so-called philosophers only or for professed thinkers. The best phi-

15

consangunity

losopher is the man who can think most *simply.*
. . . I wish that people would consider that
thought — and philosophy is no more than
good and methodical thought — is a matter *intimate* to them, a portion of their real selves . . .
that they would *value* what they think, and be
interested in it. . . . In my own opinion,' he
goes on, 'there is something depressing in this
weight of learning, with nothing that can come
into one's mind but one is told, Oh, that is the
opinion of such and such a person long ago.
. . . I can conceive of nothing more noxious
for students than to get into the habit of saying
to themselves about their ordinary philosophic
thought, Oh, somebody must have thought it
all before.'[3] Yet this is the habit most en-
couraged at our seats of learning. You must
tie your opinion to Aristotle's or Spinoza's;
you must define it by its distance from Kant's;
you must refute your rival's view by identifying
it with Protagoras's. Thus does all spontaneity of thought, all freshness of conception, get
destroyed. Everything you touch is shopworn.
The over-technicality and consequent dreari-

ness of the younger disciples at our american universities is appalling. It comes from too much following of german models and manners. Let me fervently express the hope that in this country you will hark back to the more humane english tradition. American students have to regain direct relations with our subject by painful individual effort in later life. Some of us have done so. Some of the younger ones, I fear, never will, so strong are the professional shop-habits already.

In a subject like philosophy it is really fatal to lose connexion with the open air of human nature, and to think in terms of shop-tradition only. In Germany the forms are so professionalized that anybody who has gained a teaching chair and written a book, however distorted and eccentric, has the legal right to figure forever in the history of the subject like a fly in amber. All later comers have the duty of quoting him and measuring their opinions with his opinion. Such are the rules of the professorial game — they think and write from each other and for each other and at each other exclusively. With this exclusion of the open air all true perspective gets lost, extremes and oddities count as much as sanities, and command the same attention; and if by chance any one writes popularly and about results only, with his mind directly focussed on the subject, it is reckoned *oberflächliches zeug* and *ganz unwissenschaftlich*. Professor Paulsen has recently written some feeling lines about this over-professionalism, from the reign of which in Germany his own writings, which sin by being 'literary,' have suffered loss of credit. Philosophy, he says, has long assumed in Germany the character of being an esoteric and occult science. There is a genuine fear of popularity. Simplicity of statement is deemed synonymous with hollowness and shallowness. He recalls an old professor saying to him once: 'Yes, we philosophers, whenever we wish, can go so far that in a couple of sentences we can put ourselves where nobody can follow us.' The professor said this with conscious pride, but he ought to have been ashamed of it. Great as technique is, results are greater. To teach

18

oberflachliches zeug
and ganz unwissenschaftlich

philosophy so that the pupils' interest in technique exceeds that in results is surely a vicious aberration. It is bad form, not good form, in a discipline of such universal human interest. Moreover, technique for technique, does n't David Hume's technique set, after all, the kind of pattern most difficult to follow? Is n't it the most admirable? The english mind, thank heaven, and the french mind, are still kept, by their aversion to crude technique and barbarism, closer to truth's natural probabilities. Their literatures show fewer obvious falsities and monstrosities than that of Germany. Think of the german literature of æsthetics, with the preposterousness of such an unæsthetic personage as Immanuel Kant enthroned in its centre! Think of german books on *religionsphilosophie*, with the heart's battles translated into conceptual jargon and made dialectic. The most persistent setter of questions, feeler of objections, insister on satisfactions, is the religious life. Yet all its troubles can be treated with absurdly little technicality. The wonder is that, with their way of working philosophy,

19

dialectic

individual Germans should preserve any spontaneity of mind at all. That they still manifest freshness and originality in so eminent a degree, proves the indestructible richness of the german cerebral endowment.

Let me repeat once more that a man's vision is the great fact about him. Who cares for Carlyle's reasons, or Schopenhauer's, or Spencer's? A philosophy is the expression of a man's intimate character, and all definitions of the universe are but the deliberately adopted reactions of human characters upon it. In the recent book from which I quoted the words of Professor Paulsen, a book of successive chapters by various living german philosophers,[4] we pass from one idiosyncratic personal atmosphere into another almost as if we were turning over a photograph album.

If we take the whole history of philosophy, the systems reduce themselves to a few main types which, under all the technical verbiage in which the ingenious intellect of man envelops them, are just so many visions, modes of feeling the whole push, and seeing the whole drift of life, forced on one by one's total character and experience, and on the whole *preferred* — there is no other truthful word — as one's best working attitude. Cynical characters take one general attitude, sympathetic characters another. But no general attitude is possible towards the world as a whole, until the intellect has developed considerable generalizing power and learned to take pleasure in synthetic formulas. The thought of very primitive men has hardly any tincture of philosophy. Nature can have little unity for savages. It is a Walpurgis-nacht procession, a checkered play of light and shadow, a medley of impish and elfish friendly and inimical powers. 'Close to nature' though they live, they are anything but Wordsworthians. If a bit of cosmic emotion ever thrills them, it is likely to be at midnight, when the camp smoke rises straight to the wicked full moon in the zenith, and the forest is all whispering with witchery and danger. The eeriness of the world, the mischief and the manyness, the littleness of the forces, the magical surprises, the unaccountability of every agent, these surely are the characters most impressive at that stage of culture, these communicate the thrills of curiosity and the earliest intellectual stirrings. Tempests and conflagrations, pestilences and earthquakes, reveal supramundane powers, and instigate religious terror rather than philosophy. Nature, more demonic than divine, is above all things *multifarious*. So many creatures that feed or threaten, that help or crush, so many beings to hate or love, to understand or start at — which is on top and which subordinate? Who can tell? They are co-ordinate, rather, and to adapt ourselves to them singly, to 'square' the dangerous powers and keep the others friendly, regardless of consistency or unity, is the chief problem. The symbol of nature at this stage, as Paulsen well says, is the sphinx, under whose nourishing breasts the tearing claws are visible.

But in due course of time the intellect awoke, with its passion for generalizing, simplifying, and subordinating, and then began those divergences of conception which all later experience seems rather to have deepened than to have effaced, because objective nature has contributed to both sides impartially, and has let the thinkers emphasize different parts of her, and pile up opposite imaginary supplements.

Perhaps the most interesting opposition is that which results from the clash between what I lately called the sympathetic and the cynical temper. Materialistic and spiritualistic philosophies are the rival types that result: the former defining the world so as to leave man's soul upon it as a sort of outside passenger or alien, while the latter insists that the intimate and human must surround and underlie the brutal. This latter is the spiritual way of thinking.

Now there are two very distinct types or stages in spiritualistic philosophy, and my next purpose in this lecture is to make their contrast evident. Both types attain the sought-for intimacy of view, but the one attains it somewhat less successfully than the other.

The generic term spiritualism, which I began by using merely as the opposite of materialism,

23

spiritual opposes material
cynical opposes sympathetic

thus subdivides into two species, the more intimate one of which is monistic and the less intimate dualistic. The dualistic species is the *theism* that reached its elaboration in the scholastic philosophy, while the monistic species is the *pantheism* spoken of sometimes simply as idealism, and sometimes as 'post-kantian' or 'absolute' idealism. Dualistic theism is professed as firmly as ever at all catholic seats of learning, whereas it has of late years tended to disappear at our british and american universities, and to be replaced by a monistic pantheism more or less open or disguised. I have an impression that ever since T. H. Green's time absolute idealism has been decidedly in the ascendent at Oxford. It is in the ascendent at my own university of Harvard.

Absolute idealism attains, I said, to the more intimate point of view; but the statement needs some explanation. So far as theism represents the world as God's world, and God as what Matthew Arnold called a magnified non-natural man, it would seem as if the inner quality of the world remained human, and as if our

[handwritten marginalia: monistic: Pantheism "idealism" post-Kant "absolute" idealism / dualistic: theism ending in scholastic philosophy / monistic v dualistic spiritualism]

I. THE TYPES OF THINKING

relations with it might be intimate enough—for what is best in ourselves appears then also out-side of ourselves, and we and the universe are of the same spiritual species. So far, so good, then; and one might consequently ask, What more of intimacy do you require? To which the answer is that to be like a thing is not as intimate a relation as to be substantially fused into it, to form one continuous soul and body with it; and that pantheistic idealism, making us entitatively one with God, attains this higher reach of intimacy.

monistic universe god + human ① = connect fused

The theistic conception, picturing God and his creation as entities distinct from each other, still leaves the human subject outside of the deepest reality in the universe. God is from eternity complete, it says, and sufficient unto himself; he throws off the world by a free act and as an extraneous substance, and he throws off man as a third substance, extrane-ous to both the world and himself. Between them, God says 'one,' the world says 'two,' and man says 'three,' — that is the orthodox theistic view. And orthodox theism has been

dualistic universe god ≠ human distinct

so jealous of God's glory that it has taken pains
to exaggerate everything in the notion of him
that could make for isolation and separateness.
Page upon page in scholastic books go to prove
that God is in no sense implicated by his creative act, or involved in his creation. That his
relation to the creatures he has made should
make any difference to him, carry any consequence, or qualify his being, is repudiated as
a pantheistic slur upon his self-sufficingness. I
said a moment ago that theism treats us and
God as of the same species, but from the orthodox point of view that was a slip of language.
God and his creatures are *toto genere* distinct
in the scholastic theology, they have absolutely
nothing in common; nay, it degrades God to
attribute to him any generic nature whatever;
he can be classed with nothing. There is a
sense, then, in which philosophic theism makes
us outsiders and keeps us foreigners in relation
to God, in which, at any rate, his connexion
with us appears as unilateral and not reciprocal. His action can affect us, but he can never
be affected by our reaction. Our relation, in

short, is not a strictly social relation. Of course in common men's religion the relation is believed to be social, but that is only one of the many differences between religion and theology.

This essential dualism of the theistic view has all sorts of collateral consequences. Man being an outsider and a mere subject to God, *dualistic* not his intimate partner, a character of externality invades the field. God is not heart of our heart and reason of our reason, but our magistrate, rather; and mechanically to obey his commands, however strange they may be, remains our only moral duty. Conceptions of criminal law have in fact played a great part in defining our relations with him. Our relations with speculative truth show the same externality. One of our duties is to know truth, and *dualist* rationalist thinkers have always assumed it to be our sovereign duty. But in scholastic theism we find truth already instituted and established without our help, complete apart from our knowing; and the most we can do is to acknowledge it passively and adhere to it, altho such adhesion as ours can make no jot of difference to what is adhered to. The situation here again is radically dualistic. It is not as if the world came to know itself, or God came to know himself, partly through us, as pantheistic idealists have maintained, but truth exists *per se* and absolutely, by God's grace and decree, no matter who of us knows it or is ignorant, and it would continue to exist unaltered, even though we finite knowers were all annihilated.

[handwritten in margin: law and truth comes of god, our existence is inconcequential]

It has to be confessed that this dualism and lack of intimacy has always operated as a drag and handicap on christian thought. Orthodox theology has had to wage a steady fight within the schools against the various forms of pantheistic heresy which the mystical experiences of religious persons, on the one hand, and the formal or æsthetic superiorities of monism to dualism, on the other, kept producing. God as intimate soul and reason of the universe has always seemed to some people a more worthy conception than God as external creator. So conceived, he appeared to unify the world more perfectly, he made it less finite and mechani-

[handwritten in margin: monistic over dualistic]

28

cal, and in comparison with such a God an external creator seemed more like the product of a childish fancy. I have been told by Hindoos that the great obstacle to the spread of Christianity in their country is the puerility of our dogma of creation. It has not sweep and infinity enough to meet the requirements of even the illiterate natives of India.

Assuredly most members of this audience are ready to side with Hinduism in this matter. Those of us who are sexagenarians have witnessed in our own persons one of those gradual mutations of intellectual climate, due to innumerable influences, that make the thought of a past generation seem as foreign to its successor as if it were the expression of a different race of men. The theological machinery that spoke so livingly to our ancestors, with its finite age of the world, its creation out of nothing, its juridical morality and eschatology, its relish for rewards and punishments, its treatment of God as an external contriver, an 'intelligent and moral governor,' sounds as odd to most of us as if it were some outlandish savage religion.

eschatology

A PLURALISTIC UNIVERSE

The vaster vistas which scientific evolutionism
has opened, and the rising tide of social democratic ideals, have changed the type of our
imagination, and the older monarchical theism
is obsolete or obsolescent. The place of the
divine in the world must be more organic and
intimate. An external creator and his institutions may still be verbally confessed at Church
in formulas that linger by their mere inertia,
but the life is out of them, we avoid dwelling
on them, the sincere heart of us is elsewhere.

I shall leave cynical materialism entirely
out of our discussion as not calling for treatment before this present audience, and I shall
ignore old-fashioned dualistic theism for the
same reason. Our contemporary mind having
once for all grasped the possibility of a more
intimate *weltanschauung*, the only opinions
quite worthy of arresting our attention will fall
within the general scope of what may roughly
be called the pantheistic field of vision, the
vision of God as the indwelling divine rather
than the external creator, and of human life as
part and parcel of that deep reality.

weltanschauung

I. THE TYPES OF THINKING

As we have found that spiritualism in general breaks into a more intimate and a less intimate species, so the more intimate species itself breaks into two subspecies, of which the one is more monistic, the other more pluralistic in form. I say in form, for our vocabulary gets unmanageable if we don't distinguish between form and substance here. The inner life of things must be substantially akin anyhow to the tenderer parts of man's nature in any spiritualistic philosophy. The word 'intimacy' probably covers the essential difference. Materialism holds the foreign in things to be more primary and lasting, it sends us to a lonely corner with our intimacy. The brutal aspects overlap and outwear; refinement has the feebler and more ephemeral hold on reality.

From a pragmatic point of view the difference between living against a background of foreignness and one of intimacy means the difference between a general habit of wariness and one of trust. One might call it a social difference, for after all, the common *socius* of us all is the great universe whose children we are.

materialistic qualities v. spiritual

If materialistic, we must be suspicious of this socius, cautious, tense, on guard. If spiritualistic, we may give way, embrace, and keep no ultimate fear.

The contrast is rough enough, and can be cut across by all sorts of other divisions, drawn from other points of view than that of foreignness and intimacy. We have so many different businesses with nature that no one of them yields us an all-embracing clasp. The philosophic attempt to define nature so that no one's business is left out, so that no one lies outside the door saying 'Where do *I* come in?' is sure in advance to fail. The most a philosophy can hope for is not to lock out any interest forever. No matter what doors it closes, it must leave other doors open for the interests which it neglects. I have begun by shutting ourselves up to intimacy and foreignness because that makes so generally interesting a contrast, and because it will conveniently introduce a farther contrast to which I wish this hour to lead.

The majority of men are sympathetic. Com-

paratively few are cynics because they like
cynicism, and most of our existing materialists
are such because they think the evidence of
facts impels them, or because they find the
idealists they are in contact with too private
and tender-minded; so, rather than join their
company, they fly to the opposite extreme. I
therefore propose to you to disregard materialists altogether for the present, and to consider
the sympathetic party alone.

It is normal, I say, to be sympathetic in the
sense in which I use the term. Not to demand
intimate relations with the universe, and not to
wish them satisfactory, should be accounted
signs of something wrong. Accordingly when
minds of this type reach the philosophic level,
and seek some unification of their vision, they
find themselves compelled to correct that aboriginal appearance of things by which savages
are not troubled. That sphinx-like presence,
with its breasts and claws, that first bald multifariousness, is too discrepant an object for philosophic contemplation. The intimacy and the
foreignness cannot be written down as simply

rather than being cynics or

coexisting. An order must be made; and in that order the higher side of things must dominate. The philosophy of the absolute agrees with the pluralistic philosophy which I am going to contrast with it in these lectures, in that both identify human substance with the divine substance. But whereas absolutism thinks that the said substance becomes fully divine only in the form of totality, and is not its real self in any form but the *all*-form, the pluralistic view which I prefer to adopt is willing to believe that there may ultimately never be an all-form at all, that the substance of reality may never get totally collected, that some of it may remain outside of the largest combination of it ever made, and that a distributive form of reality, the *each*-form, is logically as acceptable and empirically as probable as the all-form commonly acquiesced in as so obviously the self-evident thing. The contrast between these two forms of a reality which we will agree to suppose substantially spiritual is practically the topic of this course of lectures. You see now what I mean by pan-

34

"all form"
"each form"
is preferred

theism's two subspecies. If we give to the monistic subspecies the name of philosophy of the absolute, we may give that of radical empiricism to its pluralistic rival, and it may be well to distinguish them occasionally later by these names.

As a convenient way of entering into the study of their differences, I may refer to a recent article by Professor Jacks of Manchester College. Professor Jacks, in some brilliant pages in the 'Hibbert Journal' for last October, studies the relation between the universe and the philosopher who describes and defines it for us. You may assume two cases, he says. Either what the philosopher tells us is extraneous to the universe he is accounting for, an indifferent parasitic outgrowth, so to speak; or the fact of his philosophizing is itself one of the things taken account of in the philosophy, and self-included in the description. In the former case the philosopher means by the universe everything *except* what his own presence brings; in the latter case his philosophy is itself an intimate part of the universe, and may be a part momentous enough to give a different turn to what the other parts signify. It may be a supreme reaction of the universe upon itself by which it rises to self-comprehension. It may handle itself differently in consequence of this event.

Now both empiricism and absolutism bring the philosopher inside and make man intimate, but the one being pluralistic and the other monistic, they do so in differing ways that need much explanation. Let me then contrast the one with the other way of representing the status of the human thinker.

For monism the world is no collection, but one great all-inclusive fact outside of which is nothing—nothing is its only alternative. When the monism is idealistic, this all-enveloping fact is represented as an absolute mind that makes the partial facts by thinking them, just as we make objects in a dream by dreaming them, or personages in a story by imagining them. To *be*, on this scheme, is, on the part of a finite thing, to be an object for the absolute; and on the part of the absolute it is to be the thinker of

I. THE TYPES OF THINKING

that assemblage of objects. If we use the word
'content' here, we see that the absolute and the
world have an identical content. The absolute
is nothing but the knowledge of those objects;
the objects are nothing but what the absolute
knows. The world and the all-thinker thus
compenetrate and soak each other up without
residuum. They are but two names for the same
identical material, considered now from the
subjective, and now from the objective point of
view — gedanke and gedachtes, as we would
say if we were Germans. We philosophers naturally form part of the material, on the monistic scheme. The absolute makes us by thinking
us, and if we ourselves are enlightened enough
to be believers in the absolute, one may then
say that our philosophizing is one of the ways
in which the absolute is conscious of itself.
This is the full pantheistic scheme, the *iden-
titätsphilosophie*, the immanence of God in his
creation, a conception sublime from its tremendous unity. And yet that unity is incomplete, as closer examination will show.

The absolute and the world are one fact, I

*gedanke
gedachtes
identitasphilosophie*

said, when materially considered. Our philosophy, for example, is not numerically distinct from the absolute's own knowledge of itself, not a duplicate and copy of it, it is part of that very knowledge, is numerically identical with as much of it as our thought covers. The absolute just *is* our philosophy, along with everything else that is known, in an act of knowing which (to use the words of my gifted absolutist colleague Royce) forms in its wholeness one luminously transparent conscious moment.

But one as we are in this material sense with the absolute substance, that being only the whole of us, and we only the parts of it, yet in a formal sense something like a pluralism breaks out. When we speak of the absolute we *take* the one universal known material collectively or integrally; when we speak of its objects, of our finite selves, etc., we *take* that same identical material distributively and separately. But what is the use of a thing's *being* only once if it can be *taken* twice over, and if being taken in different ways makes different things true

we are all of us parts of the absolute, universe, etc

of it? As the absolute takes me, for example, I appear *with* everything else in its field of perfect knowledge. As I take myself, I appear *without* most other things in my field of relative ignorance. And practical differences result from its knowledge and my ignorance. Ignorance breeds mistake, curiosity, misfortune, pain, for me; I suffer those consequences. The absolute knows of those things, of course, for it knows me and my suffering, but it does n't itself suffer. It can't be ignorant, for simultaneous with its knowledge of each question goes its knowledge of each answer. It can't be patient, for it has to wait for nothing, having everything at once in its possession. It can't be surprised; it can't be guilty. No attribute connected with succession can be applied to it, for it is all at once and wholly what it is, 'with the unity of a single instant,' and succession is not of it but in it, for we are continually told that it is ' timeless.'

Things true of the world in its finite aspects, then, are not true of it in its infinite capacity. *Quâ* finite and plural its accounts of itself to itself are different from what its account to itself *quâ* infinite and one must be.

With this radical discrepancy between the absolute and the relative points of view, it seems to me that almost as great a bar to intimacy between the divine and the human breaks out in pantheism as that which we found in monarchical theism, and hoped that pantheism might not show. We humans are incurably rooted in the temporal point of view. The eternal's ways are utterly unlike our ways. 'Let us imitate the All,' said the original prospectus of that admirable Chicago quarterly called the 'Monist.' As if we could, either in thought or conduct! We are invincibly parts, let us talk as we will, and must always apprehend the absolute as if it were a foreign being. If what I mean by this is not wholly clear to you at this point, it ought to grow clearer as my lectures proceed.

II

MONISTIC IDEALISM

Inclusive,
Panthei stic
intimate
universe+god + human
connect
monistic
= idealism

LECTURE II

MONISTIC IDEALISM

LET me recall to you the programme which I indicated to you at our last meeting. After agreeing not to consider materialism in any shape, but to place ourselves straightway upon a more spiritualistic platform, I pointed out three kinds of spiritual philosophy between which we are asked to choose. The first way was that of the older dualistic theism, with ourselves represented as a secondary order of substances created by God. We found that this allowed of a degree of intimacy with the creative principle inferior to that implied in the pantheistic belief that we are substantially one with it, and that the divine is therefore the most intimate of all our possessions, heart of our heart, in fact. But we saw that this pantheistic belief could be held in two forms, a monistic form which I called philosophy of the absolute, and a pluralistic form which I called radical empiricism, the former conceiving that the divine exists authentically only

whitman

absolute)

43

Spiritualism:
A - dualistic ∨ pantheism
b monistic ∨ pluralistic
2- the philosophy of the absolute
3- radical empiricism

when the world is experienced all at once in its absolute totality, whereas radical empiricism allows that the absolute sum-total of things may never be actually experienced or realized in that shape at all, and that a disseminated, distributed, or incompletely unified appearance is the only form that reality may yet have achieved.

I may contrast the monistic and pluralistic forms in question as the 'all-form' and the 'each-form.' At the end of the last hour I animadverted on the fact that the all-form is so radically different from the each-form, which is our human form of experiencing the world, that the philosophy of the absolute, so far as insight and understanding go, leaves us almost as much outside of the divine being as dualistic theism does. I believe that radical empiricism, on the contrary, holding to the each-form, and making of God only one of the eaches, affords the higher degree of intimacy. The general thesis of these lectures I said would be a defence of the pluralistic against the monistic view. Think of the universe as existing

all-form = monistic
each-form = radical empiricism

44

II. MONISTIC IDEALISM

solely in the each-form, and you will have on the whole a more reasonable and satisfactory idea of it than if you insist on the all-form being necessary. The rest of my lectures will do little more than make this thesis more concrete, and I hope more persuasive.

It is curious how little countenance radical pluralism has ever had from philosophers. Whether materialistically or spiritualistically minded, philosophers have always aimed at cleaning up the litter with which the world apparently is filled. They have substituted economical and orderly conceptions for the first sensible tangle; and whether these were morally elevated or only intellectually neat, they were at any rate always æsthetically pure and definite, and aimed at ascribing to the world something clean and intellectual in the way of inner structure. As compared with all these rationalizing pictures, the pluralistic empiricism which I profess offers but a sorry appearance. It is a turbid, muddled, gothic sort of an affair, without a sweeping outline and with little pictorial nobility. Those of you

45

who are accustomed to the classical construc-
tions of reality may be excused if your first reaction upon it be absolute contempt—a shrug
of the shoulders as if such ideas were unworthy of explicit refutation. But one must have
lived some time with a system to appreciate
its merits. Perhaps a little more familiarity
may mitigate your first surprise at such a programme as I offer.

First, one word more than what I said last
time about the relative foreignness of the divine
principle in the philosophy of the absolute.
Those of you who have read the last two chapters of Mr. Bradley's wonderful book, 'Appearance and reality,' will remember what
an elaborately foreign aspect *his* absolute is
finally made to assume. It is neither intelligence nor will, neither a self nor a collection of
selves, neither truthful, good, nor beautiful, as
we understand these terms. It is, in short, a
metaphysical monster, all that we are permitted to say of it being that whatever it is, it is at
any rate *worth* more (worth more to itself, that
is) than if any eulogistic adjectives of ours

applied to it. It is us, and all other appearances, but none of us *as such*, for in it we are all 'transmuted,' and its own as-suchness is of another denomination altogether.

Spinoza was the first great absolutist, and the impossibility of being intimate with *his* God is universally recognized. *Quatenus infinitus est* he is other than what he is *quatenus humanam mentem constituit*. Spinoza's philosophy has been rightly said to be worked by the word *quatenus*. Conjunctions, prepositions, and adverbs play indeed the vital part in all philosophies; and in contemporary idealism the words 'as' and 'quâ' bear the burden of reconciling metaphysical unity with phenomenal diversity. Quâ absolute the world is one and perfect, quâ relative it is many and faulty, yet it is identically the self-same world — instead of talking of it as many facts, we call it one fact in many aspects.

As absolute, then, or *sub specie eternitatis*, or *quatenus infinitus est*, the world repels our sympathy because it has no history. *As such*, the absolute neither acts nor suffers, nor loves

47

quatenus infinitus est
quatenus humanam mentem
constituit

nor hates; it has no needs, desires, or aspira-
tions, no failures or successes, friends or enemies, victories or defeats. All such things per-
tain to the world quâ relative, in which our
finite experiences lie, and whose vicissitudes
alone have power to arouse our interest. What
boots it to tell me that the absolute way is the
true way, and to exhort me, as Emerson says,
to lift mine eye up to its style, and manners of
the sky, if the feat is impossible by definition?
I am finite once for all, and all the categories of
my sympathy are knit up with the finite world
as such, and with things that have a history.
'Aus dieser erde quellen meine freuden, und
ihre sonne scheinet meinen leiden.' I have
neither eyes nor ears nor heart nor mind for
anything of an opposite description, and the
stagnant felicity of the absolute's own perfection moves me as little as I move it. If we
were *readers* only of the cosmic novel, things
would be different: we should then share the
author's point of view and recognize villains
to be as essential as heroes in the plot. But
we are not the readers but the very personages

of the world-drama. In your own eyes each of you here is its hero, and the villains are your respective friends or enemies. The tale which the absolute reader finds so perfect, we spoil for one another through our several vital identifications with the destinies of the particular personages involved.

The doctrine on which the absolutists lay most stress is the absolute's 'timeless' character. For pluralists, on the other hand, time remains as real as anything, and nothing in the universe is great or static or eternal enough not to have some history. But the world that each of us feels most intimately at home with is that of beings with histories that play into our history, whom we can help in their vicissitudes even as they help us in ours. This satisfaction the absolute denies us; we can neither help nor hinder it, for it stands outside of history. It surely is a merit in a philosophy to make the very life we lead seem real and earnest. Pluralism, in exorcising the absolute, exorcises the great de-realizer of the only life we are at home in, and thus redeems the nature

49

of reality from essential foreignness. Every
end, reason, motive, object of desire or aversion, ground of sorrow or joy that we feel is
in the world of finite multifariousness, for
only in that world does anything really happen, only there do events come to pass.

In one sense this is a far-fetched and rather
childish objection, for so much of the history
of the finite is as formidably foreign to us as
the static absolute can possibly be — in fact
that entity derives its own foreignness largely
from the bad character of the finite which it
simultaneously is — that this sentimental reason for preferring the pluralistic view seems
small.[1] I shall return to the subject in my final
lecture, and meanwhile, with your permission,
I will say no more about this objection. The
more so as the necessary foreignness of the
absolute is cancelled emotionally by its attribute of *totality*, which is universally considered
to carry the further attribute of *perfection* in
its train. 'Philosophy,' says a recent american philosopher, 'is humanity's hold on totality,' and there is no doubt that most of us find

that the bare notion of an absolute all-one is inspiring. 'I yielded myself to the perfect whole,' writes Emerson; and where can you find a more mind-dilating object? A certain loyalty is called forth by the idea; even if not proved actual, it must be believed in somehow. Only an enemy of philosophy can speak lightly of it. Rationalism starts from the idea of such a whole and builds downward. Movement and change are absorbed into its immutability as forms of mere appearance. When you accept this beatific vision of what *is*, in contrast with what *goes on*, you feel as if you had fulfilled an intellectual duty. 'Reality is not in its truest nature a process,' Mr. McTaggart tells us, 'but a stable and timeless state.'[2] 'The true knowledge of God begins,' Hegel writes, 'when we know that things as they immediately are have no truth.'[3] 'The consummation of the infinite aim,' he says elsewhere, 'consists merely in removing the illusion which makes it seem yet unaccomplished. Good and absolute goodness is eternally accomplishing itself in the world: and the result is that it needs not wait upon *us*, but is already . . . accomplished. It is an illusion under which we live. . . . In the course of its process the Idea makes itself that illusion, by setting an antithesis to confront it, and its action consists in getting rid of the illusion which it has created.' ⁴

But abstract emotional appeals of any kind sound amateurish in the business that concerns us. Impressionistic philosophizing, like impressionistic watchmaking or land-surveying, is intolerable to experts. Serious discussion of the alternative before us forces me, therefore, to become more technical. The great *claim* of the philosophy of the absolute is that the absolute is no hypothesis, but a presupposition implicated in all thinking, and needing only a little effort of analysis to be seen as a logical necessity. I will therefore take it in this more rigorous character and see whether its claim is in effect so coercive.

It has seemed coercive to an enormous number of contemporaneous thinkers. Professor Henry Jones thus describes the range and influence of it upon the social and political life of

the present time:[5] 'For many years adherents
of this way of thought have deeply interested
the british public by their writings. Almost
more important than their writings is the fact
that they have occupied philosophical chairs
in almost every university in the kingdom.
Even the professional critics of idealism are
for the most part idealists — after a fashion.
And when they are not, they are as a rule more
occupied with the refutation of idealism than
with the construction of a better theory. It follows from their position of academic authority,
were it from nothing else, that idealism exer-
cises an influence not easily measured upon the
youth of the nation — upon those, that is, who
from the educational opportunities they enjoy
may naturally be expected to become the lead-
ers of the nation's thought and practice. . . .
Difficult as it is to measure the forces . . . it
is hardly to be denied that the power exercised
by Bentham and the utilitarian school has, for
better or for worse, passed into the hands of
the idealists. . . . "The Rhine has flowed into
the Thames" is the warning note rung out by

Mr. Hobhouse. Carlyle introduced it, bringing
it as far as Chelsea. Then Jowett and Thomas
Hill Green, and William Wallace and Lewis
Nettleship, and Arnold Toynbee and David
Ritchie — to mention only those teachers whose
voices now are silent — guided the waters into
those upper reaches known locally as the Isis.
John and Edward Caird brought them up the
Clyde, Hutchison Stirling up the Firth of
Forth. They have passed up the Mersey and
up the Severn and Dee and Don. They pollute
the bay of St. Andrews and swell the waters of
the Cam, and have somehow crept overland into
Birmingham. The stream of german idealism
has been diffused over the academical world of
Great Britain. The disaster is universal.'

Evidently if weight of authority were all, the
truth of absolutism would be thus decided.
But let us first pass in review the general style
of argumentation of that philosophy.

As I read it, its favorite way of meeting pluralism and empiricism is by a *reductio ad absurdum* framed somewhat as follows: You contend, it says to the pluralist, that things, though

II. MONISTIC IDEALISM

in some respects connected, are in other respects independent, so that they are not members of one all-inclusive individual fact. Well, your position is absurd on either point. For admit in fact the slightest modicum of independence, and you find (if you will only think accurately) that you have to admit more and more of it, until at last nothing but an absolute chaos, or the proved impossibility of any connexion whatever between the parts of the universe, remains upon your hands. Admit, on the other hand, the most incipient minimum of relation between any two things, and again you can't stop until you see that the absolute unity of all things is implied.

If we take the latter *reductio ad absurdum* first, we find a good example of it in Lotze's well-known proof of monism from the fact of interaction between finite things. Suppose, Lotze says in effect, and for simplicity's sake I have to paraphrase him, for his own words are too long to quote — many distinct beings *a*, *b*, *c*, etc., to exist independently of each other : *can a in that case ever act on b?*

What is it to act? Is it not to exert an influence? Does the influence detach itself from *a* and find *b*? If so, it is a third fact, and the problem is not how *a* acts, but how its 'influence' acts on *b*. By another influence perhaps? And how in the end does the chain of influences find *b* rather than *c* unless *b* is somehow prefigured in them already? And when they have found *b*, how do they make *b* respond, if *b* has nothing in common with them? Why don't they go right through *b*? The change in *b* is a *response*, due to *b*'s capacity for taking account of *a*'s influence, and that again seems to prove that *b*'s nature is somehow fitted to *a*'s nature in advance. *A* and *b*, in short, are not really as distinct as we at first supposed them, not separated by a void. Were this so they would be mutually impenetrable, or at least mutually irrelevant. They would form two universes each living by itself, making no difference to each other, taking no account of each other, much as the universe of your day dreams takes no account of mine. They must therefore belong together beforehand, be co-implicated already, their natures must have an inborn mutual reference each to each.

Lotze's own solution runs as follows: The multiple independent things supposed cannot be real in that shape, but all of them, if reciprocal action is to be possible between them, must be regarded as parts of a single real being, M. The pluralism with which our view began has to give place to a monism; and the 'transeunt' interaction, being unintelligible as such, is to be understood as an immanent operation.[6]

The words 'immanent operation' seem here to mean that the single real being M, of which *a* and *b* are members, is the only thing that changes, and that when it changes, it changes inwardly and all over at once. When part *a* in it changes, consequently, part *b* must also change, but without the whole M changing this would not occur.

A pretty argument, but a purely verbal one, as I apprehend it. *Call* your *a* and *b* distinct, they can't interact; *call* them one, they can. For taken abstractly and without qualification the words 'distinct' and 'independent' suggest only disconnection. If this be the only property of your a and b (and it is the only property your words imply), then of course, since you can't deduce their mutual influence from *it*, you can find no ground of its occurring between them. Your bare word 'separate,' contradicting your bare word 'joined,' seems to exclude connexion.

Lotze's remedy for the impossibility thus verbally found is to change the first word. If, instead of calling a and b independent, we now call them 'interdependent,' 'united,' or 'one,' he says, *these* words do not contradict any sort of mutual influence that may be proposed. If a and b are 'one,' and the one changes, a and b of course must co-ordinately change. What under the old name they could n't do, they now have license to do under the new name.

But I ask you whether giving the name of 'one' to the former 'many' makes us really understand the modus operandi of interaction any better. We have now given verbal permission to the many to change all together, if they can;

58

we have removed a verbal impossibility and
substituted a verbal possibility, but the new
name, with the possibility it suggests, tells us
nothing of the actual process by which real
things that are one can and do change at all.
In point of fact abstract oneness as such *does n't*
change, neither has it parts — any more than
abstract independence as such interacts. But
then neither abstract oneness nor abstract independence *exists;* only concrete real things
exist, which add to these properties the other
properties which they possess, to make up
what we call their total nature. To construe
any one of their abstract names as *making their
total nature impossible* is a misuse of the function of naming. The real way of rescue from
the abstract consequences of one name is not
to fly to an opposite name, equally abstract, but
rather to correct the first name by qualifying
adjectives that restore some concreteness to
the case. Don't take your 'independence' *sim-
pliciter*, as Lotze does, take it *secundum quid*.
Only when we know what the process of interaction literally and concretely *consists* in can

we tell whether beings independent *in definite respects*, distinct, for example, in origin, separate in place, different in kind, etc., can or cannot interact.

The treating of a name as excluding from the fact named what the name's definition fails positively to include, is what I call 'vicious intellectualism.' Later I shall have more to say about this intellectualism, but that Lotze's argument is tainted by it I hardly think we can deny. As well might you contend (to use an instance from Sigwart) that a person whom you have once called an 'equestrian' is thereby forever made unable to walk on his own feet.

I almost feel as if I should apologize for criticising such subtle arguments in rapid lectures of this kind. The criticisms have to be as abstract as the arguments, and in exposing their unreality, take on such an unreal sound themselves that a hearer not nursed in the intellectualist atmosphere knows not which of them to accuse. But *le vin est versé, il faut le boire*, and I must cite a couple more instances before I stop.

II. MONISTIC IDEALISM

If we are (empiricists) and go from parts to wholes, we believe that beings may first exist and feed so to speak on their own existence, and then secondarily become known to one another. But philosophers of the absolute tell us that such independence of being from being known would, if once admitted, disintegrate the universe beyond all hope of mending. The argument is one of Professor Royce's proofs that the only alternative we have is to choose the complete disunion of all things or their complete union in the absolute One.

Take, for instance, the proverb 'a cat may look at a king' and adopt the realistic view that the king's being is independent of the cat's witnessing. This assumption, which amounts to saying that it need make no essential difference to the royal object whether the feline subject cognizes him or not, that the cat may look away from him or may even be annihilated, and the king remain unchanged,—this assumption, I say, is considered by my ingenious colleague to lead to the absurd practical consequence that the two beings *can* never later acquire any possible linkages or connexions, but must remain eternally as if in different worlds. For suppose any connexion whatever to ensue, this connexion would simply be a third being additional to the cat and the king, which would itself have to be linked to both by additional links before it could connect them, and so on *ad infinitum*, the argument, you see, being the same as Lotze's about how *a*'s influence does its influencing when it influences *b*.

In Royce's own words, if the king can be without the cat knowing him, then king and cat 'can have no common features, no ties, no true relations; they are separated, each from the other, by absolutely impassable chasms. They can never come to get either ties or community of nature; they are not in the same space, nor in the same time, nor in the same natural or spiritual order.' [7] They form in short two unrelated universes, — which is the *reductio ad absurdum* required.

To escape this preposterous state of things we must accordingly revoke the original hypothesis. The king and the cat are not indifferent

reductio ad absurdum

to each other in the way supposed. But if not in that way, then in no way, for connexion in that way carries connexion in other ways; so that, pursuing the reverse line of reasoning, we end with the absolute itself as the smallest fact that can exist. Cat and king are co-involved, they are a single fact in two names, they can never have been absent from each other, and they are both equally co-implicated with all the other facts of which the universe consists.

Professor Royce's proof that whoso admits the cat's witnessing the king at all must thereupon admit the integral absolute, may be briefly put as follows: —

First, to know the king, the cat must intend *that* king, must somehow pass over and lay hold of him individually and specifically. The cat's idea, in short, must transcend the cat's own separate mind and somehow include the king, for were the king utterly outside and independent of the cat, the cat's pure other, the beast's mind could touch the king in no wise. This makes the cat much less distinct from the king than we had at first naïvely supposed.

63

There must be some prior continuity between them, which continuity Royce interprets idealistically as meaning a higher mind that owns them both as objects, and owning them can also own any relation, such as the supposed witnessing, that may obtain between them. Taken purely pluralistically, neither of them can own any part of a *between*, because, so taken, each is supposed shut up to itself: the fact of a *between* thus commits us to a higher knower.

But the higher knower that knows the two beings we start with proves to be the same knower that knows everything else. For assume any third being, the queen, say, and as the cat knew the king, so let the king know his queen, and let this second knowledge, by the same reasoning, require a higher knower as its presupposition. That knower of the king's knowing must, it is now contended, be the same higher knower that was required for the cat's knowing; for if you suppose otherwise, you have no longer the *same king*. This may not seem immediately obvious, but if you follow the intellectualistic logic employed in all these reasonings, I don't see how you can escape the admission. If it be true that the independent or indifferent cannot be related, for the abstract words 'independent' or 'indifferent' as such imply no relation, then it is just as true that the king known by the cat cannot be the king that knows the queen, for taken merely 'as such,' the abstract term 'what the cat knows' and the abstract term 'what knows the queen' are logically distinct. The king thus logically breaks into two kings, with nothing to connect them, until a higher knower is introduced to recognize them as the self-same king concerned in any previous acts of knowledge which he may have brought about. This he can do because he possesses all the terms as his own objects and can treat them as he will. Add any fourth or fifth term, and you get a like result, and so on, until at last an all-owning knower, otherwise called the absolute, is reached. The co-implicated 'through-and-through' world of monism thus stands proved by irrefutable logic, and all pluralism appears as absurd.

The reasoning is pleasing from its ingenuity,

and it is almost a pity that so straight a bridge from abstract logic to concrete fact should not bear our weight. To have the alternative forced upon us of admitting either finite things each cut off from all relation with its environment, or else of accepting the integral absolute with no environment and all relations packed within itself, would be too delicious a simplification. But the purely verbal character of the operation is undisguised. Because the *names* of finite things and their relations are disjoined, it does n't follow that the realities named need a *deus ex machina* from on high to conjoin them. The same things disjoined in one respect *appear* as conjoined in another. Naming the disjunction does n't debar us from also naming the conjunction in a later modifying statement, for the two are absolutely co-ordinate elements in the finite tissue of experience. When at Athens it was found self-contradictory that a boy could be both tall and short (tall namely in respect of a child, short in respect of a man), the absolute had not yet been thought of, but it might just as well have been invoked

66

by Socrates as by Lotze or Royce, as a relief from his peculiar intellectualistic difficulty.

Everywhere we find rationalists using the same kind of reasoning. The primal whole which is their vision must be there not only as a fact but as a logical necessity. It must be the minimum that can exist — either that absolute whole is there, or there is absolutely nothing. The logical proof alleged of the irrationality of supposing otherwise, is that you can deny the whole only in words that implicitly assert it. If you say 'parts,' of *what* are they parts? If you call them a 'many,' that very word unifies them. If you suppose them unrelated in any particular respect, that 'respect' connects them; and so on. In short you fall into hopeless contradiction. You must stay either at one extreme or the other.[8] 'Partly this and partly that,' partly rational, for instance, and partly irrational, is no admissible description of the world. If rationality be in it at all, it must be in it throughout; if irrationality be in it anywhere, that also must pervade it throughout. It must be wholly rational or wholly irrational, pure universe or pure multiverse or nulliverse; and reduced to this violent alternative, no one's choice ought long to remain doubtful. The individual absolute, with its parts co-implicated through and through, so that there is nothing in any part by which any other part can remain inwardly unaffected, is the only rational supposition. Connexions of an external sort, by which the many became merely continuous instead of being consubstantial, would be an irrational supposition.

Mr. Bradley is the pattern champion of this philosophy *in extremis,* as one might call it, for he shows an intolerance to pluralism so extreme that I fancy few of his readers have been able fully to share it. His reasoning exemplifies everywhere what I call the vice of intellectualism, for abstract terms are used by him as positively excluding all that their definition fails to include. Some Greek sophists could deny that we may say that man is good, for man, they said, means only man, and good means only good, and the word *is* can't be construed to identify such disparate meanings.

II. MONISTIC IDEALISM

Mr. Bradley revels in the same type of argument. No adjective can rationally qualify a substantive, he thinks, for if distinct from the substantive, it can't be united with it; and if not distinct, there is only one thing there, and nothing left to unite. Our whole pluralistic procedure in using subjects and predicates as we do is fundamentally irrational, an example of the desperation of our finite intellectual estate, infected and undermined as that is by the separatist discursive forms which are our only categories, but which absolute reality must somehow absorb into its unity and overcome.

Readers of 'Appearance and reality' will remember how Mr. Bradley suffers from a difficulty identical with that to which Lotze and Royce fall a prey — how shall an influence influence? how shall a relation relate? Any conjunctive relation between two phenomenal experiences a and b must, in the intellectualist philosophy of these authors, be itself a third entity; and as such, instead of bridging the one original chasm, it can only create two smaller chasms, each to be freshly bridged. Instead of hooking a to b, it needs itself to be hooked by a fresh relation r' to a and by another r'' to b. These new relations are but two more entities which themselves require to be hitched in turn by four still newer relations—so behold the vertiginous *regressus ad infinitum* in full career.

Since a *regressus ad infinitum* is deemed absurd, the notion that relations come 'between' their terms must be given up. No mere external go-between can logically connect. What occurs must be more intimate. The hooking must be a penetration, a possession. The relation must *involve* the terms, each term must involve *it*, and merging thus their being in it, they must somehow merge their being in each other, tho, as they seem still phenomenally so separate, we can never conceive exactly how it is that they are inwardly one. The absolute, however, must be supposed able to perform the unifying feat in his own inscrutable fashion.

In old times, whenever a philosopher was assailed for some particularly tough absurdity

in his system, he was wont to parry the attack
by the argument from the divine omnipotence.
'Do you mean to limit God's power?' he
would reply: 'do you mean to say that God
could not, if he would, do this or that?' This
retort was supposed to close the mouths of all
objectors of properly decorous mind. The
functions of the bradleian absolute are in this
particular identical with those of the theistic
God. Suppositions treated as too absurd to
pass muster in the finite world which we inhabit, the absolute must be able to make good
'somehow' in his ineffable way. First we hear
Mr. Bradley convicting things of absurdity;
next, calling on the absolute to vouch for them
quand même. Invoked for no other duty, that
duty it must and shall perform.

The strangest discontinuity of our world of
appearance with the supposed world of absolute reality is asserted both by Bradley and by
Royce; and both writers, the latter with great
ingenuity, seek to soften the violence of the jolt.
But it remains violent all the same, and is felt
to be so by most readers. Whoever feels the

violence strongly sees as on a diagram in just what the peculiarity of all this philosophy of the absolute consists. First, there is a healthy faith that the world must be rational and self-consistent. 'All science, all real knowledge, all experience presuppose,' as Mr. Ritchie writes, 'a coherent universe.' Next, we find a loyal clinging to the rationalist belief that sense-data and their associations are incoherent, and that only in substituting a conceptual order for their order can truth be found. Third, the substituted conceptions are treated intellectualistically, that is as mutually exclusive and discontinuous, so that the first innocent continuity of the flow of sense-experience is shattered for us without any higher conceptual continuity taking its place. Finally, since this broken state of things is intolerable, the absolute *deus ex machina* is called on to mend it in his own way, since we cannot mend it in ours.

Any other picture than this of post-kantian absolutism I am unable to frame. I see the intellectualistic criticism destroying the immediately given coherence of the phenomenal world, but unable to make its own conceptual substitutes cohere, and I see the resort to the absolute for a coherence of a higher type. The situation has dramatic liveliness, but it is inwardly incoherent throughout, and the question inevitably comes up whether a mistake may not somewhere have crept in in the process that has brought it about. May not the remedy lie rather in revising the intellectualist criticism than in first adopting it and then trying to undo its consequences by an arbitrary act of faith in an unintelligible agent. May not the flux of sensible experience itself contain a rationality that has been overlooked, so that the real remedy would consist in harking back to it more intelligently, and not in advancing in the opposite direction away from it and even away beyond the intellectualist criticism that disintegrates it, to the pseudo-rationality of the supposed absolute point of view. I myself believe that this is the real way to keep rationality in the world, and that the traditional rationalism has always been facing in the wrong direction. I hope in the end to make you share, or at any rate respect, this belief, but there is much to talk of before we get to that point.

I employed the word 'violent' just now in describing the dramatic situation in which it pleases the philosophy of the absolute to make its camp. I don't see how any one can help being struck in absolutist writings by that curious tendency to fly to violent extremes of which I have already said a word. The universe must be rational; well and good; but *how* rational? in what sense of that eulogistic but ambiguous word? — this would seem to be the next point to bring up. There are surely degrees in rationality that might be discriminated and described. Things can be consistent or coherent in very diverse ways. But no more in its conception of rationality than in its conception of relations can the monistic mind suffer the notion of more or less. Rationality is one and indivisible: if not rational thus indivisibly, the universe must be completely irrational, and no shadings or mixtures or compromises can obtain. Mr. McTaggart writes, in discussing the notion of a mixture: 'The two principles, of rationality and irrationality, to which the universe is then referred, will have to be absolutely separate and independent. For if there were any common unity to which they should be referred, it would be that unity and not its two manifestations which would be the ultimate explanation . . . and the theory, having thus become monistic,'[9] would resolve itself into the same alternative once more: is the single principle rational through and through or not?

'Can a plurality of reals be possible?' asks Mr. Bradley, and answers, 'No, impossible.' For it would mean a number of beings not dependent on each other, and this independence their plurality would contradict. For to be 'many' is to be related, the word having no meaning unless the units are somehow taken together, and it is impossible to take them in a sort of unreal void, so they must belong to a larger reality, and so carry the essence of the units beyond their proper selves, into a whole which possesses unity and is a larger system.[10]

Either absolute independence or absolute mutual dependence — this, then, is the only alternative allowed by these thinkers. Of course 'independence,' if absolute, would be preposterous, so the only conclusion allowable is that, in Ritchie's words, 'every single event is ultimately related to every other, and determined by the whole to which it belongs.' The whole complete block-universe through-and-through, therefore, or no universe at all!

Professor Taylor is so *naïf* in this habit of thinking only in extremes that he charges the pluralists with cutting the ground from under their own feet in not consistently following it themselves. What pluralists say is that a universe really connected loosely, after the pattern of our daily experience, is possible, and that for certain reasons it is the hypothesis to be preferred. What Professor Taylor thinks they naturally must or should say is that any other sort of universe is logically impossible, and that a totality of things interrelated like the world of the monists is not an hypothesis that can be seriously thought out at all.[11]

Meanwhile no sensible pluralist ever flies or wants to fly to this dogmatic extreme.

If chance is spoken of as an ingredient of the universe, absolutists interpret it to mean that double sevens are as likely to be thrown out of a dice box as double sixes are. If free-will is spoken of, that must mean that an english general is as likely to eat his prisoners to-day as a Maori chief was a hundred years ago. It is as likely — I am using Mr. McTaggart's examples — that a majority of Londoners will burn themselves alive to-morrow as that they will partake of food, as likely that I shall be hanged for brushing my hair as for committing a murder,[12] and so forth, through various suppositions that no indeterminist ever sees real reason to make.

This habit of thinking only in the most violent extremes reminds me of what Mr. Wells says of the current objections to socialism, in his wonderful little book, 'New worlds for old.' The commonest vice of the human mind is its disposition to see everything as yes or no, as black or white, its incapacity for discrimination of intermediate shades. So the critics agree to some hard and fast impossible definition of socialism, and extract absurdities from it as a conjurer gets rabbits from a hat. Socialism abolishes property, abolishes the family, and the rest. The method, Mr. Wells continues, is always the same: It is to assume that whatever the socialist postulates as desirable is wanted without limit of qualification, — for socialist read pluralist and the parallel holds good, — it is to imagine that whatever proposal is made by him is to be carried out by uncontrolled monomaniacs, and so to make a picture of the socialist dream which can be presented to the simple-minded person in doubt — 'This is socialism' — or pluralism, as the case may be. 'Surely! — SURELY! you don't want *this!* '

How often have I been replied to, when expressing doubts of the logical necessity of the absolute, of flying to the opposite extreme: 'But surely, SURELY there must be *some* connexion among things!' As if I must necessarily be an uncontrolled monomanic insanely denying any connexion whatever. The whole question revolves in very truth about the word 'some.' Radical empiricism and pluralism stand out for the legitimacy of the notion of *some:* each part of the world is in some ways connected, in some other ways not connected with its other parts, and the ways can be discriminated, for many of them are obvious, and their differences are obvious to view. Absolutism, on its side, seems to hold that 'some' is a category ruinously infected with self-contradictoriness, and that the only categories inwardly consistent and therefore pertinent to reality are 'all' and 'none.'

The question runs into the still more general one with which Mr. Bradley and later writers of the monistic school have made us abundantly familiar — the question, namely, whether all the relations with other things, possible to a being, are pre-included in its intrinsic nature and enter into its essence, or whether, in respect to some of these relations, it can *be* without reference to them, and, if it ever does enter into them, do so adventitiously and as it were by an after-thought. This is the great question as to whether 'external' relations can exist. They seem to, undoubtedly. My manuscript, for example, is 'on' the desk. The relation of being 'on' does n't seem to implicate or involve in any way the inner meaning of the manuscript or the inner structure of the desk — these objects engage in it only by their outsides, it seems only a temporary accident in their respective histories. Moreover, the 'on' fails to appear to our senses as one of those unintelligible 'betweens' that have to be separately hooked on the terms they pretend to connect. All this innocent sense-appearance, however, we are told, cannot pass muster in the eyes of reason. It is a tissue of self-contradiction which only the complete absorption of the desk and the manuscript into the higher unity of a more absolute reality can overcome.

The reasoning by which this conclusion is supported is too subtle and complicated to be properly dealt with in a public lecture, and you will thank me for not inviting you to consider it at all.[13] I feel the more free to pass it by now as I think that the cursory account of the absolutistic attitude which I have already given is sufficient for our present purpose, and that my own verdict on the philosophy of the absolute as 'not proven'—please observe that I go no farther now—need not be backed by argument at every special point. Flanking operations are less costly and in some ways more effective than frontal attacks. Possibly you will yourselves think after hearing my remaining lectures that the alternative of an universe absolutely rational or absolutely irrational is forced and strained, and that a *via media* exists which some of you may agree with me is to be preferred. *Some* rationality certainly does characterize our universe; and, weighing one kind with another, we may deem that the incomplete kinds that appear are on the whole as acceptable as the through-and-through sort of rationality on which the monistic systematizers insist.

All the said systematizers who have written since Hegel have owed their inspiration largely to him. Even when they have found no use for his particular triadic dialectic, they have drawn confidence and courage from his authoritative and conquering tone. I have said nothing about Hegel in this lecture, so I must repair the omission in the next.

III

HEGEL AND HIS METHOD

LECTURE III

HEGEL AND HIS METHOD

DIRECTLY or indirectly, that strange and powerful genius Hegel has done more to strengthen idealistic pantheism in thoughtful circles than all other influences put together. I must talk a little about him before drawing my final conclusions about the cogency of the arguments for the absolute. In no philosophy is the fact that a philosopher's vision and the technique he uses in proof of it are two different things more palpably evident than in Hegel. The vision in his case was that of a world in which reason holds all things in solution and accounts for all the irrationality that superficially appears by taking it up as a 'moment' into itself. This vision was so intense in Hegel, and the tone of authority with which he spoke from out of the midst of it was so weighty, that the impression he made has never been effaced. Once dilated to the scale of the master's eye, the disciples' sight could not contract to any lesser *hegel = dialectic method*

prospect. The technique which Hegel used to prove his vision was the so-called dialectic method, but here his fortune has been quite contrary. Hardly a recent disciple has felt his particular applications of the method to be satisfactory. Many have let them drop entirely, treating them rather as a sort of provisional stop-gap, symbolic of what might some day prove possible of execution, but having no literal cogency or value now. Yet these very same disciples hold to the vision itself as a revelation that can never pass away. The case is curious and worthy of our study.

It is still more curious in that these same disciples, altho they are usually willing to abandon any particular instance of the dialectic method to its critics, are unshakably sure that in some shape the dialectic method is the key to truth. What, then, is the dialectic method? It is itself a part of the hegelian vision or intuition, and a part that finds the strongest echo in empiricism and common sense. Great injustice is done to Hegel by treating him as primarily a reasoner. He is in

reality a naïvely observant man, only beset
with a perverse preference for the use of technical and logical jargon. He plants himself in
the empirical flux of things and gets the impression of what happens. His mind is in very
truth *impressionistic;* and his thought, when
once you put yourself at the animating centre
of it, is the easiest thing in the world to catch
the pulse of and to follow.

Any author is easy if you can catch the centre
of his vision. From the centre in Hegel come
those towering sentences of his that are com-
parable only to Luther's, as where, speaking of
the ontological proof of God's existence from
the concept of him as the *ens perfectissimum*
to which no attribute can be lacking, he says:
'It would be strange if the Notion, the very
heart of the mind, or, in a word, the concrete
totality we call God, were not rich enough to
embrace so poor a category as Being, the very
poorest and most abstract of all — for nothing
can be more insignificant than Being.' But
if Hegel's central thought is easy to catch, his
abominable habits of speech make his applica-

tion of it to details exceedingly difficult to follow. His passion for the slipshod in the way of sentences, his unprincipled playing fast and loose with terms; his dreadful vocabulary, calling what completes a thing its 'negation,' for example; his systematic refusal to let you know whether he is talking logic or physics or psychology, his whole deliberately adopted policy of ambiguity and vagueness, in short: all these things make his present-day readers wish to tear their hair—or his — out in desperation. Like Byron's corsair, he has left a name 'to other times, linked with one virtue and a thousand crimes.'

The virtue was the vision, which was really in two parts. The first part was that reason is all-inclusive, the second was that things are 'dialectic.' Let me say a word about this second part of Hegel's vision.

The impression that any *naïf* person gets who plants himself innocently in the flux of things is that things are off their balance. Whatever equilibriums our finite experiences attain to are but provisional. Martinique volcanoes shatter our wordsworthian equilibrium with nature. Accidents, either moral, mental, or physical, break up the slowly built-up equilibriums men reach in family life and in their civic and professional relations. Intellectual enigmas frustrate our scientific systems, and the ultimate cruelty of the universe upsets our religious attitudes and outlooks. Of no special system of good attained does the universe recognize the value as sacred. Down it tumbles, over it goes, to feed the ravenous appetite for destruction, of the larger system of history in which it stood for a moment as a landing-place and stepping-stone. This dogging of everything by its negative, its fate, its undoing, this perpetual moving on to something future which shall supersede the present, this is the hegelian intuition of the essential provision-ality, and consequent unreality, of everything empirical and finite. Take any concrete finite thing and try to hold it fast. You cannot, for so held, it proves not to be concrete at all, but an arbitrary extract or abstract which you have made from the remainder of empirical

reality. The rest of things invades and overflows both it and you together, and defeats your
rash attempt. Any partial view whatever of the
world tears the part out of its relations, leaves
out some truth concerning it, is untrue of
it, falsifies it. The full truth about anything
involves more than that thing. In the end
nothing less than the whole of everything can
be the truth of anything at all.

Taken so far, and taken in the rough, Hegel
is not only harmless, but accurate. There is a
dialectic movement in things, if such it please
you to call it, one that the whole constitution
of concrete life establishes; but it is one that
can be described and accounted for in terms
of the pluralistic vision of things far more naturally than in the monistic terms to which
Hegel finally reduced it. Pluralistic empiricism knows that everything is in an environment, a surrounding world of other things,
and that if you leave it to work there it will
inevitably meet with friction and opposition
from its neighbors. Its rivals and enemies will
destroy it unless it can buy them off by com-

promising some part of its original pretensions.

But Hegel saw this undeniable characteristic of the world we live in in a non-empirical
light. Let the *mental idea* of the thing work *equilibrium*
in your thought all alone, he fancied, and just
the same consequences will follow. It will be
negated by the opposite ideas that dog it, and
can survive only by entering, along with them,
into some kind of treaty. This treaty will be
an instance of the so-called 'higher synthesis'
of everything with its negative; and Hegel's
originality lay in transporting the process from
the sphere of percepts to that of concepts and
treating it as the universal method by which
every kind of life, logical, physical, or psychological, is mediated. Not to the sensible facts
as such, then, did Hegel point for the secret of
what keeps existence going, but rather to the
conceptual way of treating them. Concepts
were not in his eyes the static self-contained
things that previous logicians had supposed,
but were germinative, and passed beyond themselves into each other by what he called their

immanent dialectic. In ignoring each other as they do, they virtually exclude and deny each other, he thought, and thus in a manner introduce each other. So the dialectic logic, according to him, had to supersede the 'logic of identity' in which, since Aristotle, all Europe had been brought up.

This view of concepts is Hegel's revolutionary performance; but so studiously vague and ambiguous are all his expressions of it that one can hardly tell whether it is the concepts as such, or the sensible experiences and elements conceived, that Hegel really means to work with. The only thing that is certain is that whatever you may say of his procedure, some one will accuse you of misunderstanding it. I make no claim to understanding it, I treat it merely impressionistically.

So treating it, I regret that he should have called it by the name of logic. Clinging as he did to the vision of a really living world, and refusing to be content with a chopped-up intellectualist picture of it, it is a pity that he should have adopted the very word that intel-

92

III. HEGEL AND HIS METHOD

lectualism had already pre-empted. But he clung fast to the old rationalist contempt for the immediately given world of sense and all its squalid particulars, and never tolerated the notion that the form of philosophy might be empirical only. His own system had to be a product of eternal reason, so the word 'logic,' with its suggestions of coercive necessity, was the only word he could find natural. He pretended therefore to be using the *a priori* method, and to be working by a scanty equipment of ancient logical terms — position, negation, reflection, universal, particular, individual, and the like. But what he really worked by was his own empirical perceptions, which exceeded and overflowed his miserably insufficient logical categories in every instance of their use.

What he did with the category of negation was his most original stroke. The orthodox opinion is that you can advance logically through the field of concepts only by going from the same to the same. Hegel felt deeply the sterility of this law of conceptual thought;

he saw that in a fashion negation also relates
things; and he had the brilliant idea of transcending the ordinary logic by treating advance
from the different to the different as if it were
also a necessity of thought. 'The so-called
maxim of identity,' he wrote, 'is supposed to
be accepted by the consciousness of every one.
But the language which such a law demands,
"a planet is a planet, magnetism is magnetism,
mind is mind," deserves to be called silliness.
No mind either speaks or thinks or forms conceptions in accordance with this law, and no
existence of any kind whatever conforms to it.
We must never view identity as abstract identity, to the exclusion of all difference. That is
the touchstone for distinguishing all bad philosophy from what alone deserves the name
of philosophy. If thinking were no more than
registering abstract identities, it would be a
most superfluous performance. Things and
concepts are identical with themselves only
in so far as at the same time they involve
distinction.' [1]

The distinction that Hegel has in mind here

superfluous ?

is naturally in the first instance distinction from all other things or concepts. But in his hands this quickly develops into contradiction of them, and finally, reflected back upon itself, into self-contradiction; and the immanent self-contradictoriness of all finite concepts thenceforth becomes the propulsive logical force that moves the world.[2] 'Isolate a thing from all its relations,' says Dr. Edward Caird,[3] expounding Hegel, 'and try to assert it by itself; you find that it has negated itself as well as its relations. The thing in itself is nothing.' Or, to quote Hegel's own words: 'When we suppose an existent A, and another, B, B is at first defined as the other. But A is just as much the other of B. Both are others in the same fashion. . . . " Other " is the other by itself, therefore the other of every other, consequently the other of itself, the simply unlike itself, the self-negator, the self-alterer,' etc.[4] Hegel writes elsewhere: 'The finite, as implicitly other than what it is, is forced to surrender its own immediate or natural being, and to turn suddenly into its opposite. . . . Dialectic is the universal

95

and irresistible power before which nothing can stay. . . . *Summum jus, summa injuria* — to drive an abstract right to excess is to commit injustice. . . . Extreme anarchy and extreme despotism lead to one another. Pride comes before a fall. Too much wit outwits itself. Joy brings tears, melancholy a sardonic smile.'[5] To which one well might add that most human institutions, by the purely technical and professional manner in which they come to be administered, end by becoming obstacles to the very purposes which their founders had in view.

Once catch well the knack of this scheme of thought and you are lucky if you ever get away from it. It is all you can see. Let any one pronounce anything, and your feeling of a contradiction being implied becomes a habit, almost a motor habit in some persons who symbolize by a stereotyped gesture the position, sublation, and final reinstatement involved. If you say 'two' or 'many,' your speech bewrayeth you, for the very name collects them into one. If you express doubt, your expression contradicts its content, for the doubt itself is not doubted but affirmed. If you say 'disorder,' what is that but a certain bad kind of order? if you say 'indetermination,' you are determining just *that*. If you say 'nothing but the unexpected happens,' the unexpected becomes what you expect. If you say 'all things are relative,' to what is the all of them itself relative? If you say 'no more,' you have said more already, by implying a region in which no more is found; to know a limit as such is consequently already to have got beyond it; and so forth, throughout as many examples as one cares to cite.

Whatever you posit appears thus as one-sided, and negates its other, which, being equally one-sided, negates *it;* and, since this situation remains unstable, the two contradictory terms have together, according to Hegel, to engender a higher truth of which they both appear as indispensable members, mutually mediating aspects of that higher concept or situation in thought.

Every higher total, however provisional and relative, thus reconciles the contradictions which its parts, abstracted from it, prove implicitly to contain. Rationalism, you remember, is what I called the way of thinking that methodically subordinates parts to wholes, so Hegel here is rationalistic through and through. The only whole by which *all* contradictions are reconciled is for him the absolute whole of wholes, the all-inclusive reason to which Hegel himself gave the name of the absolute Idea, but which I shall continue to call 'the absolute' purely and simply, as I have done hitherto.

Empirical instances of the way in which higher unities reconcile contradictions are innumerable, so here again Hegel's vision, taken merely impressionistically, agrees with countless facts. Somehow life does, out of its total resources, find ways of satisfying opposites at once. This is precisely the paradoxical aspect which much of our civilization presents. Peace we secure by armaments, liberty by laws and constitutions; simplicity and naturalness are the consummate result of artificial breeding and training; health, strength, and wealth are increased only by lavish use, expense, and wear.

Our mistrust of mistrust engenders our commercial system of credit; our tolerance of anarchistic and revolutionary utterances is the only way of lessening their danger; our charity has to say no to beggars in order not to defeat its own desires; the true epicurean has to observe great sobriety; the way to certainty lies through radical doubt; virtue signifies not innocence but the knowledge of sin and its overcoming; by obeying nature, we command her, etc. The ethical and the religious life are full of such contradictions held in solution. You hate your enemy? — well, forgive him, and thereby heap coals of fire on his head; to realize yourself, renounce yourself; to save your soul, first lose it; in short, die to live.

From such massive examples one easily generalizes Hegel's vision. Roughly, his 'dialectic' picture is a fair account of a good deal of the world. It sounds paradoxical, but whenever you once place yourself at the point of view of any higher synthesis, you see exactly how it does in a fashion take up opposites into itself. As an example, consider the conflict between

99

our carnivorous appetites and hunting instincts and the sympathy with animals which our refinement is bringing in its train. We have found how to reconcile these opposites most effectively by establishing game-laws and close seasons and by keeping domestic herds. The creatures preserved thus are preserved for the sake of slaughter, truly, but if not preserved for that reason, not one of them would be alive at all. Their will to live and our will to kill them thus harmoniously combine in this peculiar higher synthesis of domestication.

Merely as a reporter of certain empirical aspects of the actual, Hegel, then, is great and true. But he aimed at being something far greater than an empirical reporter, so I must say something about that essential aspect of his thought. Hegel was dominated by the notion of a truth that should prove incontrovertible, binding on every one, and certain, which should be *the* truth, one, indivisible, eternal, objective, and necessary, to which all our particular thinking must lead as to its consummation. This is the dogmatic ideal, the postulate, uncriticised, undoubted, and unchallenged, of all rationalizers in philosophy. '*I have never doubted*,' a recent Oxford writer says, that truth is universal and single and timeless, a single content or significance, one and whole and complete.⁶ Advance in thinking, in the hegelian universe, has, in short, to proceed by the apodictic words *must be* rather than by those inferior hypothetic words *may be*, which are all that empiricists can use.

Now Hegel found that his idea of an immanent movement through the field of concepts by way of 'dialectic' negation played most beautifully into the hands of this rationalistic demand for something absolute and *inconcussum* in the way of truth. It is easy to see how. If you affirm anything, for example that A is, and simply leave the matter thus, you leave it at the mercy of any one who may supervene and say 'not A, but B is.' If he does say so, your statement does n't refute him, it simply contradicts him, just as his contradicts you. The only way of making your affirmation about A *self-securing* is by getting it into a form which will by implication negate all possible negations in advance. The mere absence of negation is not enough; it must be present, but present with its fangs drawn. What you posit as A must already have cancelled the alternative or made it innocuous, by having negated it in advance. Double negation is the only form of affirmation that fully plays into the hands of the dogmatic ideal. Simply and innocently affirmative statements are good enough for empiricists, but unfit for rationalist use, lying open as they do to every accidental contradictor, and exposed to every puff of doubt. The *final* truth must be something to which there is no imaginable alternative, because it contains all its possible alternatives inside of itself as moments already taken account of and overcome. Whatever involves its own alternatives as elements of itself is, in a phrase often repeated, its 'own other,' made so by the *methode der absoluten negativität.*

Formally, this scheme of an organism of truth that has already fed as it were on its own liability to death, so that, death once dead for it,

there's no more dying then, is the very fulfilment of the rationalistic aspiration. That one
and only whole, with all its parts involved in it,
negating and making one another impossible if
abstracted and taken singly, but necessitating
and holding one another in place if the whole
of them be taken integrally, is the literal ideal
sought after; it is the very diagram and picture
of that notion of *the* truth with no outlying
alternative, to which nothing can be added, nor
from it anything withdrawn, and all variations
from which are absurd, which so dominates
the human imagination. Once we have taken
in the features of this diagram that so successfully solves the world-old problem, the older
ways of proving the necessity of judgments
cease to give us satisfaction. Hegel's way we
think must be the right way. The true must be
essentially the self-reflecting self-contained re-
current, that which secures itself by including
its own other and negating it; that makes a
spherical system with no loose ends hanging
out for foreignness to get a hold upon; that is
forever rounded in and closed, not strung along

rectilinearly and open at its ends like that universe of simply collective or additive form
which Hegel calls the world of the bad infinite,
and which is all that empiricism, starting with
simply posited single parts and elements, is
ever able to attain to.

No one can possibly deny the sublimity of
this hegelian conception. It is surely in the
grand style, if there be such a thing as a grand
style in philosophy. For us, however, it remains, so far, a merely formal and diagram-
matic conception; for with the actual content
of absolute truth, as Hegel materially tries to
set it forth, few disciples have been satisfied,
and I do not propose to refer at all to the concreter parts of his philosophy. The main thing
now is to grasp the generalized vision, and feel
the authority of the abstract scheme of a statement self-secured by involving double negation.
Absolutists who make no use of Hegel's own
technique are really working by his method.
You remember the proofs of the absolute
which I instanced in my last lecture, Lotze's
and Royce's proofs by *reductio ad absurdum*, to

the effect that any smallest connexion rashly supposed in things will logically work out into absolute union, and any minimal disconnexion into absolute disunion, —these are really arguments framed on the hegelian pattern. The truth is that which you implicitly affirm in the very attempt to deny it; it is that from which every variation refutes itself by proving self-contradictory. This is the supreme insight of rationalism, and to-day the best *must-be's* of rationalist argumentation are but so many attempts to communicate it to the hearer.

Thus, you see, my last lecture and this lecture make connexion again and we can consider Hegel and the other absolutists to be supporting the same system. The next point I wish to dwell on is the part played by what I have called vicious intellectualism in this wonderful system's structure.

Rationalism in general thinks it gets the fulness of truth by turning away from sensation to conception, conception obviously giving the more universal and immutable picture. Intellectualism in the vicious sense I have already defined as the habit of assuming that a concept *ex*cludes from any reality conceived by its means everything not included in the concept's definition. I called such intellectualism illegitimate as I found it used in Lotze's, Royce's, and Bradley's proofs of the absolute (which absolute I consequently held to be nonproven by their arguments), and I left off by asserting my own belief that a pluralistic and incompletely integrated universe, describable only by the free use of the word 'some,' is a legitimate hypothesis.

Now Hegel himself, in building up his method of double negation, offers the vividest possible example of this vice of intellectualism. Every idea of a finite thing is of course a concept of *that* thing and not a concept of anything else. But Hegel treats this not being a concept of anything else as if it were *equivalent to the concept of anything else not being*, or in other words as if it were a denial or negation of everything else. Then, as the other things, thus implicitly contradicted by the thing first conceived, also by the same law contradict *it*, the pulse of dialectic commences to beat and the famous triads begin to grind out the cosmos. If any one finds the process here to be a luminous one, he must be left to the illumination, he must remain an undisturbed hegelian. What others feel as the intolerable ambiguity, verbosity, and unscrupulousness of the master's way of deducing things, he will probably ascribe — since divine oracles are notoriously hard to interpret — to the 'difficulty' that habitually accompanies profundity. For my own part, there seems something grotesque and *saugrenu* in the pretension of a style so disobedient to the first rules of sound communication between minds, to be the authentic mother-tongue of reason, and to keep step more accurately than any other style does with the absolute's own ways of thinking. I do not therefore take Hegel's technical apparatus seriously at all. I regard him rather as one of those numerous original seers who can never learn how to articulate. His would-be coercive logic counts for nothing in my eyes; but that does not in the least impugn the philosophic importance of his conception of the absolute, if we take it merely hypothetically as one of the great types of cosmic vision.

Taken thus hypothetically, I wish to discuss it briefly. But before doing so I must call your attention to an odd peculiarity in the hegelian procedure. The peculiarity is one which will come before us again for a final judgment in my seventh lecture, so at present I only note it in passing. Hegel, you remember, considers that the immediate finite data of experience are 'untrue' because they are not their own others. They are negated by what is external to them. The absolute is true because it and it only has no external environment, and has attained to being its own other. (These words sound queer enough, but those of you who know something of Hegel's text will follow them.) Granting his premise that to be true a thing must in some sort be its own other, everything hinges on whether he is right in holding that the several pieces of finite experience themselves cannot be said to be in any wise *their* own others. When conceptually or intellectualistically treated, they of course cannot be their own others. Every abstract concept as such excludes what it does n't include, and if such concepts are adequate substitutes for reality's concrete pulses, the latter must square themselves with intellectualistic logic, and no one of them in any sense can claim to be its own other. If, however, the conceptual treatment of the flow of reality should prove for any good reason to be inadequate and to have a practical rather than a theoretical or speculative value, then an independent empirical look into the constitution of reality's pulses might possibly show that some of them *are* their own others, and indeed are so in the self-same sense in which the absolute is maintained to be so by Hegel. When we come to my sixth lecture, on Professor Bergson, I shall in effect defend this very view, strengthening my thesis by his authority. I am unwilling to say anything more about the point at this time, and what I have just said of it is only a sort of surveyor's note of where our present position lies in the general framework of these lectures.

Let us turn now at last to the great question

109

of fact, *Does the absolute exist or not?* to which all our previous discussion has been preliminary. I may sum up that discussion by saying that whether there really be an absolute or not, no one makes himself absurd or self-contradictory by doubting or denying it. The charges of self-contradiction, where they do not rest on purely verbal reasoning, rest on a vicious intellectualism. I will not recapitulate my criticisms. I will simply ask you to change the *venue,* and to discuss the absolute now as if it were only an open hypothesis. As such, is it more probable or more improbable?

But first of all I must parenthetically ask you to distinguish the notion of the absolute carefully from that of another object with which it is liable to become heedlessly entangled. That other object is the 'God' of common people in their religion, and the creator-God of orthodox christian theology. Only thoroughgoing monists or pantheists believe in the absolute. The God of our popular Christianity is but one member of a pluralistic system. He and we stand outside of each other, just as

the devil, the saints, and the angels stand outside of both of us. I can hardly conceive of
anything more different from the absolute than
the God, say, of David or of Isaiah. *That* God
is an essentially finite being *in* the cosmos, not
with the cosmos in him, and indeed he has a
very local habitation there, and very one-sided
local and personal attachments. If it should
prove probable that the absolute does not exist,
it will not follow in the slightest degree that a
God like that of David, Isaiah, or Jesus may
not exist, or may not be the most important existence in the universe for us to acknowledge.
I pray you, then, not to confound the two ideas
as you listen to the criticisms I shall have to
proffer. I hold to the finite God, for reasons
which I shall touch on in the seventh of these
lectures; but I hold that his rival and compet-
itor —I feel almost tempted to say his enemy
— the absolute, is not only not forced on us by
logic, but that it is an improbable hypothesis.

The great claim made for the absolute is that
by supposing it we make the world appear
more rational. Any hypothesis that does that

will always be accepted as more probably true than an hypothesis that makes the world appear irrational. Men are once for all so made that they prefer a rational world to believe in and to live in. But rationality has at least four dimensions, intellectual, æsthetical, moral, and practical; and to find a world rational to the maximal degree *in all these respects simultaneously* is no easy matter. Intellectually, the world of mechanical materialism is the most rational, for we subject its events to mathematical calculation. But the mechanical world is ugly, as arithmetic is ugly, and it is nonmoral. Morally, the theistic world is rational enough, but full of intellectual frustrations. The practical world of affairs, in its turn, so supremely rational to the politician, the military man, or the man of conquering business-faculty that he never would vote to change the type of it, is irrational to moral and artistic temperaments; so that whatever demand for rationality we find satisfied by a philosophic hypothesis, we are liable to find some other demand for rationality unsatisfied by the same hypothesis.

The rationality we gain in one coin we thus pay for in another; and the problem accordingly seems at first sight to resolve itself into that of getting a conception which will yield the largest *balance* of rationality rather than one which will yield perfect rationality of every description. In general, it may be said that if a man's conception of the world lets loose any action in him that is easy, or any faculty which he is fond of exercising, he will deem it rational in so far forth, be the faculty that of computing, fighting, lecturing, classifying, framing schematic tabulations, getting the better end of a bargain, patiently waiting and enduring, preaching, joke-making, or what you like. Albeit the absolute is defined as being necessarily an embodiment of objectively perfect rationality, it is fair to its english advocates to say that those who have espoused the hypothesis most concretely and seriously have usually avowed the irrationality to their own minds of certain elements in it.

Probably the weightiest contribution to our feeling of the rationality of the universe which

113

the notion of the absolute brings is the assur-
ance that however disturbed the surface may
be, at bottom all is well with the cosmos —
central peace abiding at the heart of endless
agitation. This conception is rational in many
ways, beautiful æsthetically, beautiful intellectually (could we only follow it into detail), and
beautiful morally, if the enjoyment of security
can be accounted moral. Practically it is less
beautiful; for, as we saw in our last lecture, in
representing the deepest reality of the world
as static and without a history, it loosens the
world's hold upon our sympathies and leaves
the soul of it foreign. Nevertheless it does give
peace, and that kind of rationality is so para-
mountly demanded by men that to the end of
time there will be absolutists, men who choose
belief in a static eternal, rather than admit that
the finite world of change and striving, even
with a God as one of the strivers, is itself eternal. For such minds Professor Royce's words
will always be the truest: ' The very presence
of ill in the temporal order is the condition of
the perfection of the eternal order. . . . We

long for the absolute only in so far as in us the absolute also longs, and seeks through our very temporal striving, the peace that is nowhere in time, but only, and yet absolutely, in eternity. Were there no longing in time there would be no peace in eternity. . . . God [*i. e.* the absolute] who here in me aims at what I now temporally miss, not only possesses in the eternal world the goal after which I strive, but comes to possess it even through and because of my sorrow. Through this my tribulation the absolute triumph then is won. . . . In the absolute I am fulfilled. Yet my very fulfilment demands and therefore can transcend this sorrow.'[7] Royce is particularly felicitous in his ability to cite parts of finite experience to which he finds his picture of this absolute experience analogous. But it is hard to portray the absolute at all without rising into what might be called the 'inspired' style of language — I use the word not ironically, but prosaically and descriptively, to designate the only literary form that goes with the kind of emotion that the absolute arouses. One can follow the pathway of reasoning soberly enough,[8] but the picture itself has to be effulgent. This admirable faculty of transcending, whilst inwardly preserving, every contrariety, is the absolute's characteristic form of rationality. We are but syllables in the mouth of the Lord; if the whole sentence is divine, each syllable is absolutely what it should be, in spite of all appearances. In making up the balance for or against absolutism, this emotional value weights heavily the credit side of the account.

The trouble is that we are able to see so little into the positive detail of it, and that if once admitted not to be coercively proven by the intellectualist arguments, it remains only a hypothetic possibility.

On the debit side of the account the absolute, taken seriously, and not as a mere name for our right occasionally to drop the strenuous mood and take a moral holiday, introduces all those tremendous irrationalities into the universe which a frankly pluralistic theism escapes, but which have been flung as a reproach at every form of monistic theism or pantheism.

It introduces a speculative 'problem of evil' namely, and leaves us wondering why the perfection of the absolute should require just such particular hideous forms of life as darken the day for our human imaginations. If they were forced on it by something alien, and to 'overcome' them the absolute had still to keep hold of them, we could understand its feeling of triumph, though we, so far as we were ourselves among the elements overcome, could acquiesce but sullenly in the resultant situation, and would never just have chosen it as the most rational one conceivable. But the absolute is represented as a being without environment, upon which nothing alien can be forced, and which has spontaneously chosen from within to give itself the spectacle of all that evil rather than a spectacle with less evil in it.[9] Its perfection is represented as the source of things, and yet the first effect of that perfection is the tremendous imperfection of all finite experience. In whatever sense the word 'rationality' may be taken, it is vain to contend that the impression made on our finite minds by such

117

a way of representing things is altogether
rational. Theologians have felt its irrationality acutely, and the 'fall,' the predestination,
and the election which the situation involves
have given them more trouble than anything
else in their attempt to pantheize Christianity.
The whole business remains a puzzle, both
intellectually and morally.

Grant that the spectacle or world-romance
offered to itself by the absolute is in the absolute's eyes perfect. Why would not the world
be more perfect by having the affair remain in
just those terms, and by not having any finite
spectators to come in and add to what was
perfect already their innumerable imperfect
manners of seeing the same spectacle? Suppose the entire universe to consist of one superb
copy of a book, fit for the ideal reader. Is
that universe improved or deteriorated by having myriads of garbled and misprinted separate
leaves and chapters also created, giving false
impressions of the book to whoever looks at
them? To say the least, the balance of rationality is not obviously in favor of such added

118

mutilations. So this question becomes urgent: Why, the absolute's own total vision of things being so rational, was it necessary to comminute it into all these coexisting inferior fragmentary visions?

Leibnitz in his theodicy represents God as limited by an antecedent reason in things which makes certain combinations logically incompatible, certain goods impossible. He surveys in advance all the universes he might create, and by an act of what Leibnitz calls his antecedent will he chooses our actual world as the one in which the evil, unhappily necessary anyhow, is at its minimum. It is the best of all the worlds that are possible, therefore, but by no means the most abstractly desirable world. Having made this mental choice, God next proceeds to what Leibnitz calls his act of consequent or decretory will: he says '*Fiat*' and the world selected springs into objective being, with all the finite creatures in it to suffer from its imperfections without sharing in its creator's atoning vision.

Lotze has made some penetrating remarks

119

on this conception of Leibnitz's, and they exactly fall in with what I say of the absolutist conception. The world projected out of the creative mind by the *fiat*, and existing in detachment from its author, is a sphere of being where the parts realize themselves only singly. If the divine value of them is evident only when they are collectively looked at, then, Lotze rightly says, the world surely becomes poorer and not richer for God's utterance of the *fiat*. He might much better have remained contented with his merely antecedent choice of the scheme, without following it up by a creative decree. The scheme *as such* was admirable; it could only lose by being translated into reality.[10] Why, I similarly ask, should the absolute ever have lapsed from the perfection of its own integral experience of things, and refracted itself into all our finite experiences?

It is but fair to recent english absolutists to say that many of them have confessed the imperfect rationality of the absolute from this point of view. Mr. McTaggart, for example, writes: 'Does not our very failure to perceive

the perfection of the universe destroy it ? . . .
In so far as we do not see the perfection of the
universe, we are not perfect ourselves. And as
we are parts of the universe, that cannot be
perfect.'[11]

And Mr. Joachim finds just the same difficulty. Calling the hypothesis of the absolute
by the name of the 'coherence theory of truth,'
he calls the problem of understanding how the
complete coherence of all things in the absolute
should involve as a necessary moment in its
self-maintenance the self-assertion of the finite
minds, a self-assertion which in its extreme
form is error, — he calls this problem, I say,
an insoluble puzzle. If truth be the universal
fons et origo, how does error slip in ? 'The coherence theory of truth,' he concludes, 'may
thus be said to suffer shipwreck at the very
entrance of the harbor.'[12] Yet in spite of this
rather bad form of irrationality, Mr. Joachim
stoutly asserts his 'immediate certainty'[13] of the
theory shipwrecked, the correctness of which
he says he has 'never doubted.' This candid confession of a fixed attitude of faith in

the absolute, which even one's own criticisms and perplexities fail to disturb, seems to me very significant. Not only empiricists, but absolutists also, would all, if they were as candid as this author, confess that the prime thing in their philosophy is their vision of a truth possible, which they then employ their reasoning to convert, as best it can, into a certainty or probability.

I can imagine a believer in the absolute retorting at this point that *he* at any rate is not dealing with mere probabilities, but that the nature of things logically requires the multitudinous erroneous copies, and that therefore the universe cannot be the absolute's book alone. For, he will ask, is not the absolute defined as the total consciousness of everything that is? Must not its field of view consist of parts? And what can the parts of a total consciousness be unless they be fractional consciousnesses? Our finite minds *must* therefore coexist with the absolute mind. We are its constituents, and it cannot live without us. — But if any one of you feels tempted to retort in this wise, let me remind you that you are frankly employing pluralistic weapons, and thereby giving up the absolutist cause. The notion that the absolute is made of constituents on which its being depends is the rankest empiricism. The absolute as such has *objects*, not constituents, and if the objects develop selfhoods upon their own several accounts, those selfhoods must be set down as facts additional to the absolute consciousness, and not as elements implicated in its definition. The absolute is a rationalist conception. Rationalism goes from wholes to parts, and always assumes wholes to be self-sufficing.[14]

My conclusion, so far, then, is this, that altho the hypothesis of the absolute, in yielding a certain kind of religious peace, performs a most important rationalizing function, it nevertheless, from the intellectual point of view, remains decidedly irrational. The *ideally* perfect whole is certainly that whole of which the *parts also are perfect*—if we can depend on logic for anything, we can depend on it for that definition. The absolute is defined as the ideally perfect whole, yet most of its parts, if not all, are admittedly imperfect. Evidently the conception lacks internal consistency, and yields us a problem rather than a solution. It creates a speculative puzzle, the so-called mystery of evil and of error, from which a pluralistic metaphysic is entirely free.

In any pluralistic metaphysic, the problems that evil presents are practical, not speculative. Not why evil should exist at all, but how we can lessen the actual amount of it, is the sole question we need there consider. 'God,' in the religious life of ordinary men, is the name not of the whole of things, heaven forbid, but only of the ideal tendency in things, believed in as a superhuman person who calls us to co-operate in his purposes, and who furthers ours if they are worthy. He works in an external environment, has limits, and has enemies. When John Mill said that the notion of God's omnipotence must be given up, if God is to be kept as a religious object, he was surely accurately right; yet so prevalent is the lazy monism that idly haunts the region of God's name, that so simple and truthful a saying was generally treated as a paradox: God, it was said, *could* not be finite. I believe that the only God worthy of the name *must* be finite, and I shall return to this point in a later lecture. If the absolute exist in addition — and the hypothesis must, in spite of its irrational features, still be left open — then the absolute is only the wider cosmic whole of which our God is but the most ideal portion, and which in the more usual human sense is hardly to be termed a religious hypothesis at all. 'Cosmic emotion' is the better name for the reaction it may awaken.

Observe that all the irrationalities and puzzles which the absolute gives rise to, and from which the finite God remains free, are due to the fact that the absolute has nothing, absolutely nothing, outside of itself. The finite God whom I contrast with it may conceivably have *almost* nothing outside of himself; he may already have triumphed over and absorbed all but the minutest fraction of the universe; but that fraction, however small, reduces him to the status of a relative being, and in principle the universe is saved from all the irrationalities incidental to absolutism. The only irrationality left would be the irrationality of which pluralism as such is accused, and of this I hope to say a word more later.

I have tired you with so many subtleties in this lecture that I will add only two other counts to my indictment.

First, then, let me remind you that *the absolute is useless for deductive purposes*. It gives us absolute safety if you will, but it is compatible with every relative danger. You cannot enter the phenomenal world with the notion of it in your grasp, and name beforehand any detail which you are likely to meet there. Whatever the details of experience may prove to be, *after the fact of them* the absolute will adopt them. It is an hypothesis that functions retrospectively only, not prospectively. *That*, whatever it may be, will have been in point of fact the sort of world which the absolute was pleased to offer to itself as a spectacle.

Again, the absolute is always represented

idealistically, as the all-knower. Thinking this
view consistently out leads one to frame an
almost ridiculous conception of the absolute
mind, owing to the enormous mass of unprofit-
able information which it would then seem
obliged to carry. One of the many *reductiones
ad absurdum* of pluralism by which idealism
thinks it proves the absolute One is as follows:
Let there be many facts; but since on idealist
principles facts exist only by being known, the
many facts will therefore mean many knowers.
But that there are so many knowers is itself
a fact, which in turn requires *its* knower, so
the one absolute knower has eventually to be
brought in. *All* facts lead to him. If it be a
fact that this table is not a chair, not a rhi-
noceros, not a logarithm, not a mile away from
the door, not worth five hundred pounds ster-
ling, not a thousand centuries old, the absolute must even now be articulately aware of all
these negations. Along with what everything
is it must also be conscious of everything which
it is not. This infinite atmosphere of explicit
negativity — observe that it has to be explicit —

around everything seems to us so useless an encumbrance as to make the absolute still more foreign to our sympathy. Furthermore, if it be a fact that certain ideas are silly, the absolute has to have already thought the silly ideas to establish them in silliness. The rubbish in its mind would thus appear easily to outweigh in amount the more desirable material. One would expect it fairly to burst with such an obesity, plethora, and superfœtation of useless information.[15]

I will spare you further objections. The sum of it all is that the absolute is not forced on our belief by logic, that it involves features of irrationality peculiar to itself, and that a thinker to whom it does not come as an 'immediate certainty' (to use Mr. Joachim's words), is in no way bound to treat it as anything but an emotionally rather sublime hypothesis. As such, it might, with all its defects, be, on account of its peace-conferring power and its formal grandeur, more rational than anything else in the field. But meanwhile the strung-along unfinished world in time is its rival: *reality MAY exist in distributive form, in the shape not of an all but of a set of eaches, just as it seems to* — this is the anti-absolutist hypothesis. *Prima facie* there is this in favor of the eaches, that they are at any rate real enough to have made themselves at least *appear* to every one, whereas the absolute has as yet appeared immediately to only a few mystics, and indeed to them very ambiguously. The advocates of the absolute assure us that any distributive form of being is infected and undermined by self-contradiction. If we are unable to assimilate their arguments, and we have been unable, the only course we can take, it seems to me, is to let the absolute bury the absolute, and to seek reality in more promising directions, even among the details of the finite and the immediately given.

If these words of mine sound in bad taste to some of you, or even sacrilegious, I am sorry. Perhaps the impression may be mitigated by what I have to say in later lectures.

IV

CONCERNING FECHNER

LECTURE IV

CONCERNING FECHNER

THE prestige of the absolute has rather crumbled in our hands. The logical proofs of it miss fire; the portraits which its best court-painters show of it are featureless and foggy in the extreme; and, apart from the cold comfort of assuring us that with *it* all is well, and that to see that all is well with us also we need only rise to its eternal point of view, it yields us no relief whatever. It introduces, on the contrary, into philosophy and theology certain poisonous difficulties of which but for its intrusion we never should have heard.

But if we drop the absolute out of the world, must we then conclude that the world contains nothing better in the way of consciousness than our consciousness? Is our whole instinctive belief in higher presences, our persistent inner turning towards divine companionship, to count for nothing? Is it but the pathetic illusion of beings with incorrigibly social and imaginative minds?

Such a negative conclusion would, I believe, be desperately hasty, a sort of pouring out of the child with the bath. Logically it is possible to believe in superhuman beings without identifying them with the absolute at all. The treaty of offensive and defensive alliance which certain groups of the christian clergy have recently made with our transcendentalist philosophers seems to me to be based on a well-meaning but baleful mistake. Neither the Jehovah of the old testament nor the heavenly father of the new has anything in common with the absolute except that they are all three greater than man; and if you say that the notion of the absolute is what the gods of Abraham, of David, and of Jesus, after first developing into each other, were inevitably destined to develop into in more reflective and modern minds, I reply that although in certain specifically philosophical minds this may have been the case, in minds more properly to be termed religious the development has followed quite another path. The whole history of evangelical Christianity is there to prove it. I propose in these lectures to plead for that other line of development. To set the doctrine of the absolute in its proper framework, so that it shall not fill the whole welkin and exclude all alternative possibilities of higher thought — as it seems to do for many students who approach it with a limited previous acquaintance with philosophy —I will contrast it with a system which, abstractly considered, seems at first to have much in common with absolutism, but which, when taken concretely and temperamentally, really stands at the opposite pole. I refer to the philosophy of Gustav Theodor Fechner, a writer but little known as yet to English readers, but destined, I am persuaded, to wield more and more influence as time goes on.

It is the intense concreteness of Fechner, his fertility of detail, which fills me with an admiration which I should like to make this audience share. Among the philosophic cranks of my acquaintance in the past was a lady all the tenets of whose system I have forgotten except one. Had she been born in the Ionian Archipelago some three thousand years ago, that one doctrine would probably have made her name sure of a place in every university curriculum and examination paper. The world, she said, is composed of only two elements, the Thick, namely, and the Thin. No one can deny the truth of this analysis, as far as it goes (though in the light of our contemporary knowledge of nature it has itself a rather 'thin' sound), and it is nowhere truer than in that part of the world called philosophy. I am sure, for example, that many of you, listening to what poor account I have been able to give of transcendental idealism, have received an impression of its arguments being strangely thin, and of the terms it leaves us with being shiveringly thin wrappings for so thick and burly a world as this. Some of you of course will charge the thinness to my exposition; but thin as that has been, I believe the doctrines reported on to have been thinner. From Green to Haldane the absolute proposed to us to straighten out the confusions of the thicket of experience in which our life is passed remains a pure abstraction which hardly any one tries to make a whit concreter. If we open

Green, we get nothing but the transcendental ego of apperception (Kant's name for the fact that to be counted in experience a thing has to be witnessed), blown up into a sort of timeless soap-bubble large enough to mirror the whole universe. Nature, Green keeps insisting, consists only in relations, and these imply the action of a mind that is eternal; a self-distinguishing consciousness which itself escapes from the relations by which it determines other things. Present to whatever is in succession, it is not in succession itself. If we take the Cairds, they tell us little more of the principle of the universe — it is always a return into the identity of the self from the difference of its objects. It separates itself from them and so becomes conscious of them in their separation from one another, while at the same time it binds them together as elements in one higher self-consciousness.

This seems the very quintessence of thinness; and the matter hardly grows thicker when we gather, after enormous amounts of reading, that the great enveloping self in question is absolute reason as such, and that as such it is characterized by the habit of using certain jejune 'categories' with which to perform its eminent relating work. The whole active material of natural fact is tried out, and only the barest intellectualistic formalism remains.

Hegel tried, as we saw, to make the system concreter by making the relations between things 'dialectic,' but if we turn to those who use his name most worshipfully, we find them giving up all the particulars of his attempt, and simply praising his intention — much as in our manner we have praised it ourselves. Mr. Haldane, for example, in his wonderfully clever Gifford lectures, praises Hegel to the skies, but what he tells of him amounts to little more than this, that 'the categories in which the mind arranges its experiences, and gives meaning to them, the universals in which the particulars are grasped in the individual, are a logical chain, in which the first presupposes the last, and the last is its presupposition and its truth.' He hardly tries at all to thicken this thin logical scheme. He says indeed that absolute mind in

itself, and absolute mind in its hetereity or otherness, under the distinction which it sets up of
itself from itself, have as their real *prius* absolute mind in synthesis; and, this being absolute
mind's true nature, its dialectic character must
show itself in such concrete forms as Goethe's
and Wordsworth's poetry, as well as in religious
forms. 'The nature of God, the nature of absolute mind, is to exhibit the triple movement
of dialectic, and so the nature of God as presented in religion must be a triplicity, a trinity.'
But beyond thus naming Goethe and Wordsworth and establishing the trinity, Mr. Haldane's Hegelianism carries us hardly an inch
into the concrete detail of the world we actually
inhabit.

Equally thin is Mr. Taylor, both in his principles and in their results. Following Mr. Bradley, he starts by assuring us that reality cannot
be self-contradictory, but to be related to anything really outside of one's self is to be self-
contradictory, so the ultimate reality must be
a single all-inclusive systematic whole. Yet all
he can say of this whole at the end of his excel-

lently written book is that the notion of it 'can make no addition to our information and can of itself supply no motives for practical endeavor.'

Mr. McTaggart treats us to almost as thin a fare. 'The main practical interest of Hegel's philosophy,' he says, 'is to be found in the abstract certainty which the logic gives us that all reality is rational and righteous, even when we cannot see in the least how it is so. . . . Not that it shows us how the facts around us are good, not that it shows us how we can make them better, but that it proves that they, like other reality, are *sub specie eternitatis*, perfectly good, and *sub specie temporis*, destined to become perfectly good.'

Here again, no detail whatever, only the abstract certainty that whatever the detail may prove to be, it will be good. Common non-dialectical men have already this certainty as a result of the generous vital enthusiasm about the universe with which they are born. The peculiarity of transcendental philosophy is its sovereign contempt for merely vital functions like enthusiasm, and its pretension to turn our simple and immediate trusts and faiths into the form of logically mediated certainties, to question which would be absurd. But the whole basis on which Mr. McTaggart's own certainty so solidly rests, settles down into the one nutshell of an assertion into which he puts Hegel's gospel, namely, that in every bit of experience and thought, however finite, the whole of reality (the absolute idea, as Hegel calls it) is 'implicitly present.'

This indeed is Hegel's *vision*, and Hegel thought that the details of his dialectic proved its truth. But disciples who treat the details of the proof as unsatisfactory and yet cling to the vision, are surely, in spite of their pretension to a more rational consciousness, no better than common men with their enthusiasms or deliberately adopted faiths. We have ourselves seen some of the weakness of the monistic proofs. Mr. McTaggart picks plenty of holes of his own in Hegel's logic, and finally concludes that 'all true philosophy must be mystical, not indeed in its methods but in its final conclusions,'

which is as much as to say that the rationalistic
methods leave us in the lurch, in spite of all
their superiority, and that in the end vision
and faith must eke them out. But how abstract
and thin is here the vision, to say nothing of the
faith! The whole of reality, explicitly absent
from our finite experiences, must nevertheless
be present in them all implicitly, altho no one
of us can ever see how — the bare word 'implicit' here bearing the whole pyramid of the
monistic system on its slender point. Mr. Joachim's monistic system of truth rests on an even
slenderer point.—'*I have never doubted,*' he
says, 'that universal and timeless truth is a
single content or significance, one and whole
and complete,' and he candidly confesses the
failure of rationalistic attempts 'to raise this
immediate certainty' to the level of reflective
knowledge. There is, in short, no mediation
for him between the Truth in capital letters
and all the little 'lower-case' truths — and
errors — which life presents. The psychological fact that he never has 'doubted' is enough.

The whole monistic pyramid, resting on

points as thin as these, seems to me to be a *machtspruch*, a product of will far more than one of reason. Unity is good, therefore things *shall* cohere; they *shall* be one; there *shall* be categories to make them one, no matter what empirical disjunctions may appear. In Hegel's own writings, the *shall-be* temper is ubiquitous and towering; it overrides verbal and logical resistances alike. Hegel's error, as Professor Royce so well says, 'lay not in introducing logic into passion,' as some people charge, 'but in conceiving the logic of passion as the only logic. . . . He is [thus] suggestive,' Royce says, 'but never final. His system as a system has crumbled, but his vital comprehension of our life remains forever.'[1]

That vital comprehension we have already seen. It is that there is a sense in which real things are not merely their own bare selves, but may vaguely be treated as also their own others, and that ordinary logic, since it denies this, must be overcome. Ordinary logic denies this because it substitutes concepts for real things, and concepts *are* their own bare selves and

143

nothing else. What Royce calls Hegel's 'system' was Hegel's attempt to make us believe that he was working by concepts and grinding out a higher style of logic, when in reality sensible experiences, hypotheses, and passion furnished him with all his results.

What I myself may mean by things being their own others, we shall see in a later lecture. It is now time to take our look at Fechner, whose thickness is a refreshing contrast to the thin, abstract, indigent, and threadbare appearance, the starving, school-room aspect, which the speculations of most of our absolutist philosophers present.

There is something really weird and uncanny in the contrast between the abstract pretensions of rationalism and what rationalistic methods concretely can do. If the 'logical prius' of our mind were really the 'implicit presence' of the whole 'concrete universal,' the whole of reason, or reality, or spirit, or the absolute idea, or whatever it may be called, in all our finite thinking, and if this reason worked (for example) by the dialectical method, does n't it seem odd that in the greatest instance of rationalization mankind has known, in 'science,' namely, the dialectical method should never once have been tried? Not a solitary instance of the use of it in science occurs to my mind. Hypotheses, and deductions from these, controlled by sense-observations and analogies with what we know elsewhere, are to be thanked for all of science's results.

Fechner used no methods but these latter ones in arguing for his metaphysical conclusions about reality — but let me first rehearse a few of the facts about his life.

Born in 1801, the son of a poor country pastor in Saxony, he lived from 1817 to 1887, when he died, seventy years therefore, at Leipzig, a typical *gelehrter* of the old-fashioned german stripe. His means were always scanty, so his only extravagances could be in the way of thought, but these were gorgeous ones. He passed his medical examinations at Leipzig University at the age of twenty-one, but decided, instead of becoming a doctor, to devote himself to physical science. It was ten years before he was made professor of physics, although he soon was authorized to lecture. Meanwhile, he had to make both ends meet, and this he did by voluminous literary labors. He translated, for example, the four volumes of Biot's treatise on physics, and the six of Thénard's work on chemistry, and took care of their enlarged editions later. He edited repertories of chemistry and physics, a pharmaceutical journal, and an encyclopædia in eight volumes, of which he wrote about one third. He published physical treatises and experimental investigations of his own, especially in electricity. Electrical measurements, as you know, are the basis of electrical science, and Fechner's measurements in galvanism, performed with the simplest self-made apparatus, are classic to this day. During this time he also published a number of half-philosophical, half-humorous writings, which have gone through several editions, under the name of Dr. Mises, besides poems, literary and artistic essays, and other occasional articles.

But overwork, poverty, and an eye-trouble
produced by his observations on after-images
in the retina (also a classic piece of investiga-
tion) produced in Fechner, then about thirty-
eight years old, a terrific attack of nervous
prostration with painful hyperæsthesia of all
the functions, from which he suffered three
years, cut off entirely from active life. Present-
day medicine would have classed poor Fechner's malady quickly enough, as partly a habit-
neurosis, but its severity was such that in his
day it was treated as a visitation incomprehen-
sible in its malignity; and when he suddenly
began to get well, both Fechner and others
treated the recovery as a sort of divine miracle.
This illness, bringing Fechner face to face with
inner desperation, made a great crisis in his
life. 'Had I not then clung to the faith,' he
writes, 'that clinging to faith would somehow
or other work its reward, *so hätte ich jene zeit
nicht ausgehalten.*' His religious and cosmo-
logical faiths saved him — thenceforward one
great aim with him was to work out and communicate these faiths to the world. He did so

on the largest scale; but he did many other things too ere he died.

A book on the atomic theory, classic also; four elaborate mathematical and experimental volumes on what he called psychophysics — many persons consider Fechner to have practically founded scientific psychology in the first of these books; a volume on organic evolution, and two works on experimental æsthetics, in which again Fechner is considered by some judges to have laid the foundations of a new science, must be included among these other performances. Of the more religious and philosophical works, I shall immediately give a further account.

All Leipzig mourned him when he died, for he was the pattern of the ideal german scholar, as daringly original in his thought as he was homely in his life, a modest, genial, laborious slave to truth and learning, and withal the owner of an admirable literary style of the vernacular sort. The materialistic generation, that in the fifties and sixties called his speculations fantastic, had been replaced by one with greater liberty of imagination, and a Preyer, a Wundt, a Paulsen, and a Lasswitz could now speak of Fechner as their master.

His mind was indeed one of those multitudinously organized cross-roads of truth which are occupied only at rare intervals by children of men, and from which nothing is either too far or too near to be seen in due perspective. Patientest observation, exactest mathematics, shrewdest discrimination, humanest feeling, flourished in him on the largest scale, with no apparent detriment to one another. He was in fact a philosopher in the 'great' sense, altho he cared so much less than most philosophers care for abstractions of the 'thin' order. For him the abstract lived in the concrete, and the hidden motive of all he did was to bring what he called the daylight view of the world into ever greater evidence, that daylight view being this, that the whole universe in its different spans and wave-lengths, exclusions and envelopments, is everywhere alive and conscious. It has taken fifty years for his chief book, 'Zend-avesta,' to pass into a sec-

ond edition (1901). 'One swallow,' he cheer-
fully writes, 'does not make a summer. But
the first swallow would not come unless the
summer were coming; and for me that summer
means my daylight view some time prevailing.'

The original sin, according to Fechner, of
both our popular and our scientific thinking, is
our inveterate habit of regarding the spiritual
not as the rule but as an exception in the midst
of nature. Instead of believing our life to be
fed at the breasts of the greater life, our individuality to be sustained by the greater individuality, which must necessarily have more consciousness and more independence than all
that it brings forth, we habitually treat whatever lies outside of our life as so much slag
and ashes of life only; or if we believe in a
Divine Spirit, we fancy him on the one side as
bodiless, and nature as soulless on the other.
What comfort, or peace, Fechner asks, can come
from such a doctrine? The flowers wither at
its breath, the stars turn into stone; our own
body grows unworthy of our spirit and sinks to
a tenement for carnal senses only. The book

of nature turns into a volume on mechanics, in which whatever has life is treated as a sort of anomaly; a great chasm of separation yawns between us and all that is higher than ourselves; and God becomes a thin nest of abstractions.

Fechner's great instrument for vivifying the daylight view is analogy; not a rationalistic argument is to be found in all his many pages — only reasonings like those which men continually use in practical life. For example: My house is built by some one, the world too is built by some one. The world is greater than my house, it must be a greater some one who built the world. My body moves by the influence of my feeling and will; the sun, moon, sea, and wind, being themselves more powerful, move by the influence of some more powerful feeling and will. I live now, and change from one day to another; I shall live hereafter, and change still more, etc.

Bain defines genius as the power of seeing analogies. The number that Fechner could perceive was prodigious; but he insisted on the differences as well. Neglect to make allowance for these, he said, is the common fallacy in analogical reasoning. Most of us, for example, reasoning justly that, since all the minds we know are connected with bodies, therefore God's mind should be connected with a body, proceed to suppose that that body must be just an animal body over again, and paint an altogether human picture of God. But all that the analogy comports is *a* body — the particular features of *our* body are adaptations to a habitat so different from God's that if God have a physical body at all, it must be utterly different from ours in structure. Throughout his writings Fechner makes difference and analogy walk abreast, and by his extraordinary power of noticing both, he converts what would ordinarily pass for objections to his conclusions into factors of their support.

The vaster orders of mind go with the vaster orders of body. The entire earth on which we live must have, according to Fechner, its own collective consciousness. So must each sun, moon, and planet; so must the whole solar system have its own wider consciousness, in which the consciousness of our earth plays one part. So has the entire starry system as such its consciousness; and if that starry system be not the sum of all that *is*, materially considered, then that whole system, along with whatever else may be, is the body of that absolutely totalized consciousness of the universe to which men give the name of God.

Speculatively Fechner is thus a monist in his theology; but there is room in his universe for every grade of spiritual being between man and the final all-inclusive God; and in suggesting what the positive content of all this super-humanity may be, he hardly lets his imagination fly beyond simple spirits of the planetary order. The earth-soul he passionately believes in; he treats the earth as our special human guardian angel; we can pray to the earth as men pray to their saints; but I think that in his system, as in so many of the actual historic theologies, the supreme God marks only a sort of limit of enclosure of the worlds above man. He is left thin and abstract in his majesty, men preferring to carry on their personal transactions with the many less remote and abstract messengers and mediators whom the divine order provides.

I shall ask later whether the abstractly monistic turn which Fechner's speculations took was necessitated by logic. I believe it not to have been required. Meanwhile let me lead you a little more into the detail of his thought. Inevitably one does him miserable injustice by summarizing and abridging him. For altho the type of reasoning he employs is almost childlike for simplicity, and his bare conclusions can be written on a single page, the *power* of the man is due altogether to the profuseness of his concrete imagination, to the multitude of the points which he considers successively, to the cumulative effect of his learning, of his thoroughness, and of the ingenuity of his detail, to his admirably homely style, to the sincerity with which his pages glow, and finally to the impression he gives of a man who doesn't live at second-hand, but who *sees*, who in fact speaks as one having authority, and not as if he were

one of the common herd of professorial philosophic scribes.

Abstractly set down, his most important
conclusion for my purpose in these lectures is
that the constitution of the world is identical
throughout. In ourselves, visual consciousness
goes with our eyes, tactile consciousness with
our skin. But altho neither skin nor eye knows
aught of the sensations of the other, they come
together and figure in some sort of relation and
combination in the more inclusive consciousness which each of us names his *self*. Quite
similarly, then, says Fechner, we must suppose
that my consciousness of myself and yours of
yourself, altho in their immediacy they keep
separate and know nothing of each other, are
yet known and used together in a higher consciousness, that of the human race, say, into
which they enter as constituent parts. Similarly, the whole human and animal kingdoms
come together as conditions of a consciousness of still wider scope. This combines in the
soul of the earth with the consciousness of the
vegetable kingdom, which in turn contributes

its share of experience to that of the whole solar system, and so on from synthesis to synthesis and height to height, till an absolutely universal consciousness is reached.

A vast analogical series, in which the basis of the analogy consists of facts directly observable in ourselves.

The supposition of an earth-consciousness meets a strong instinctive prejudice which Fechner ingeniously tries to overcome. Man's mind is the highest consciousness upon the earth, we think — the earth itself being in all ways man's inferior. How should its consciousness, if it have one, be superior to his?

What are the marks of superiority which we are tempted to use here? If we look more carefully into them, Fechner points out that the earth possesses each and all of them more perfectly than we. He considers in detail the points of difference between us, and shows them all to make for the earth's higher rank. I will touch on only a few of these points.

One of them of course is independence of other external beings. External to the earth are only the other heavenly bodies. All the things on which we externally depend for life —air, water, plant and animal food, fellow men, etc. — are included in her as her constituent parts. She is self-sufficing in a million respects in which we are not so. We depend on her for almost everything, she on us for but a small portion of her history. She swings us in her orbit from winter to summer and revolves us from day into night and from night into day.

Complexity in unity is another sign of superiority. The total earth's complexity far exceeds that of any organism, for she includes all our organisms in herself, along with an infinite number of things that our organisms fail to include. Yet how simple and massive are the phases of her own proper life! As the total bearing of any animal is sedate and tranquil compared with the agitation of its blood corpuscles, so is the earth a sedate and tranquil being compared with the animals whom she supports.

To develop from within, instead of being fashioned from without, is also counted as something superior in men's eyes. An egg is a higher style of being than a piece of clay which an external modeler makes into the image of a bird. Well, the earth's history develops from within. It is like that of a wonderful egg which the sun's heat, like that of a mother-hen, has stimulated to its cycles of evolutionary change.

Individuality of type, and difference from other beings of its type, is another mark of rank. The earth differs from every other planet, and as a class planetary beings are extraordinarily distinct from other beings.

Long ago the earth was called an animal; but a planet is a higher class of being than either man or animal; not only quantitatively greater, like a vaster and more awkward whale or elephant, but a being whose enormous size requires an altogether different plan of life. Our animal organization comes from our inferiority. Our need of moving to and fro, of stretching our limbs and bending our bodies, shows only our defect. What are our legs but crutches, by means of which, with restless efforts, we go hunting after the things we have not inside of ourselves. But the earth is no such cripple; why should she who already possesses within herself the things we so painfully pursue, have limbs analogous to ours? Shall she mimic a small part of herself? What need has she of arms, with nothing to reach for? of a neck, with no head to carry? of eyes or nose when she finds her way through space without either, and has the millions of eyes of all her animals to guide their movements on her surface, and all their noses to smell the flowers that grow? For, as we are ourselves a part of the earth, so our organs are her organs. She is, as it were, eye and ear over her whole extent — all that we see and hear in separation she sees and hears at once. She brings forth living beings of countless kinds upon her surface, and their multitudinous conscious relations with each other she takes up into her higher and more general conscious life.

Most of us, considering the theory that the whole terrestrial mass is animated as our bodies are, make the mistake of working the analogy too literally, and allowing for no differences. If the earth be a sentient organism, we say, where are her brain and nerves ? What corresponds to her heart and lungs ? In other words, we expect functions which she already performs through us, to be performed outside of us again, and in just the same way. But we see perfectly well how the earth performs some of these functions in a way unlike our way. If you speak of circulation, what need has she of a heart when the sun keeps all the showers of rain that fall upon her and all the springs and brooks and rivers that irrigate her, going ? What need has she of internal lungs, when her whole sensitive surface is in living commerce with the atmosphere that clings to it ?

The organ that gives us most trouble is the brain. All the consciousness we directly know seems tied to brains. — Can there be consciousness, we ask, where there is no brain ? But our brain, which primarily serves to correlate our muscular reactions with the external objects on which we depend, performs a function which the earth performs in an entirely different way. She has no proper muscles or limbs of her own, and the only objects external to her are the other stars. To these her whole mass reacts by most exquisite alterations in its total gait, and by still more exquisite vibratory responses in its substance. Her ocean reflects the lights of heaven as in a mighty mirror, her atmosphere refracts them like a monstrous lens, the clouds and snow-fields combine them into white, the woods and flowers disperse them into colors. Polarization, interference, absorption, awaken sensibilities in matter of which our senses are too coarse to take any note.

For these cosmic relations of hers, then, she no more needs a special brain than she needs eyes or ears. *Our* brains do indeed unify and correlate innumerable functions. Our eyes know nothing of sound, our ears nothing of light, but, having brains, we can feel sound and light together, and compare them. We account for this by the fibres which in the brain connect the optical with the acoustic centre, but just how these fibres bring together not only the sensations, but the centres, we fail to see. But if fibres are indeed all that is needed to do that trick, has not the earth pathways, by which you and I are physically continuous, more than enough to do for our two minds what the brain-fibres do for the sounds and sights in a single mind? Must every higher means of unification between things be a literal *brain*-fibre, and go by that name? Cannot the earth-mind know otherwise the contents of our minds together?

Fechner's imagination, insisting on the differences as well as on the resemblances, thus tries to make our picture of the whole earth's life more concrete. He revels in the thought of its perfections. To carry her precious freight through the hours and seasons what form could be more excellent than hers — being as it is horse, wheels, and wagon all in one. Think of her beauty — a shining ball, sky-blue and sun-lit over one half, the other bathed in starry night, reflecting the heavens from all her waters, myriads of lights and shadows in the folds of her mountains and windings of her valleys, she would be a spectacle of rainbow glory, could one only see her from afar as we see parts of her from her own mountain-tops. Every quality of landscape that has a name would then be visible in her at once—all that is delicate or graceful, all that is quiet, or wild, or romantic, or desolate, or cheerful, or luxuriant, or fresh. That landscape is her face — a peopled landscape, too, for men's eyes would appear in it like diamonds among the dewdrops. Green would be the dominant color, but the blue atmosphere and the clouds would enfold her as a bride is shrouded in her veil — a veil the vapory transparent folds of which the earth, through her ministers the winds, never tires of laying and folding about herself anew.

Every element has its own living denizens. Can the celestial ocean of ether, whose waves are light, in which the earth herself floats, not have hers, higher by as much as their element is higher, swimming without fins, flying without wings, moving, immense and tranquil, as by a half-spiritual force through the half-spiritual sea which they inhabit, rejoicing in the exchange of luminous influence with one another, following the slightest pull of one another's attraction, and harboring, each of them, an inexhaustible inward wealth?

Men have always made fables about angels, dwelling in the light, needing no earthly food or drink, messengers between ourselves and God. Here are actually existent beings, dwelling in the light and moving through the sky, needing neither food nor drink, intermediaries between God and us, obeying his commands. So, if the heavens really are the home of angels, the heavenly bodies must be those very angels, for other creatures *there* are none. Yes! the earth is our great common guardian angel, who watches over all our interests combined.

In a striking page Fechner relates one of his moments of direct vision of this truth.

'On a certain spring morning I went out to walk. The fields were green, the birds sang, the dew glistened, the smoke was rising, here and there a man appeared; a light as of transfiguration lay on all things. It was only a little bit of the earth; it was only one moment of her existence; and yet as my look embraced her more and more it seemed to me not only so beautiful an idea, but so true and clear a fact, that she is an angel, an angel so rich and fresh and flower-like, and yet going her round in the skies so firmly and so at one with herself, turning her whole living face to Heaven, and carrying me along with her into that Heaven, that I asked myself how the opinions of men could ever have so spun themselves away from life so far as to deem the earth only a dry clod, and to seek for angels above it or about it in the emptiness of the sky, — only to find them nowhere. . . . But such an experience as this passes for fantastic. The earth is a globular body, and what more she may be, one can find in mineralogical cabinets.'[2]

Where there is no vision the people perish. Few professorial philosophers have any vision. Fechner had vision, and that is why one can read him over and over again, and each time bring away a fresh sense of reality.

His earliest book was a vision of what the inner life of plants may be like. He called it 'Nanna.' In the development of animals the nervous system is the central fact. Plants develop centrifugally, spread their organs abroad. For that reason people suppose that they can have no consciousness, for they lack the unity which the central nervous system provides. But the plant's consciousness may be of another type, being connected with other structures. Violins and pianos give out sounds because they have strings. Does it follow that nothing but strings can give out sound? How then about flutes and organ-pipes? Of course their sounds are of a different quality, and so may the consciousness of plants be of a quality correlated exclusively with the kind of organization that they possess. Nutrition, respiration, propagation take place in them without nerves. In us these functions are conscious only in unusual states, normally their consciousness is eclipsed by that which goes with the brain. No such eclipse occurs in plants, and their lower consciousness may therefore be all the more lively. With nothing to do but to drink the light and air with their leaves, to let their cells proliferate, to feel their rootlets draw the sap, is it conceiv-

able that they should not consciously suffer if
water, light, and air are suddenly withdrawn?
or that when the flowering and fertilization
which are the culmination of their life take
place, they should not feel their own existence
more intensely and enjoy something like what
we call pleasure in ourselves? Does the water-
lily, rocking in her triple bath of water, air, and
light, relish in no wise her own beauty? When
the plant in our room turns to the light, closes
her blossoms in the dark, responds to our wa-
tering or pruning by increase of size or change
of shape and bloom, who has the right to say
she does not feel, or that she plays a purely passive part? Truly plants can foresee nothing,
neither the scythe of the mower, nor the hand
extended to pluck their flowers. They can
neither run away nor cry out. But this only
proves how different their modes of feeling
life must be from those of animals that live
by eyes and ears and locomotive organs, it does
not prove that they have no mode of feeling
life at all.

How scanty and scattered would sensation

167

be on our globe, if the feeling-life of plants were blotted from existence. Solitary would consciousness move through the woods in the shape of some deer or other quadruped, or fly about the flowers in that of some insect, but can we really suppose that the Nature through which God's breath blows is such a barren wilderness as this?

I have probably by this time said enough to acquaint those of you who have never seen these metaphysical writings of Fechner with their more general characteristics, and I hope that some of you may now feel like reading them yourselves.[3] The special thought of Fechner's with which in these lectures I have most practical concern, is his belief that the more inclusive forms of consciousness are in part *constituted* by the more limited forms. Not that they are the mere sum of the more limited forms. As our mind is not the bare sum of our sights plus our sounds plus our pains, but in adding these terms together also finds relations among them and weaves them into schemes and forms and objects of which no one

168

sense in its separate estate knows anything, so the earth-soul traces relations between the contents of my mind and the contents of yours of which neither of our separate minds is conscious. It has schemes, forms, and objects proportionate to its wider field, which our mental fields are far too narrow to cognize. By ourselves we are simply out of relation with each other, for it we are both of us there, and *different* from each other, which is a positive relation. What we are without knowing, it knows that we are. We are closed against its world, but that world is not closed against us. It is as if the total universe of inner life had a sort of grain or direction, a sort of valvular structure, permitting knowledge to flow in one way only, so that the wider might always have the narrower under observation, but never the narrower the wider.

Fechner's great analogy here is the relation of the senses to our individual minds. When our eyes are open their sensations enter into our general mental life, which grows incessantly by the addition of what they see. Close

the eyes, however, and the visual additions
stop, nothing but thoughts and memories of
the past visual experiences remain — in combination of course with the enormous stock of
other thoughts and memories, and with the
data coming in from the senses not yet closed.
Our eye-sensations of themselves know nothing of this enormous life into which they fall.
Fechner thinks, as any common man would
think, that they are taken into it directly when
they occur, and form part of it just as they are.
They don't stay outside and get represented
inside by their copies. It is only the memories and concepts of them that are copies;
the sensible perceptions themselves are taken
in or walled out in their own proper persons
according as the eyes are open or shut.

Fechner likens our individual persons on
the earth unto so many sense-organs of the
earth's soul. We add to its perceptive life so
long as our own life lasts. It absorbs our perceptions, just as they occur, into its larger
sphere of knowledge, and combines them with
the other data there. When one of us dies, it

is as if an eye of the world were closed, for all *perceptive* contributions from that particular quarter cease. But the memories and conceptual relations that have spun themselves round the perceptions of that person remain in the larger earth-life as distinct as ever, and form new relations and grow and develop throughout all the future, in the same way in which our own distinct objects of thought, once stored in memory, form new relations and develop throughout our whole finite life. This is Fechner's theory of immortality, first published in the little 'Büchlein des lebens nach dem tode,' in 1836, and re-edited in greatly improved shape in the last volume of his 'Zend-avesta.'

We rise upon the earth as wavelets rise upon the ocean. We grow out of her soil as leaves grow from a tree. The wavelets catch the sunbeams separately, the leaves stir when the branches do not move. They realize their own events apart, just as in our own consciousness, when anything becomes emphatic, the background fades from observation. Yet the event works back upon the background, as the wavelet works upon the waves, or as the leaf's movements work upon the sap inside the branch. The whole sea and the whole tree are registers of what has happened, and are different for the wave's and the leaf's action having occurred. A grafted twig may modify its scion to the roots:—so our outlived private experiences, impressed on the whole earth-mind as memories, lead the immortal life of ideas there, and become parts of the great system, fully distinguished from one another, just as we ourselves when alive were distinct, realizing themselves no longer isolatedly, but along with one another as so many partial systems, entering thus into new combinations, being affected by the perceptive experiences of those living then, and affecting the living in their turn — altho they are so seldom recognized by living men to do so.

If you imagine that this entrance after the death of the body into a common life of higher type means a merging and loss of our distinct personality, Fechner asks you whether a visual sensation of our own exists in any sense *less for itself* or *less distinctly*, when it enters into our higher relational consciousness and is there distinguished and defined.

— But here I must stop my reporting and send you to his volumes. Thus is the universe alive, according to this philosopher! I think you will admit that he makes it more *thickly* alive than do the other philosophers who, following rationalistic methods solely, gain the same results, but only in the thinnest outlines. Both Fechner and Professor Royce, for example, believe ultimately in one all-inclusive mind. Both believe that we, just as we stand here, are constituent parts of that mind. No other *content* has it than us, with all the other creatures like or unlike us, and the relations which it finds between us. Our eaches, collected into one, are substantively identical with its all, tho the all is perfect while no each is perfect, so that we have to admit that new qualities as well as unperceived relations accrue from the collective form. It is thus superior to the distributive form. But having reached this result, Royce (tho his treatment of the subject on its moral side seems to me infinitely richer and thicker than that of any other contemporary idealistic philosopher) leaves us very much to our own devices. Fechner, on the contrary, tries to trace the superiorities due to the more collective form in as much detail as he can. He marks the various intermediary stages and halting places of collectivity, — as we are to our separate senses, so is the earth to us, so is the solar system to the earth, etc., — and if, in order to escape an infinitely long summation, he posits a complete God as the all-container and leaves him about as indefinite in feature as the ideal-ists leave their absolute, he yet provides us with a very definite gate of approach to him in the shape of the earth-soul, through which in the nature of things we must first make connexion with all the more enveloping superhuman realms, and with which our more immediate religious commerce at any rate has to be car-ried on.

Ordinary monistic idealism leaves everything intermediary out. It recognizes only the extremes, as if, after the first rude face of the phenomenal world in all its particularity, nothing but the supreme in all its perfection could be found. First, you and I, just as we are in this room; and the moment we get below that surface, the unutterable absolute itself! Does n't this show a singularly indigent imagination? Is n't this brave universe made on a richer pattern, with room in it for a long hierarchy of beings? Materialistic science makes it infinitely richer in terms, with its molecules, and ether, and electrons, and what not. Absolute idealism, thinking of reality only under intellectual forms, knows not what to do with *bodies* of any grade, and can make no use of any psychophysical analogy or correspondence. The resultant thinness is startling when compared with the thickness and articulation of such a universe as Fechner paints. May not satisfaction with the rationalistic absolute as the alpha and omega, and treatment of it in all its abstraction as an adequate religious object, argue a certain native poverty of mental demand? Things reveal themselves soonest to those who most passionately want them, for our need sharpens our wit. To a mind content with little, the much in the universe may always remain hid.

To be candid, one of my reasons for saying so much about Fechner has been to make the thinness of our current transcendentalism appear more evident by an effect of contrast. Scholasticism ran thick; Hegel himself ran thick; but english and american transcendentalisms run thin. If philosophy is more a matter of passionate vision than of logic, — and I believe it is, logic only finding reasons for the vision afterwards, — must not such thinness come either from the vision being defective in the disciples, or from their passion, matched with Fechner's or with Hegel's own passion, being as moonlight unto sunlight or as water unto wine?[4]

But I have also a much deeper reason for making Fechner a part of my text. His *assumption that conscious experiences freely compound and separate themselves*, the same assumption

by which absolutism explains the relation of
our minds to the eternal mind, and the same
by which empiricism explains the composition
of the human mind out of subordinate mental elements, is not one which we ought to let
pass without scrutiny. I shall scrutinize it in
the next lecture.

V

THE COMPOUNDING OF
CONSCIOUSNESS

LECTURE V

THE COMPOUNDING OF CONSCIOUSNESS

In my last lecture I gave a miserably scanty outline of the way of thinking of a philosopher remarkable for the almost unexampled richness of his imagination of details. I owe to Fechner's shade an apology for presenting him in a manner so unfair to the most essential quality of his genius; but the time allotted is too short to say more about the particulars of his work, so I proceed to the programme I suggested at the end of our last hour. I wish to discuss the assumption that states of consciousness, so-called, can separate and combine themselves freely, and keep their own identity unchanged while forming parts of simultaneous fields of experience of wider scope.

Let me first explain just what I mean by this. While you listen to my voice, for example, you are perhaps inattentive to some bodily sensation due to your clothing or your posture.

Yet that sensation would seem probably to be there, for in an instant, by a change of attention, you can have it in one field of consciousness with the voice. It seems as if it existed first in a separate form, and then as if, without itself changing, it combined with your other co-existent sensations. It is after this analogy that pantheistic idealism thinks that we exist in the absolute. The absolute, it thinks, makes the world by knowing the whole of it at once in one undivided eternal act.[1] To 'be,' *really* to be, is to be as it knows us to be, along with everything else, namely, and clothed with the fulness of our meaning. Meanwhile we *are* at the same time not only really and as it knows us, but also apparently, for to our separate single selves we appear *without* most other things and unable to declare with any fulness what our own meaning is. Now the classic doctrine of pantheistic idealism, from the Upanishads down to Josiah Royce, is that the finite knowers, in spite of their apparent ignorance, are one with the knower of the all. In the most limited moments of our private experience, the absolute idea, as Dr. McTaggart told us, is implicitly contained. The moments, as Royce says, exist only in relation to it. They are true or erroneous only through its overshadowing presence. Of the larger self that alone eternally is, they are the organic parts. They *are*, only inasmuch as they are implicated in its being.

There is thus in reality but this one self, consciously inclusive of all the lesser selves, *logos*, problem-solver, and all-knower; and Royce ingeniously compares the ignorance that in our persons breaks out in the midst of its complete knowledge and isolates me from you and both of us from it, to the inattention into which our finite minds are liable to fall with respect to such implicitly present details as those corporeal sensations to which I made allusion just now. Those sensations stand to our total private minds in the same relation in which our private minds stand to the absolute mind. Privacy means ignorance — I still quote Royce — and ignorance means inattention. We are finite because our wills, as such, are only fragments of the absolute will; because will means interest, and an incomplete will means an incomplete interest; and because incompleteness of interest means inattention to much that a fuller interest would bring us to perceive.[2]

In this account Royce makes by far the manliest of the post-hegelian attempts to read some empirically apprehensible content into the notion of our relation to the absolute mind.

I have to admit, now that I propose to you to scrutinize this assumption rather closely, that trepidation seizes me. The subject is a subtle and abstruse one. It is one thing to delve into subtleties by one's self with pen in hand, or to study out abstruse points in books, but quite another thing to make a popular lecture out of them. Nevertheless I must not flinch from my task here, for I think that this particular point forms perhaps the vital knot of the present philosophic situation, and I imagine that the times are ripe, or almost ripe, for a serious attempt to be made at its untying.

It may perhaps help to lessen the arduousness of the subject if I put the first part of what

V. COMPOUNDING OF CONSCIOUSNESS

I have to say in the form of a direct personal confession.

In the year 1890 I published a work on psychology in which it became my duty to discuss the value of a certain explanation of our higher mental states that had come into favor among the more biologically inclined psychologists. Suggested partly by the association of ideas, and partly by the analogy of chemical compounds, this opinion was that complex mental states are resultants of the self-compounding of simpler ones. The Mills had spoken of mental chemistry; Wundt of a 'psychic synthesis,' which might develop properties not contained in the elements; and such writers as Spencer, Taine, Fiske, Barratt, and Clifford had propounded a great evolutionary theory in which, in the absence of souls, selves, or other principles of unity, primordial units of mind-stuff or mind-dust were represented as summing themselves together in successive stages of compounding and re-compounding, and thus engendering our higher and more complex states of mind. The elementary feeling of A, let us say, and the elementary feeling of B, when they occur in certain conditions, combine, according to this doctrine, into a feeling of A-plus-B, and this in turn combines with a similarly generated feeling of C-plus-D, until at last the whole alphabet may appear together in one field of awareness, without any other witnessing principle or principles beyond the feelings of the several letters themselves, being supposed to exist. What each of them witnesses separately, 'all' of them are supposed to witness in conjunction. But their distributive knowledge does n't *give rise* to their collective knowledge by any act, it *is* their collective knowledge. The lower forms of consciousness 'taken together' *are* the higher. It, 'taken apart,' consists of nothing and *is* nothing but them. This, at least, is the most obvious way of understanding the doctrine, and is the way I understood it in the chapter in my psychology.

Superficially looked at, this seems just like the combination of H_2 and O into water, but looked at more closely, the analogy halts badly.

V. COMPOUNDING OF CONSCIOUSNESS

When a chemist tells us that two atoms of hydrogen and one of oxygen combine themselves of their own accord into the new compound substance 'water,' he knows (if he believes in the mechanical view of nature) that this is only an elliptical statement for a more complex fact. That fact is that when H_2 and O, instead of keeping far apart, get into closer quarters, say into the position H-O-H, they *affect surrounding bodies differently :* they now wet our skin, dissolve sugar, put out fire, etc., which they didn't in their former positions. 'Water' is but *our name* for what acts thus peculiarly. But if the skin, sugar, and fire were absent, no witness would speak of water at all. He would still talk of the H and O distributively, merely noting that they acted now in the new position H-O-H.

In the older psychologies the soul or self took the place of the sugar, fire, or skin. The lower feelings produced *effects on it*, and their apparent compounds were only its reactions. As you tickle a man's face with a feather, and he laughs, so when you tickle his intellectual principle with a retinal feeling, say, and a muscular feeling at once, it laughs responsively by its category of 'space,' but it would be false to treat the space as simply made of those simpler feelings. It is rather a new and unique psychic creation which their combined action on the mind is able to evoke.

I found myself obliged, in discussing the mind-dust theory, to urge this last alternative view. The so-called mental compounds are simple psychic reactions of a higher type. The form itself of them, I said, is something new. We can't say that awareness of the alphabet as such is nothing more than twenty-six awarenesses, each of a separate letter; for those are twenty-six distinct awarenesses, of single letters *without* others, while their so-called sum is one awareness, of every letter *with* its comrades. There is thus something new in the collective consciousness. It knows the same letters, indeed, but it knows them in this novel way. It is safer, I said (for I fought shy of admitting a self or soul or other agent of combination), to treat the consciousness of the alphabet as a twenty-seventh fact, the substitute and not the sum of the twenty-six simpler consciousnesses, and to say that while under certain physiological conditions they alone are produced, other more complex physiological conditions result in its production instead. Do not talk, therefore, I said, of the higher states *consisting* of the simpler, or *being* the same with them; talk rather of their *knowing the same things*. They are different mental facts, but they apprehend, each in its own peculiar way, the same objective A, B, C, and D.

The theory of combination, I was forced to conclude, is thus untenable, being both logically nonsensical and practically unnecessary. Say what you will, twelve thoughts, each of a single word, are not the self-same mental thing as one thought of the whole sentence. The higher thoughts, I insisted, are psychic units, not compounds; but for all that, they may know together as a collective multitude the very same objects which under other conditions are known separately by as many simple thoughts.

189

For many years I held rigorously to this view,[3] and the reasons for doing so seemed to me during all those years to apply also to the opinion that the absolute mind stands to our minds in the relation of a whole to its parts. If untenable in finite psychology, that opinion ought to be untenable in metaphysics also. The great transcendentalist metaphor has always been, as I lately reminded you, a grammatical sentence. Physically such a sentence is of course composed of clauses, these of words, the words of syllables, and the syllables of letters. We may take each word in, yet not understand the sentence; but if suddenly the meaning of the whole sentence flashes, the sense of each word is taken up into that whole meaning. Just so, according to our transcendentalist teachers, the absolute mind thinks the whole sentence, while we, according to our rank as thinkers, think a clause, a word, a syllable, or a letter. Most of us are, as I said, mere syllables in the mouth of Allah. And as Allah comes first in the order of being, so comes first the entire sentence, the *logos* that forms the eternal absolute thought. Students of language tell us that speech began with men's efforts to make *statements*. The rude synthetic vocal utterances first used for this effect slowly got stereotyped, and then much later got decomposed into grammatical parts. It is not as if men had first invented letters and made syllables of them, then made words of the syllables and sentences of the words; — they actually followed the reverse order. So, the transcendentalists affirm, the complete absolute thought is the pre-condition of our thoughts, and we finite creatures *are* only in so far as it owns us as its verbal fragments.

The metaphor is so beautiful, and applies, moreover, so literally to such a multitude of the minor wholes of experience, that by merely hearing it most of us are convinced that it must apply universally. We see that no smallest raindrop can come into being without a whole shower, no single feather without a whole bird, neck and crop, beak and tail, coming into being simultaneously: so we unhesitatingly lay down the law that no part of anything can be except so far as the whole also is. And then, since everything whatever is part of the whole universe, and since (if we are idealists) nothing, whether part or whole, exists except for a witness, we proceed to the conclusion that the unmitigated absolute as witness of the whole is the one sole ground of being of every partial fact, the fact of our own existence included. We think of ourselves as being only a few of the feathers, so to speak, which help to constitute that absolute bird. Extending the analogy of certain wholes, of which we have familiar experience, to the whole of wholes, we easily become absolute idealists.

But if, instead of yielding to the seductions of our metaphor, be it sentence, shower, or bird, we analyze more carefully the notion suggested by it that we are constituent parts of the absolute's eternal field of consciousness, we find grave difficulties arising. First, the difficulty I found with the mind-dust theory. If the absolute makes us by knowing us, how can we exist otherwise than *as* it knows us? But it knows each of us indivisibly from everything else. Yet if to exist means nothing but to be experienced, as idealism affirms, we surely exist otherwise, for we experience *ourselves* ignorantly and in division. We indeed differ from the absolute not only by defect, but by excess. Our ignorances, for example, bring curiosities and doubts by which it cannot be troubled, for it owns eternally the solution of every problem. Our impotence entails pains, our imperfection sins, which its perfection keeps at a distance. What I said of the alphabet-form and the letters holds good of the absolute experience and our experiences. Their relation, whatever it may be, seems not to be that of identity.

It is impossible to reconcile the peculiarities of our experience with our being only the absolute's mental objects. A God, as distinguished from the absolute, creates things by projecting them beyond himself as so many substances, each endowed with *perseity*, as the scholastics call it. But objects of thought are not things *per se*. They are there only *for* their thinker, and only *as* he thinks them. How, then, can they become severally alive on their own accounts and think themselves quite otherwise than as he thinks them? It is as if the characters in a novel were to get up from the pages, and walk away and transact business of their own outside of the author's story.

A third difficulty is this: The bird-metaphor is physical, but we see on reflection that in the *physical* world there is no real compounding. 'Wholes' are not realities there, parts only are realities. 'Bird' is only our *name* for the physical fact of a certain grouping of organs, just as 'Charles's Wain' is our name for a certain grouping of stars. The 'whole,' be it bird or constellation, is nothing but our vision, nothing but an effect on our sensorium when a lot of things act on it together. It is not realized by any organ or any star, or experienced apart from the consciousness of an onlooker.[4] In the physical world taken by itself there *is* thus no 'all,' there are only the 'eaches' — at least that is the 'scientific' view.

In the mental world, on the contrary, wholes do in point of fact realize themselves *per se*. The meaning of the whole sentence is just as much a real experience as the feeling of each word is; the absolute's experience *is* for itself, as much as yours is for yourself or mine for myself. So the feather-and-bird analogy won't work unless you make the absolute into a distinct sort of mental agent with a vision produced in it *by* our several minds analogous to the 'bird'-vision which the feathers, beak, etc., produce *in* those same minds. The 'whole,' which is *its* experience, would then be its unifying reaction on our experiences, and not those very experiences self-combined. Such a view as this would go with theism, for the theistic God is a separate being; but it would not go with pantheistic idealism, the very essence of which is to insist that we are literally *parts* of God, and he only ourselves in our totality — the word 'ourselves' here standing of course for all the universe's finite facts.

I am dragging you into depths unsuitable, I fear, for a rapid lecture. Such difficulties as these have to be teased out with a needle, so to speak, and lecturers should take only bird's-eye views. The practical upshot of the matter, however, so far as I am concerned, is this, that if I had been lecturing on the absolute a very few years ago, I should unhesitatingly have urged these difficulties, and developed them at still greater length, to show that the hypothesis of the absolute was not only non-coercive from the logical point of view, but self-contradictory as well, its notion that parts and whole are only two names for the same thing not bearing critical scrutiny. If you stick to purely physical terms like stars, there *is* no whole. If you call the whole mental, then the so-called whole, instead of being one fact with the parts, appears rather as the integral reaction on those parts of an independent higher witness, such as the theistic God is supposed to be.

So long as this was the state of my own mind, I could accept the notion of self-compounding in the supernal spheres of experience no more easily than in that chapter on mind-dust I had accepted it in the lower spheres. I found myself compelled, therefore, to call the absolute impossible ; and the untrammelled freedom with which pantheistic or monistic idealists stepped over the logical barriers which Lotze

and others had set down long before I had — I
had done little more than quote these previous critics in my chapter—surprised me not
a little, and made me, I have to confess, both
resentful and envious. Envious because in the
bottom of my heart I wanted the same freedom
myself, for motives which I shall develop later;
and resentful because my absolutist friends
seemed to me to be stealing the privilege of
blowing both hot and cold. To establish their
absolute they used an intellectualist type of
logic which they disregarded when employed
against it. It seemed to me that they ought at
least to have mentioned the objections that
had stopped me so completely. I had yielded
to them against my 'will to believe,' out of
pure logical scrupulosity. They, professing to
loathe the will to believe and to follow purest
rationality, had simply ignored them. The
method was easy, but hardly to be called candid. Fechner indeed was candid enough, for
he had never thought of the objections, but
later writers, like Royce, who should presum-
ably have heard them, had passed them by in

silence. I felt as if these philosophers were
granting their will to believe in monism too
easy a license. My own conscience would permit me no such license.

So much for the personal confession by
which you have allowed me to introduce the
subject. Let us now consider it more objectively.

The fundamental difficulty I have found is
the number of contradictions which idealistic
monists seem to disregard. In the first place
they attribute to all existence a mental or
experiential character, but I find their simultaneous belief that the higher and the lower in
the universe are entitatively identical, incompatible with this character. Incompatible in
consequence of the generally accepted doctrine
that, whether Berkeley were right or not in
saying of material existence that its *esse* is
sentiri, it is undoubtedly right to say of *mental*
existence that its *esse* is *sentiri* or *experiri*. If I
feel pain, it is just pain that I feel, however
I may have come by the feeling. No one pretends that pain as such only appears like pain,

but in itself is different, for to be as a mental experience *is* only to appear to some one.

The idealists in question ought then to do one of two things, but they do neither. They ought either to refute the notion that as mental states appear, so they are; or, still keeping that notion, they ought to admit a distinct agent of unification to do the work of the all-knower, just as our respective souls or selves in popular philosophy do the work of partial knowers. Otherwise it is like a joint-stock company all shareholders and no treasurer or director. If our finite minds formed a billion facts, then its mind, knowing our billion, would make a universe composed of a billion and one facts. But transcendental idealism is quite as unfriendly to active principles called souls as physiological psychology is, Kant having, as it thinks, definitively demolished them. And altho some disciples speak of the transcendental ego of apperception (which they celebrate as Kant's most precious legacy to posterity) as if it were a combining agent, the drift of monistic authority is certainly in the direction of treating

199

it as only an all-witness, whose field of vision we finite witnesses do not cause, but constitute rather. We are the letters, it is the alphabet; we are the features, it is the face; not indeed as if either alphabet or face were something additional to the letters or the features, but rather as if it were only another name for the very letters or features themselves. The all-form assuredly differs from the each-form, but the *matter* is the same in both, and the each-form only an unaccountable appearance.

But this, as you see, contradicts the other idealist principle, of a mental fact being just what it appears to be. If their forms of appearance are so different, the all and the eaches cannot be identical.

The way out (unless, indeed, we are willing to discard the logic of identity altogether) would seem to be frankly to write down the all and the eaches as two distinct orders of witness, each minor witness being aware of its own 'content' solely, while the greater witness knows the minor witnesses, knows their whole content pooled together, knows their relations to one another, and knows of just how much each one of them is ignorant.

The two types of witnessing are here palpably non-identical. We get a pluralism, not a monism, out of them. In my psychology-chapter I had resorted openly to such pluralism, treating each total field of consciousness as a distinct entity, and maintaining that the higher fields merely supersede the lower functionally by knowing more about the same objects.

The monists themselves writhe like worms on the hook to escape pluralistic or at least dualistic language, but they cannot escape it. They speak of the eternal and the temporal 'points of view'; of the universe in its infinite 'aspect' or in its finite 'capacity'; they say that '*quâ* absolute' it is one thing, '*quâ* relative' another; they contrast its 'truth' with its 'appearances'; they distinguish the total from the partial way of 'taking' it, etc.; but they forget that, on idealistic principles, to make such distinctions is tantamount to making different beings, or at any rate that varying points of view, aspects, appearances, ways of taking, and the like, are meaningless phrases unless we suppose outside of the unchanging content of reality a diversity of witnesses who experience or take it variously, the absolute mind being just the witness that takes it most completely.

For consider the matter one moment longer, if you can. Ask what this notion implies, of appearing differently from different points of view. If there be no outside witness, a thing can appear only to itself, the eaches or parts to their several selves temporally, the all or whole to itself eternally. Different 'selves' thus break out inside of what the absolutist insists to be intrinsically one fact. But how can what is *actually* one be *effectively* so many ? Put your witnesses anywhere, whether outside or inside of what is witnessed, in the last resort your witnesses must on idealistic principles be distinct, for what is witnessed is different.

I fear that I am expressing myself with terrible obscurity — some of you, I know, are groaning over the logic-chopping. Be a pluralist or be a monist, you say, for heaven's sake,

no matter which, so long as you stop arguing.
It reminds one of Chesterton's epigram that
the only thing that ever drives human beings
insane is logic. But whether I be sane or insane,
you cannot fail, even tho you be transcendentalists yourselves, to recognize to some degree
by my trouble the difficulties that beset monistic idealism. What boots it to call the parts and
the whole the same body of experience, when in
the same breath you have to say that the all 'as
such' means one sort of experience and each
part 'as such' means another?

Difficulties, then, so far, but no stable solution as yet, for I have been talking only criti-
cally. You will probably be relieved to hear,
then, that having rounded this corner, I shall
begin to consider what may be the possibilities
of getting farther.

To clear the path, I beg you first to note one
point. What has so troubled my logical conscience is not so much the absolute by itself
as the whole class of suppositions of which it
is the supreme example, collective experiences
namely, claiming identity with their constitu-

ent parts, yet experiencing things quite differently from these latter. If *any* such collective experience can be, then of course, so far as the mere logic of the case goes, the absolute may be. In a previous lecture I have talked against the absolute from other points of view. In this lecture I have meant merely to take it as the example most prominent at Oxford of the thing which has given me such logical perplexity. I don't logically see how a collective experience of any grade whatever can be treated as logically identical with a lot of distributive experiences. They form two different concepts. The absolute happens to be the only collective experience concerning which Oxford idealists have urged the identity, so I took it as my prerogative instance. But Fechner's earth-soul, or any stage of being below or above that, would have served my purpose just as well: the same logical objection applies to these collective experiences as to the absolute.

So much, then, in order that you may not be confused about my strategical objective. The real point to defend against the logic that I have used is the identity of the collective and distributive anyhow, not the particular example of such identity known as the absolute.

So now for the directer question. Shall we say that every complex mental fact is a separate psychic entity succeeding upon a lot of other psychic entities which are erroneously called its parts, and superseding them in function, but not literally being composed of them? This was the course I took in my psychology; and if followed in theology, we should have to deny the absolute as usually conceived, and replace it by the 'God' of theism. We should also have to deny Fechner's 'earth-soul' and all other superhuman collections of experience of every grade, so far at least as these are held to be compounded of our simpler souls in the way which Fechner believed in; and we should have to make all these denials in the name of the incorruptible logic of self-identity, teaching us that to call a thing and its other the same is to commit the crime of self-contradiction.

But if we realize the whole philosophic situation thus produced, we see that it is almost intolerable. Loyal to the logical kind of rationality, it is disloyal to every other kind. It makes the universe discontinuous. These fields of experience that replace each other so punctually, each knowing the same matter, but in ever-widening contexts, from simplest feeling up to absolute knowledge, *can* they have no *being* in common when their cognitive function is so manifestly common? The regular succession of them is on such terms an unintelligible miracle. If you reply that their common *object* is of itself enough to make the many witnesses continuous, the same implacable logic follows you—how *can* one and the same object appear so variously? Its diverse appearances break it into a plurality; and our world of objects then falls into discontinuous pieces quite as much as did our world of subjects. The resultant irrationality is really intolerable.

I said awhile ago that I was envious of Fechner and the other pantheists because I myself wanted the same freedom that I saw them unscrupulously enjoying, of letting mental fields compound themselves and so make the universe more continuous, but that my conscience held me prisoner. In my heart of hearts, however, I knew that my situation was absurd and could be only provisional. That secret of a continuous life which the universe knows by heart and acts on every instant cannot be a contradiction incarnate. If logic says it is one, so much the worse for logic. Logic being the lesser thing, the static incomplete abstraction, must succumb to reality, not reality to logic. Our intelligence cannot wall itself up alive, like a pupa in its chrysalis. It must at any cost keep on speaking terms with the universe that engendered it. Fechner, Royce, and Hegel seem on the truer path. Fechner has never heard of logic's veto, Royce hears the voice but cannily ignores the utterances, Hegel hears them but to spurn them — and all go on their way rejoicing. Shall we alone obey the veto?

Sincerely, and patiently as I could, I struggled with the problem for years, covering hundreds of sheets of paper with notes and memoranda and discussions with myself over the difficulty. How can many consciousnesses be at the same time one consciousness? How can one and the same identical fact experience itself so diversely? The struggle was vain; I found myself in an *impasse*. I saw that I must either forswear that 'psychology without a soul' to which my whole psychological and kantian education had committed me, — I must, in short, bring back distinct spiritual agents to know the mental states, now singly and now in combination, in a word bring back scholasticism and common sense — or else I must squarely confess the solution of the problem impossible, and then either give up my intellectualistic logic, the logic of identity, and adopt some higher (or lower) form of rationality, or, finally, face the fact that life is logically irrational.

Sincerely, this is the actual trilemma that confronts every one of us. Those of you who are scholastic-minded, or simply common-sense minded, will smile at the elaborate groans of my parturient mountain resulting in nothing but this mouse. Accept the spiritual agents, for heaven's sake, you will say, and leave off your ridiculous pedantry. Let but our ' souls' combine our sensations by their intellectual faculties, and let but ' God ' replace the pantheistic world-soul, and your wheels will go round again — you will enjoy both life and logic together.

This solution is obvious and I know that many of you will adopt it. It is comfortable, and all our habits of speech support it. Yet it is not for idle or fantastical reasons that the notion of the substantial soul, so freely used by common men and the more popular philosophies, has fallen upon such evil days, and has no prestige in the eyes of critical thinkers. It only shares the fate of other unrepresentable substances and principles. They are without exception all so barren that to sincere inquirers they appear as little more than names masquerading — Wo die begriffe fehlen da stellt ein wort zur rechten zeit sich ein. You see no deeper into the fact that a hundred sensations get compounded or known together by thinking that a 'soul' does the compounding than you see into a man's living eighty years by thinking of him as an octogenarian, or into our having five fingers by calling us pentadactyls. Souls have worn out both themselves and their welcome, that is the plain truth. Philosophy ought to get the manifolds of experience unified on principles less empty. Like the word 'cause,' the word 'soul' is but a theoretic stop-gap — it marks a place and claims it for a future explanation to occupy.

This being our post-humian and post-kantian state of mind, I will ask your permission to leave the soul wholly out of the present discussion and to consider only the residual dilemma. Some day, indeed, souls may get their innings again in philosophy — I am quite ready to admit that possibility — they form a category of thought too natural to the human mind to expire without prolonged resistance. But if the belief in the soul ever does come to life after the many funeral-discourses which humian and kantian criticism have preached over it, I am sure it will be only when some one has found in the term a pragmatic significance that has hitherto eluded observation.

V. COMPOUNDING OF CONSCIOUSNESS

When that champion speaks, as he well may speak some day, it will be time to consider souls more seriously.

Let us leave out the soul, then, and confront what I just called the residual dilemma. Can we, on the one hand, give up the logic of identity? — can we, on the other, believe human experience to be fundamentally irrational? Neither is easy, yet it would seem that we must do one or the other.

Few philosophers have had the frankness fairly to admit the necessity of choosing between the 'horns' offered. Reality must be rational, they have said, and since the ordinary intellectualist logic is the only usual test of rationality, reality and logic must agree 'somehow.' Hegel was the first non-mystical writer to face the dilemma squarely and throw away the ordinary logic, saving a pseudo-rationality for the universe by inventing the higher logic of the 'dialectic process.' Bradley holds to the intellectualist logic, and by dint of it convicts the human universe of being irrationality incarnate. But what must be and can be, is, he says; there must and can be relief from *that* irrationality; and the absolute must already have got the relief in secret ways of its own, impossible for us to guess at. *We* of course get no relief, so Bradley's is a rather ascetic doctrine. Royce and Taylor accept similar solutions, only they emphasize the irrationality of our finite universe less than Bradley does; and Royce in particular, being unusually 'thick' for an idealist, tries to bring the absolute's secret forms of relief more sympathetically home to our imagination.

Well, what must we do in this tragic predicament? For my own part, I have finally found myself compelled to *give up the logic*, fairly, squarely, and irrevocably. It has an imperishable use in human life, but that use is not to make us theoretically acquainted with the essential nature of reality — just what it is I can perhaps suggest to you a little later. Reality, life, experience, concreteness, immediacy, use what word you will, exceeds our logic, overflows and surrounds it. If you like to employ words eulogistically, as most men do, and so encourage confusion, you may say that reality obeys a higher logic, or enjoys a higher rationality. But I think that even eulogistic words should be used rather to distinguish than to commingle meanings, so I prefer bluntly to call reality if not irrational then at least non-rational in its constitution, — and by reality here I mean reality where things *happen*, all temporal reality without exception. I myself find no good warrant for even suspecting the existence of any reality of a higher denomination than that distributed and strung-along and flowing sort of reality which we finite beings swim in. That is the sort of reality given us, and that is the sort with which logic is so incommensurable. If there be any higher sort of reality — the 'absolute,' for example — that sort, by the confession of those who believe in it, is still less amenable to ordinary logic; it transcends logic and is therefore still less rational in the intellectualist sense, so it cannot help us to save our logic as an adequate definer and confiner of existence.

These sayings will sound queer and dark,

probably they will sound quite wild or childish in the absence of explanatory comment.
Only the persuasion that I soon can explain
them, if not satisfactorily to all of you, at least
intelligibly, emboldens me to state them thus
baldly as a sort of programme. Please take
them as a thesis, therefore, to be defended
by later pleading.

I told you that I had long and sincerely
wrestled with the dilemma. I have now to
confess (and this will probably re-animate
your interest) that I should not now be eman-
cipated, not now subordinate logic with so very
light a heart, or throw it out of the deeper
regions of philosophy to take its rightful and
respectable place in the world of simple human
practice, if I had not been influenced by a
comparatively young and very original french
writer, Professor Henri Bergson. Reading his
works is what has made me bold. If I had not
read Bergson, I should probably still be black-
ening endless pages of paper privately, in the
hope of making ends meet that were never
meant to meet, and trying to discover some

mode of conceiving the behavior of reality which should leave no discrepancy between it and the accepted laws of the logic of identity. It is certain, at any rate, that without the confidence which being able to lean on Bergson's authority gives me I should never have ventured to urge these particular views of mine upon this ultra-critical audience.

I must therefore, in order to make my own views more intelligible, give some preliminary account of the bergsonian philosophy. But here, as in Fechner's case, I must confine myself only to the features that are essential to the present purpose, and not entangle you in collateral details, however interesting otherwise. For our present purpose, then, the essential contribution of Bergson to philosophy is his criticism of intellectualism. In my opinion he has killed intellectualism definitively and without hope of recovery. I don't see how it can ever revive again in its ancient platonizing rôle of claiming to be the most authentic, intimate, and exhaustive definer of the nature of reality. Others, as Kant for example, have denied intellectualism's pretensions to define reality *an sich* or in its absolute capacity; but Kant still leaves it laying down laws — and laws from which there is no appeal — to all our human experience; while what Bergson denies is that its methods give any adequate account of this human experience in its very finiteness. Just how Bergson accomplishes all this I must try to tell in my imperfect way in the next lecture; but since I have already used the words 'logic,' 'logic of identity,' 'intellectualistic logic,' and 'intellectualism' so often, and sometimes used them as if they required no particular explanation, it will be wise at this point to say at greater length than heretofore in what sense I take these terms when I claim that Bergson has refuted their pretension to decide what reality can or cannot be. Just what I mean by intellectualism is therefore what I shall try to give a fuller idea of during the remainder of this present hour.

In recent controversies some participants have shown resentment at being classed as intellectualists. I mean to use the word disparagingly, but shall be sorry if it works offence. Intellectualism has its source in the faculty which gives us our chief superiority to the brutes, our power, namely, of translating the crude flux of our merely feeling-experience into a conceptual order. An immediate experience, as yet unnamed or classed, is a mere *that* that we undergo, a thing that asks, '*What* am I?' When we name and class it, we say for the first time what it is, and all these whats are abstract names or concepts. Each concept means a particular *kind* of thing, and as things seem once for all to have been created in kinds, a far more efficient handling of a given bit of experience begins as soon as we have classed the various parts of it. Once classed, a thing can be treated by the law of its class, and the advantages are endless. Both theoretically and practically this power of framing abstract concepts is one of the sublimest of our human prerogatives. We come back into the concrete from our journey into these abstractions, with an increase both of vision and of power. It is no wonder that earlier thinkers, forgetting that

concepts are only man-made extracts from the
temporal flux, should have ended by treating
them as a superior type of being, bright,
changeless, true, divine, and utterly opposed
in nature to the turbid, restless lower world.
The latter then appears as but their corruption
and falsification.

Intellectualism in the vicious sense began
when Socrates and Plato taught that what a
thing really is, is told us by its *definition*. Ever
since Socrates we have been taught that reality
consists of essences, not of appearances, and
that the essences of things are known whenever
we know their definitions. So first we identify
the thing with a concept and then we identify
the concept with a definition, and only then,
inasmuch as the thing *is* whatever the definition expresses, are we sure of apprehending the
real essence of it or the full truth about it.

So far no harm is done. The misuse of concepts begins with the habit of employing them
privatively as well as positively, using them not
merely to assign properties to things, but to
deny the very properties with which the things

sensibly present themselves. Logic can extract all its possible consequences from any definition, and the logician who is *unerbittlich consequent* is often tempted, when he cannot extract a certain property from a definition, to deny that the concrete object to which the definition applies can possibly possess that property. The definition that fails to yield it must exclude or negate it. This is Hegel's regular method of establishing his system.

It is but the old story, of a useful practice first becoming a method, then a habit, and finally a tyranny that defeats the end it was used for. Concepts, first employed to make things intelligible, are clung to even when they make them unintelligible. Thus it comes that when once you have conceived things as 'independent,' you must proceed to deny the possibility of any connexion whatever among them, because the notion of connexion is not contained in the definition of independence. For a like reason you must deny any possible forms or modes of unity among things which you have begun by defining as a 'many.' We have cast a glance at Hegel's and Bradley's use of this sort of reasoning, and you will remember Sigwart's epigram that according to it a horseman can never in his life go on foot, or a photographer ever do anything but photograph.

The classic extreme in this direction is the denial of the possibility of change, and the consequent branding of the world of change as unreal, by certain philosophers. The definition of A is changeless, so is the definition of B. The one definition cannot change into the other, so the notion that a concrete thing A should change into another concrete thing B is made out to be contrary to reason. In Mr. Bradley's difficulty in seeing how sugar can be sweet intellectualism outstrips itself and becomes openly a sort of verbalism. Sugar is just sugar and sweet is just sweet; neither is the other; nor can the word 'is' ever be understood to join any subject to its predicate rationally. Nothing 'between' things can connect them, for 'between' is just that third thing, 'between,' and would need itself to be connected to the

first and second things by two still finer betweens, and so on ad infinitum.

The particular intellectualistic difficulty that
had held my own thought so long in a vise was,
as we have seen at such tedious length, the impossibility of understanding how 'your' experience and 'mine,' which 'as such' are defined as
not conscious of each other, can nevertheless
at the same time be members of a world-expe-
rience defined expressly as having all its parts
co-conscious, or known together. The definitions are contradictory, so the things defined
can in no way be united. You see how unintelligible intellectualism here seems to make the
world of our most accomplished philosophers.
Neither as they use it nor as we use it does it
do anything but make nature look irrational
and seem impossible.

In my next lecture, using Bergson as my
principal topic, I shall enter into more concrete
details and try, by giving up intellectualism
frankly, to make, if not the world, at least my
own general thesis, less unintelligible.

VI

BERGSON AND HIS CRITIQUE OF
INTELLECTUALISM

LECTURE VI

BERGSON AND HIS CRITIQUE OF INTELLECTUALISM

I GAVE you a very stiff lecture last time, and I fear that this one can be little less so. The best way of entering into it will be to begin immediately with Bergson's philosophy, since I told you that that was what had led me personally to renounce the intellectualistic method and the current notion that logic is an adequate measure of what can or cannot be.

Professor Henri Bergson is a young man, comparatively, as influential philosophers go, having been born at Paris in 1859. His career has been the perfectly routine one of a successful french professor. Entering the école normale supérieure at the age of twenty-two, he spent the next seventeen years teaching at *lycées*, provincial or parisian, until his fortieth year, when he was made professor at the said école normale. Since 1900 he has been professor at the Collège de France, and member of the Institute since 1900.

So far as the outward facts go, Bergson's career has then been commonplace to the utmost. Neither one of Taine's famous principles of explanation of great men, *the race, the environment, or the moment,* no, nor all three together, will explain that peculiar way of looking at things that constitutes his mental individuality. Originality in men dates from nothing previous, other things date from it, rather. I have to confess that Bergson's originality is so profuse that many of his ideas baffle me entirely. I doubt whether any one understands him all over, so to speak; and I am sure that he would himself be the first to see that this must be, and to confess that things which he himself has not yet thought out clearly, had yet to be mentioned and have a tentative place assigned them in his philosophy. Many of us are profusely original, in that no man can understand us — violently peculiar ways of looking at things are no great rarity. The rarity is when great peculiarity of vision is allied with great lucidity and unusual command of all the classic expository apparatus. Bergson's resources in the way of erudition are remarkable, and in the way of expression they are simply phenomenal. This is why in France, where *l'art de bien dire* counts for so much and is so sure of appreciation, he has immediately taken so eminent a place in public esteem. Old-fashioned professors, whom his ideas quite fail to satisfy, nevertheless speak of his talent almost with bated breath, while the youngsters flock to him as to a master.

If anything can make hard things easy to follow, it is a style like Bergson's. A 'straightforward' style, an american reviewer lately called it ; failing to see that such straightforwardness means a flexibility of verbal resource that follows the thought without a crease or wrinkle, as elastic silk underclothing follows the movements of one's body. The lucidity of Bergson's way of putting things is what all readers are first struck by. It seduces you and bribes you in advance to become his disciple. It is a miracle, and he a real magician.

M. Bergson, if I am rightly informed, came into philosophy through the gateway of mathematics. The old antinomies of the infinite were, I imagine, the irritant that first woke his faculties from their dogmatic slumber. You all remember Zeno's famous paradox, or sophism, as many of our logic books still call it, of Achilles and the tortoise. Give that reptile ever so small an advance and the swift runner Achilles can never overtake him, much less get ahead of him; for if space and time are infinitely divisible (as our intellects tell us they must be), by the time Achilles reaches the tortoise's starting-point, the tortoise has already got ahead of *that* starting-point, and so on *ad infinitum*, the interval between the pursuer and the pursued growing endlessly minuter, but never becoming wholly obliterated. The common way of showing up the sophism here is by pointing out the ambiguity of the expression 'never can overtake.' What the word 'never' falsely suggests, it is said, is an infinite duration of time; what it really means is the inexhaustible number of the steps of which the overtaking must consist. But if these steps are infinitely short, a finite time will suffice for them; and in point of fact they do rapidly converge, whatever be the original interval or the contrasted speeds, toward infinitesimal shortness. This proportionality of the shortness of the times to that of the spaces required frees us, it is claimed, from the sophism which the word 'never' suggests.

But this criticism misses Zeno's point entirely. Zeno would have been perfectly willing to grant that if the tortoise can be overtaken at all, he can be overtaken in (say) twenty seconds, but he would still have insisted that he can't be overtaken at all. Leave Achilles and the tortoise out of the account altogether, he would have said — they complicate the case unnecessarily. Take any single process of change whatever, take the twenty seconds themselves elapsing. If time be infinitely divisible, and it must be so on intellectualist principles, they simply cannot elapse, their end cannot be reached; for no matter how much of them has already elapsed, before the remainder, however minute, can have wholly elapsed, the earlier half of it must first have elapsed. And this ever re-arising need of making the

earlier half elapse *first* leaves time with always
something to do *before* the last thing is done,
so that the last thing never gets done. Expressed in bare numbers, it is like the conver-
gent series $\frac{1}{2}$ plus $\frac{1}{4}$ plus $\frac{1}{8}$ . . . , of which the
limit is one. But this limit, simply because it
is a limit, stands outside the series, the value
of which approaches it indefinitely but never
touches it. If in the natural world there were
no other way of getting things save by such successive addition of their logically involved fractions, no complete units or whole things would
ever come into being, for the fractions' sum
would always leave a remainder. But in point
of fact nature does n't make eggs by making
first half an egg, then a quarter, then an eighth,
etc., and adding them together. She either
makes a whole egg at once or none at all, and so
of all her other units. It is only in the sphere of
change, then, where one phase of a thing must
needs come into being before another phase
can come that Zeno's paradox gives trouble.

And it gives trouble then only if the succession of steps of change be infinitely divisi-

ble. If a bottle had to be emptied by an infinite number of successive decrements, it is mathematically impossible that the emptying should ever positively terminate. In point of fact, however, bottles and coffee-pots empty themselves by a finite number of decrements, each of definite amount. Either a whole drop emerges or nothing emerges from the spout. If all change went thus drop-wise, so to speak, if real time sprouted or grew by units of duration of determinate amount, just as our perceptions of it grow by pulses, there would be no zenonian paradoxes or kantian antinomies to trouble us. All our sensible experiences, as we get them immediately, do thus change by discrete pulses of perception, each of which keeps us saying 'more, more, more,' or 'less, less, less,' as the definite increments or diminutions make themselves felt. The discreteness is still more obvious when, instead of old things changing, they cease, or when altogether new things come. Fechner's term of the 'threshold,' which has played such a part in the psychology of perception, is only one way of naming the quantitative discreteness in the change of all our sensible experiences. They come to us in drops. Time itself comes in drops.

Our ideal decomposition of the drops which are all that we feel into still finer fractions is but an incident in that great transformation of the perceptual order into a conceptual order of which I spoke in my last lecture. It is made in the interest of our rationalizing intellect solely. The times directly *felt* in the experiences of living subjects have originally no common measure. Let a lump of sugar melt in a glass, to use one of M. Bergson's instances. We feel the time to be long while waiting for the process to end, but who knows how long or how short it feels to the sugar? All *felt* times coexist and overlap or compenetrate each other thus vaguely, but the artifice of plotting them on a common scale helps us to reduce their aboriginal confusion, and it helps us still more to plot, against the same scale, the successive possible steps into which nature's various changes may be resolved, either sensibly or conceivably. We thus straighten out the aboriginal privacy and vagueness, and can date things publicly, as it were, and by each other. The notion of one objective and 'evenly flowing' time, cut into numbered instants, applies itself as a common measure to all the steps and phases, no matter how many, into which we cut the processes of nature. They are now definitely contemporary, or later or earlier one than another, and we can handle them mathematically, as we say, and far better, practically as well as theoretically, for having thus correlated them one to one with each other on the common schematic or conceptual time-scale.

Motion, to take a good example, is originally a turbid sensation, of which the native shape is perhaps best preserved in the phenomenon of vertigo. In vertigo we feel that movement *is*, and is more or less violent or rapid, more or less in this direction or that, more or less alarming or sickening. But a man subject to vertigo may gradually learn to co-ordinate his felt motion with his real position and that of other things, and intellectualize it enough to succeed at last in walking without staggering. The

mathematical mind similarly organizes motion
in its way, putting it into a logical definition:
motion is now conceived as 'the occupancy of
serially successive points of space at serially
successive instants of time.' With such a definition we escape wholly from the turbid privacy
of sense. But do we not also escape from
sense-reality altogether? Whatever motion
really may be, it surely is not static; but the
definition we have gained is of the absolutely
static. It gives a set of one-to-one relations between space-points and time-points, which relations themselves are as fixed as the points are.
It gives *positions* assignable ad infinitum, but
how the body gets from one position to another
it omits to mention. The body gets there by
moving, of course; but the conceived positions,
however numerously multiplied, contain no
element of movement, so Zeno, using nothing
but them in his discussion, has no alternative
but to say that our intellect repudiates motion
as a non-reality. Intellectualism here does
what I said it does — it makes experience less
instead of more intelligible.

VI. BERGSON AND INTELLECTUALISM

We of course need a stable scheme of concepts, stably related with one another, to lay hold of our experiences and to co-ordinate them withal. When an experience comes with sufficient saliency to stand out, we keep the thought of it for future use, and store it in our conceptual system. What does not of itself stand out, we learn to *cut* out; so the system grows completer, and new reality, as it comes, gets named after and conceptually strung upon this or that element of it which we have already established. The immutability of such an abstract system is its great practical merit; the same identical terms and relations in it can always be recovered and referred to — change itself is just such an unalterable concept. But all these abstract concepts are but as flowers gathered, they are only moments dipped out from the stream of time, snap-shots taken, as by a kinetoscopic camera, at a life that in its original coming is continuous. Useful as they are as samples of the garden, or to re-enter the stream with, or to insert in our revolving lantern, they have no value but these practical values.

You cannot explain by them what makes any single phenomenon be or go — you merely dot out the path of appearances which it traverses. For you cannot make continuous being out of discontinuities, and your concepts are discontinuous. The stages into which you analyze a change are *states*, the change itself goes on between them. It lies along their intervals, inhabits what your definition fails to gather up, and thus eludes conceptual explanation altogether.

'When the mathematician,' Bergson writes, 'calculates the state of a system at the end of a time t, nothing need prevent him from supposing that betweenwhiles the universe vanishes, in order suddenly to appear again at the due moment in the new configuration. It is only the t-th moment that counts — that which flows throughout the intervals, namely real time, plays no part in his calculation. . . . In short, the world on which the mathematician operates is a world which dies and is born anew at every instant, like the world which Descartes thought of when he spoke of a continued creation.' To know adequately what really *happens* we ought, Bergson insists, to see into the intervals, but the mathematician sees only their extremities. He fixes only a few results, he dots a curve and then interpolates, he substitutes a tracing for a reality.

This being so undeniably the case, the history of the way in which philosophy has dealt with it is curious. The ruling tradition in philosophy has always been the platonic and aristotelian belief that fixity is a nobler and worthier thing than change. Reality must be one and unalterable. Concepts, being themselves fixities, agree best with this fixed nature of truth, so that for any knowledge of ours to be quite true it must be knowledge by universal concepts rather than by particular experiences, for these notoriously are mutable and corruptible. This is the tradition known as rationalism in philosophy, and what I have called intellectualism is only the extreme application of it. In spite of sceptics and empiricists, in spite of Protagoras, Hume, and James Mill, rationalism has never been seriously questioned, for its sharpest critics have always had a tender place in their hearts for it, and have obeyed some of its mandates. They have not been consistent; they have played fast and loose with the enemy; and Bergson alone has been radical.

To show what I mean by this, let me contrast his procedure with that of some of the transcendentalist philosophers whom I have lately mentioned. Coming after Kant, these pique themselves on being 'critical,' on building in fact upon Kant's 'critique' of pure reason. What that critique professed to establish was this, that concepts do not apprehend reality, but only such appearances as our senses feed out to them. They give immutable intellectual forms to these appearances, it is true, but the reality *an sich* from which in ultimate resort the sense-appearances have to come remains forever unintelligible to our intellect. Take motion, for example. Sensibly, motion comes in drops, waves, or pulses; either some actual amount of it, or none, being apprehended. This amount is the datum or *gabe* which reality feeds out to our intellectual faculty; but our intellect makes of it a task or *aufgabe* — this pun is one of the most memorable of Kant's formulas — and insists that in every pulse of it an infinite number of successive minor pulses shall be ascertainable. These minor pulses *we* can indeed *go on* to ascertain or to compute indefinitely if we have patience; but it would contradict the definition of an infinite number to suppose the endless series of them to have actually counted *themselves* out piecemeal. Zeno made this manifest; so the infinity which our intellect requires of the sense-datum is thus a future and potential rather than a past and actual infinity of structure. The datum after it has made itself must be decompos*able* ad infinitum by our conception, but of the steps by which that structure actually got composed we know nothing. Our intellect casts, in short, no ray of light on the processes by which experiences *get made*.

Kant's monistic successors have in general found the data of immediate experience even more self-contradictory, when intellectually

239

treated, than Kant did. Not only the character of infinity involved in the relation of various empirical data to their 'conditions,' but the very notion that empirical things should be related to one another at all, has seemed to them, when the intellectualistic fit was upon them, full of paradox and contradiction. We saw in a former lecture numerous instances of this from Hegel, Bradley, Royce, and others. We saw also where the solution of such an intolerable state of things was sought for by these authors. Whereas Kant had placed it outside of and *before* our experience, in the *dinge an sich* which are the causes of the latter, his monistic successors all look for it either *after* experience, as its absolute completion, or else consider it to be even now implicit within experience as its ideal signification. Kant and his successors look, in short, in diametrically opposite directions. Do not be misled by Kant's admission of theism into his system. His God is the ordinary dualistic God of Christianity, to whom his philosophy simply opens the door; he has nothing whatsoever in common with the 'absolute spirit' set up by his successors. So far as this absolute spirit is logically derived from Kant, it is not from his God, but from entirely different elements of his philosophy. First from his notion that an unconditioned totality of the conditions of any experience must be assignable; and then from his other notion that the presence of some witness, or ego of apperception, is the most universal of all the conditions in question. The post-kantians make of the witness-condition what is called a concrete universal, an individualized all-witness or world-self, which shall imply in its rational constitution each and all of the other conditions put together, and therefore necessitate each and all of the conditioned experiences.

Abridgments like this of other men's opinions are very unsatisfactory, they always work injustice; but in this case those of you who are familiar with the literature will see immediately what I have in mind; and to the others, if there be any here, it will suffice to say that what I am trying so pedantically to point out is only the fact that monistic idealists after Kant have invariably sought relief from the supposed contradictions of our world of sense by looking forward toward an *ens rationis* conceived as its integration or logical completion, while he looked backward toward non-rational *dinge an sich* conceived as its cause. Pluralistic empiricists, on the other hand, have remained in the world of sense, either naïvely and because they overlooked the intellectualistic contradictions, or because, not able to ignore them, they thought they could refute them by a superior use of the same intellectualistic logic. Thus it is that John Mill pretends to refute the Achilles-tortoise fallacy.

The important point to notice here is the intellectualist logic. Both sides treat it as authoritative, but they do so capriciously: the absolutists smashing the world of sense by its means, the empiricists smashing the absolute — for the absolute, they say, is the quintessence of all logical contradictions. Neither side attains consistency. The Hegelians have to invoke a higher logic to supersede the purely destructive efforts of their first logic. The empiricists use their logic against the absolute, but refuse to use it against finite experience. Each party uses it or drops it to suit the vision it has faith in, but neither impugns in principle its general theoretic authority.

Bergson alone challenges its theoretic authority in principle. He alone denies that mere conceptual logic can tell us what is impossible or possible in the world of being or fact; and he does so for reasons which at the same time that they rule logic out from lordship over the whole of life, establish a vast and definite sphere of influence where its sovereignty is indisputable. Bergson's own text, felicitous as it is, is too intricate for quotation, so I must use my own inferior words in explaining what I mean by saying this.

In the first place, logic, giving primarily the relations between concepts as such, and the relations between natural facts only secondarily or so far as the facts have been already identified with concepts and defined by them, must of course stand or fall with the conceptual method. But the conceptual method is a transformation which the flux of life undergoes at our hands in the interests of practice essentially and only subordinately in the interests of theory. We live forward, we understand backward, said a danish writer; and to understand life by concepts is to arrest its movement, cutting it up into bits as if with scissors, and immobilizing these in our logical herbarium where, comparing them as dried specimens, we can ascertain which of them statically includes or excludes which other. This treatment supposes life to have already accomplished itself, for the concepts, being so many views taken after the fact, are retrospective and post mortem. Nevertheless we can draw conclusions from them and project them into the future. We cannot learn from them how life made itself go, or how it will make itself go; but, on the supposition that its ways of making itself go are unchanging, we can calculate what positions of imagined arrest it will exhibit hereafter under given conditions. We can compute, for instance, at what point Achilles will be, and where the tortoise will be, at the end of the twentieth minute. Achilles may then be at a point far ahead; but the full detail of how he will have managed practically to get there our logic never gives us — we have seen, indeed, that it finds that its results contradict the facts of nature. The computations which the other sciences make differ in no respect from those of mathematics. The concepts used are all of them dots through which, by interpolation or extrapolation, curves are drawn, while along the curves other dots are found as consequences. The latest refinements of logic dispense with the curves altogether, and deal solely with the dots and their correspondences each to each in various series. The authors of these recent improvements tell us expressly that their aim is to abolish the last vestiges of intuition, *videlicet* of concrete reality, from the field of reasoning, which then will operate literally on mental dots or bare abstract units of discourse, and on the ways in which they may be strung in naked series.

This is all very esoteric, and my own understanding of it is most likely misunderstanding.
So I speak here only by way of brief reminder
to those who know. For the rest of us it is
enough to recognize this fact, that altho by
means of concepts cut out from the sensible
flux of the past, we can re-descend upon the
future flux and, making another cut, say what
particular thing is likely to be found there; and
that altho in this sense concepts give us knowledge, and may be said to have some theoretic
value (especially when the particular thing
foretold is one in which we take no present
practical interest); yet in the deeper sense of
giving *insight* they have no theoretic value, for
they quite fail to connect us with the inner life
of the flux, or with the causes that govern its
direction. Instead of being interpreters of
reality, concepts negate the inwardness of reality altogether. They make the whole notion
of a causal influence between finite things in-
comprehensible. No real activities and indeed
no real connexions of any kind can obtain if we
follow the conceptual logic; for to be distin-

guishable, according to what I call intellectualism, is to be incapable of connexion. The work begun by Zeno, and continued by Hume, Kant, Herbart, Hegel, and Bradley, does not stop till sensible reality lies entirely disintegrated at the feet of 'reason.'

Of the 'absolute' reality which reason proposes to substitute for sensible reality I shall have more to say presently. Meanwhile you see what Professor Bergson means by insisting that the function of the intellect is practical rather than theoretical. Sensible reality is too concrete to be entirely manageable—look at the narrow range of it which is all that any animal, living in it exclusively as he does, is able to compass. To get from one point in it to another we have to plough or wade through the whole intolerable interval. No detail is spared us; it is as bad as the barbed-wire complications at Port Arthur, and we grow old and die in the process. But with our faculty of abstracting and fixing concepts we are there in a second, almost as if we controlled a fourth dimension, skipping the intermediaries as by a divine winged power, and getting at the exact point we require without entanglement with any context. What we do in fact is to *harness up* reality in our conceptual systems in order to drive it the better. This process is practical because all the termini to which we drive are *particular* termini, even when they are facts of the mental order. But the sciences in which the conceptual method chiefly celebrates its triumphs are those of space and matter, where the transformations of external things are dealt with. To deal with moral facts conceptually, we have first to transform them, substitute brain-diagrams or physical metaphors, treat ideas as atoms, interests as mechanical forces, our conscious 'selves' as 'streams,' and the like. Paradoxical effect! as Bergson well remarks, if our intellectual life were not practical but destined to reveal the inner natures. One would then suppose that it would find itself most at home in the domain of its own intellectual realities. But it is precisely there that it finds itself at the end of its tether. We know the inner movements of our spirit only perceptually.

We feel them live in us, but can give no distinct account of their elements, nor definitely predict their future; while things that lie along the world of space, things of the sort that we literally *handle*, are what our intellects cope with most successfully. Does not this confirm us in the view that the original and still surviving function of our intellectual life is to guide us in the practical adaptation of our expectancies and activities?

One can easily get into a verbal mess at this point, and my own experience with 'pragmatism' makes me shrink from the dangers that lie in the word 'practical,' and far rather than stand out against you for that word, I am quite willing to part company with Professor Bergson, and to ascribe a primarily theoretical function to our intellect, provided you on your part then agree to discriminate 'theoretic' or scientific knowledge from the deeper 'speculative' knowledge aspired to by most philosophers, and concede that theoretic knowledge, which is knowledge *about* things, as distinguished from living or sympathetic acquaintance with them, touches only the outer surface of reality.[1] The surface which theoretic knowledge taken in this sense covers may indeed be enormous in extent; it may dot the whole diameter of space and time with its conceptual creations; but it does not penetrate a millimeter into the solid dimension. That inner dimension of reality is occupied by the *activities* that keep it going, but the intellect, speaking through Hume, Kant & Co., finds itself obliged to deny, and persists in denying, that activities have any intelligible existence. What exists for *thought*, we are told, is at most the results that we illusorily ascribe to such activities, strung along the surfaces of space and time by *regel der verknüpfung*, laws of nature which state only coexistences and successions.[1]

Thought deals thus solely with surfaces. It can name the thickness of reality, but it cannot fathom it, and its insufficiency here is essential and permanent, not temporary.

The only way in which to apprehend reality's thickness is either to experience it directly by

being a part of reality one's self, or to evoke
it in imagination by sympathetically divining
some one else's inner life. But what we thus
immediately experience or concretely divine is
very limited in duration, whereas abstractly we
are able to conceive eternities. Could we feel a
million years concretely as we now feel a passing
minute, we should have very little employment
for our conceptual faculty. We should know the
whole period fully at every moment of its pas-
sage, whereas we must now construct it labori-
ously by means of concepts which we project.
Direct acquaintance and conceptual knowledge
are thus complementary of each other; each
remedies the other's defects. If what we care
most about be the synoptic treatment of phenomena, the vision of the far and the gathering
of the scattered like, we must follow the conceptual method. But if, as metaphysicians, we
are more curious about the inner nature of
reality or about what really makes it go, we
must turn our backs upon our winged concepts
altogether, and bury ourselves in the thickness
of those passing moments over the surface of

which they fly, and on particular points of which they occasionally rest and perch.

Professor Bergson thus inverts the traditional platonic doctrine absolutely. Instead of intellectual knowledge being the profounder, he calls it the more superficial. Instead of being the only adequate knowledge, it is grossly inadequate, and its only superiority is the practical one of enabling us to make short cuts through experience and thereby to save time. The one thing it cannot do is to reveal the nature of things — which last remark, if not clear already, will become clearer as I proceed. Dive back into the flux itself, then, Bergson tells us, if you wish to *know* reality, that flux which Platonism, in its strange belief that only the immutable is excellent, has always spurned; turn your face toward sensation, that flesh-bound thing which rationalism has always loaded with abuse. — This, you see, is exactly the opposite remedy from that of looking forward into the absolute, which our idealistic contemporaries prescribe. It violates our mental habits, being a kind of passive and receptive listening quite contrary to that effort to react noisily and verbally on everything, which is our usual intellectual pose.

What, then, are the peculiar features in the perceptual flux which the conceptual translation so fatally leaves out?

The essence of life is its continuously changing character; but our concepts are all discontinuous and fixed, and the only mode of making them coincide with life is by arbitrarily supposing positions of arrest therein. With such arrests our concepts may be made congruent. But these concepts are not *parts* of reality, not real positions taken by it, but *suppositions* rather, notes taken by ourselves, and you can no more dip up the substance of reality with them than you can dip up water with a net, however finely meshed.

When we conceptualize, we cut out and fix, and exclude everything but what we have fixed. A concept means a *that-and-no-other*. Conceptually, time excludes space; motion and rest exclude each other; approach excludes contact; presence excludes absence; unity excludes plurality; independence excludes relativity; 'mine' excludes 'yours'; this connexion excludes that connexion—and so on indefinitely; whereas in the real concrete sensible flux of life experiences compenetrate each other so that it is not easy to know just what is excluded and what not. Past and future, for example, conceptually separated by the cut to which we give the name of present, and defined as being the opposite sides of that cut, are to some extent, however brief, co-present with each other throughout experience. The literally present moment is a purely verbal supposition, not a position; the only present ever realized concretely being the 'passing moment' in which the dying rearward of time and its dawning future forever mix their lights. Say 'now' and it *was* even while you say it.

It is just intellectualism's attempt to substitute static cuts for units of experienced duration that makes real motion so unintelligible. The conception of the first half of the interval between Achilles and the tortoise excludes that of the last half, and the mathematical neces-

sity of traversing it separately before the last
half is traversed stands permanently in the way
of the last half ever being traversed. Meanwhile the living Achilles (who, for the purposes
of this discussion, is only the abstract name of
one phenomenon of impetus, just as the tortoise is of another) asks no leave of logic. The
velocity of his acts is an indivisible nature in
them like the expansive tension in a spring
compressed. We define it conceptually as $\frac{s}{t}$,
but the s and t are only artificial cuts made
after the fact, and indeed most artificial when
we treat them in both runners as the same
tracts of 'objective' space and time, for the
experienced spaces and times in which the
tortoise inwardly lives are probably as different as his velocity from the same things in
Achilles. The impetus of Achilles is one concrete fact, and carries space, time, and conquest
over the inferior creature's motion indivisibly
in it. He perceives nothing, while running, of
the mathematician's homogeneous time and
space, of the infinitely numerous succession
of cuts in both, or of their order. End and

beginning come for him in the one onrush, and all that he actually experiences is that, in the midst of a certain intense effort of his own, the rival is in point of fact outstripped.

We are so inveterately wedded to the conceptual decomposition of life that I know that this will seem to you like putting muddiest confusion in place of clearest thought, and relapsing into a molluscoid state of mind. Yet I ask you whether the absolute superiority of our higher thought is so very clear, if all that it can find is impossibility in tasks which sense-experience so easily performs.

What makes you call real life confusion is that it presents, as if they were dissolved in one another, a lot of differents which conception breaks life's flow by keeping apart. But *are* not differents actually dissolved in one another? Has n't every bit of experience its quality, its duration, its extension, its intensity, its urgency, its clearness, and many aspects besides, no one of which can exist in the isolation in which our verbalized logic keeps it? They exist only *durcheinander*. Reality always is, in M. Bergson's phrase, an endosmosis or conflux of the same with the different: they compenetrate and telescope. For conceptual logic, the same is nothing but the same, and all sames with a third thing are the same with each other. Not so in concrete experience. Two spots on our skin, each of which feels the same as a third spot when touched along with it, are felt as different from each other. Two tones, neither distinguishable from a third tone, are perfectly distinct from each other. The whole process of life is due to life's violation of our logical axioms. Take its continuity as an example. Terms like A and C appear to be connected by intermediaries, by B for example. Intellectualism calls this absurd, for 'B-connected-with-A' is, 'as such,' a different term from 'B-connected-with-C.' But real life laughs at logic's veto. Imagine a heavy log which takes two men to carry it. First A and B take it. Then C takes hold and A drops off; then D takes hold and B drops off, so that C and D now bear it; and so on. The log meanwhile never drops, and keeps its sameness throughout the journey. Even so it is with all our experiences. Their changes are not complete annihilations followed by complete creations of something absolutely novel. There is partial decay and partial growth, and all the while a nucleus of relative constancy from which what decays drops off, and which takes into itself whatever is grafted on, until at length something wholly different has taken its place. In such a process we are as sure, in spite of intellectualist logic with its 'as suches,' that it *is* the same nucleus which is able now to make connexion with what goes and again with what comes, as we are sure that the same point can lie on diverse lines that intersect there. Without being one throughout, such a universe is continuous. Its members interdigitate with their next neighbors in manifold directions, and there are no clean cuts between them anywhere.

The great clash of intellectualist logic with sensible experience is where the experience is that of influence exerted. Intellectualism denies (as we saw in lecture ii) that finite things

can act on one another, for all things, once
translated into concepts, remain shut up to
themselves. To act on anything means to get
into it somehow; but that would mean to get
out of one's self and be one's other, which is
self-contradictory, etc. Meanwhile each of us
actually *is* his own other to that extent, livingly
knowing how to perform the trick which logic
tells us can't be done. My thoughts animate
and actuate this very body which you see and
hear, and thereby influence your thoughts. The
dynamic current somehow does get from me
to you, however numerous the intermediary
conductors may have to be. Distinctions may
be insulators in logic as much as they like, but
in life distinct things can and do commune
together every moment.

The conflict of the two ways of knowing is
best summed up in the intellectualist doctrine
that 'the same cannot exist in many relations.'
This follows of course from the concepts of the
two relations being so distinct that 'what-is-
in-the-one' means 'as such' something distinct from what 'what-is-in-the-other' means.

It is like Mill's ironical saying, that we should not think of Newton as both an Englishman and a mathematician, because an Englishman as such is not a mathematician and a mathematician as such is not an Englishman. But the real Newton was somehow both things at once; and throughout the whole finite universe each real thing proves to be many differents without undergoing the necessity of breaking into disconnected editions of itself.

These few indications will perhaps suffice to put you at the bergsonian point of view. The immediate experience of life solves the problems which so baffle our conceptual intelligence: How can what is manifold be one? how can things get out of themselves? how be their own others? how be both distinct and connected? how can they act on one another? how be for others and yet for themselves? how be absent and present at once? The intellect asks these questions much as we might ask how anything can both separate and unite things, or how sounds can grow more alike by continuing to grow more different. If you already know space

sensibly, you can answer the former question
by pointing to any interval in it, long or short;
if you know the musical scale, you can answer
the latter by sounding an octave; but then you
must first have the sensible knowledge of these
realities. Similarly Bergson answers the intellectualist conundrums by pointing back to our
various finite sensational experiences and saying, 'Lo, even thus; even so are these other
problems solved livingly.'

When you have broken the reality into concepts you never can reconstruct it in its wholeness. Out of no amount of discreteness can you
manufacture the concrete. But place yourself
at a bound, or *d'emblée,* as M. Bergson says, inside of the living, moving, active thickness of
the real, and all the abstractions and distinctions are given into your hand: you can now
make the intellectualist substitutions to your
heart's content. Install yourself in phenomenal
movement, for example, and velocity, succession, dates, positions, and innumerable other
things are given you in the bargain. But with
only an abstract succession of dates and posi-

tions you can never patch up movement itself. It slips through their intervals and is lost.

So it is with every concrete thing, however complicated. Our intellectual handling of it is a retrospective patchwork, a post-mortem dissection, and can follow any order we find most expedient. We can make the thing seem self-contradictory whenever we wish to. But place yourself at the point of view of the thing's interior *doing,* and all these back-looking and conflicting conceptions lie harmoniously in your hand. Get at the expanding centre of a human character, the *élan vital* of a man, as Bergson calls it, by living sympathy, and at a stroke you see how it makes those who see it from without interpret it in such diverse ways. It is something that breaks into both honesty and dishonesty, courage and cowardice, stupidity and insight, at the touch of varying circumstances, and you feel exactly why and how it does this, and never seek to identify it stably with any of these single abstractions. Only your intellectualist does that, — and you now also feel why *he* must do it to the end.

Place yourself similarly at the centre of a man's philosophic vision and you understand at once all the different things it makes him write or say. But keep outside, use your postmortem method, try to build the philosophy up out of the single phrases, taking first one and then another and seeking to make them fit, and of course you fail. You crawl over the thing like a myopic ant over a building, tumbling into every microscopic crack or fissure, finding nothing but inconsistencies, and never suspecting that a centre exists. I hope that some of the philosophers in this audience may occasionally have had something different from this intellectualist type of criticism applied to their own works!

What really *exists* is not things made but things in the making. Once made, they are dead, and an infinite number of alternative conceptual decompositions can be used in defining them. But put yourself *in the making* by a stroke of intuitive sympathy with the thing and, the whole range of possible decompositions coming at once into your possession, you are no longer troubled with the question which of them is the more absolutely true. Reality *falls* in passing into conceptual analysis; it *mounts* in living its own undivided life—it buds and bourgeons, changes and creates. Once adopt the movement of this life in any given instance and you know what Bergson calls the *devenir réel* by which the thing evolves and grows. Philosophy should seek this kind of living understanding of the movement of reality, not follow science in vainly patching together fragments of its dead results.

Thus much of M. Bergson's philosophy is sufficient for my purpose in these lectures, so here I will stop, leaving unnoticed all its other constituent features, original and interesting tho they be. You may say, and doubtless some of you now are saying inwardly, that his re-manding us to sensation in this wise is only a regress, a return to that ultra-crude empiricism which your own idealists since Green have buried ten times over. I confess that it is indeed a return to empiricism, but I think that the return in such accomplished shape only proves the latter's immortal truth. What won't stay buried must have some genuine life. *Am anfang war die tat;* fact is a *first;* to which all our conceptual handling comes as an inadequate second, never its full equivalent. When I read recent transcendentalist literature — I must partly except my colleague Royce! — I get nothing but a sort of marking of time, champing of jaws, pawing of the ground, and resettling into the same attitude, like a weary horse in a stall with an empty manger. It is but turning over the same few threadbare categories, bringing the same objections, and urging the same answers and solutions, with never a new fact or a new horizon coming into sight. But open Bergson, and new horizons loom on every page you read. It is like the breath of the morning and the song of birds. It tells of reality itself, instead of merely reiterating what dusty-minded professors have written about what other previous professors have thought. Nothing in Bergson is shop-worn or at second hand.

That he gives us no closed-in system will of

course be fatal to him in intellectualist eyes. He only evokes and invites; but he first annuls the intellectualist veto, so that we now join step with reality with a philosophical conscience never quite set free before. As a french disciple of his well expresses it: 'Bergson claims of us first of all a certain inner catastrophe, and not every one is capable of such a logical revolution. But those who have once found themselves flexible enough for the execution of such a psychological change of front, discover somehow that they can never return again to their ancient attitude of mind. They are now Bergsonians . . . and possess the principal thoughts of the master all at once. They have understood in the fashion in which one loves, they have caught the whole melody and can thereafter admire at their leisure the originality, the fecundity, and the imaginative genius with which its author develops, transposes, and varies in a thousand ways by the orchestration of his style and dialectic, the original theme.'[2]

This, scant as it is, is all I have to say about

VI. BERGSON AND INTELLECTUALISM

Bergson on this occasion — I hope it may send some of you to his original text. I must now turn back to the point where I found it advisable to appeal to his ideas. You remember my own intellectualist difficulties in the last lecture, about how a lot of separate consciousnesses can at the same time be one collective thing. How, I asked, can one and the same identical content of experience, of which on idealist principles the *esse* is to be felt, be felt so diversely if itself be the only feeler? The usual way of escape by 'quatenus' or 'as such' won't help us here if we are radical intellectualists, I said, for appearance-together is as such *not* appearance-apart, the world *quâ* many is not the world *quâ* one, as absolutism claims. If we hold to Hume's maxim, which later intellectualism uses so well, that whatever things are distinguished are as separate as if there were no manner of connexion between them, there seemed no way out of the difficulty save by stepping outside of experience altogether and invoking different spiritual agents, selves or souls, to realize the diversity required. But this rescue by 'scholastic entities' I was unwilling to accept any more than pantheistic idealists accept it.

Yet, to quote Fechner's phrase again, 'nichts wirkliches kann unmöglich sein,' the actual cannot be impossible, and what *is* actual at every moment of our lives is the sort of thing which I now proceed to remind you of. You can hear the vibration of an electric contact-maker, smell the ozone, see the sparks, and feel the thrill, co-consciously as it were or in one field of experience. But you can also isolate any one of these sensations by shutting out the rest. If you close your eyes, hold your nose, and remove your hand, you can get the sensation of sound alone, but it seems still the same sensation that it was; and if you restore the action of the other organs, the sound coalesces with the feeling, the sight, and the smell sensations again. Now the natural way of talking of all this[3] is to say that certain sensations are experienced, now singly, and now together with other sensations, in a common conscious field. Fluctuations of attention give analogous results. We let a sensation in or keep it out by changing our attention; and similarly we let an item of memory in or drop it out. [Please don't raise the question here of how these changes *come to pass*. The immediate condition is probably cerebral in every instance, but it would be irrelevant now to consider it, for now we are thinking only of results, and I repeat that the natural way of thinking of them is that which intellectualist criticism finds so absurd.]

The absurdity charged is that the self-same should function so differently, now with and now without something else. But this it sensibly seems to do. This very desk which I strike with my hand strikes in turn your eyes. It functions at once as a physical object in the outer world and as a mental object in our sundry mental worlds. The very body of mine that *my* thought actuates is the body whose gestures are *your* visual object and to which you give my name. The very log which John helped to carry is the log now borne by James. The very girl you love is simultane-

ously entangled elsewhere. The very place behind me is in front of you. Look where you
will, you gather only examples of the same amid
the different, and of different relations existing
as it were in solution in the same thing. *Quâ*
this an experience is not the same as it is *quâ*
that, truly enough; but the *quâs* are conceptual
shots of ours at its post-mortem remains, and
in its sensational immediacy everything is all
at once whatever different things it is at once
at all. It is before C and after A, far from
you and near to me, without this associate and
with that one, active and passive, physical and
mental, a whole of parts and part of a higher
whole, all simultaneously and without interference or need of doubling-up its being, so
long as we keep to what I call the 'immediate'
point of view, the point of view in which we
follow our sensational life's continuity, and to
which all living language conforms. It is only
when you try — to continue using the hegelian
vocabulary — to 'mediate' the immediate, or
to substitute concepts for sensational life, that
intellectualism celebrates its triumph and the

immanent-self-contradictoriness of all this smooth-running finite experience gets proved.

Of the oddity of inventing as a remedy for the inconveniences resulting from this situation a supernumerary conceptual object called an absolute, into which you pack the self-same contradictions unreduced, I will say something in the next lecture. The absolute is said to perform its feats by taking up its other into itself. But that is exactly what is done when every individual morsel of the sensational stream takes up the adjacent morsels by coalescing with them. This is just what we mean by the stream's sensible continuity. No element *there* cuts itself off from any other element, as concepts cut themselves from concepts. No part *there* is so small as not to be a place of conflux. No part there is not really *next* its neighbors; which means that there is literally nothing between; which means again that no part goes exactly so far and no farther; that no part absolutely excludes another, but that they compenetrate and are cohesive; that if you tear out one, its roots bring out more with them; that whatever is real is telescoped and diffused into other reals; that, in short, every minutest thing is already its hegelian 'own other,' in the fullest sense of the term.

Of course this *sounds* self-contradictory, but as the immediate facts don't sound at all, but simply *are*, until we conceptualize and name them vocally, the contradiction results only from the conceptual or discursive form being substituted for the real form. But if, as Bergson shows, that form is superimposed for practical ends only, in order to let us jump about over life instead of wading through it; and if it cannot even pretend to reveal anything of what life's inner nature is or ought to be; why then we can turn a deaf ear to its accusations. The resolve to turn the deaf ear is the inner crisis or 'catastrophe' of which M. Bergson's disciple whom I lately quoted spoke. We are so subject to the philosophic tradition which treats *logos* or discursive thought generally as the sole avenue to truth, that to fall back on raw unverbalized life as more of a revealer, and to think of concepts as the merely practical things which

VI. BERGSON AND INTELLECTUALISM

Bergson calls them, comes very hard. It is putting off our proud maturity of mind and becoming again as foolish little children in the eyes of reason. But difficult as such a revolution is, there is no other way, I believe, to the possession of reality, and I permit myself to hope that some of you may share my opinion after you have heard my next lecture.

VII

THE CONTINUITY OF EXPERIENCE

LECTURE VII

THE CONTINUITY OF EXPERIENCE

I FEAR that few of you will have been able to obey Bergson's call upon you to look towards the sensational life for the fuller knowledge of reality, or to sympathize with his attempt to limit the divine right of concepts to rule our mind absolutely. It is too much like looking downward and not up. Philosophy, you will say, does n't lie flat on its belly in the middle of experience, in the very thick of its sand and gravel, as this Bergsonism does, never getting a peep at anything from above. Philosophy is essentially the vision of things from above. It does n't simply feel the detail of things, it comprehends their intelligible plan, sees their forms and principles, their categories and rules, their order and necessity. It takes the superior point of view of the architect. Is it conceivable that it should ever forsake that point of view and abandon itself to a slovenly life of immediate feeling? To say nothing of

your traditional Oxford devotion to Aristotle
and Plato, the leaven of T. H. Green probably works still too strongly here for his anti-
sensationalism to be outgrown quickly. Green
more than any one realized that knowledge
about things was knowledge of their relations;
but nothing could persuade him that our sensational life could contain any relational element. He followed the strict intellectualist
method with sensations. What they were not
expressly defined as including, they must exclude. Sensations are not defined as relations,
so in the end Green thought that they could get
related together only by the action on them from
above of a 'self-distinguishing' absolute and
eternal mind, present to that which is related,
but not related itself. 'A relation,' he said, 'is
not contingent with the contingency of feeling.
It is permanent with the permanence of the
combining and comparing thought which alone
constitutes it.'[1] In other words, relations are
purely conceptual objects, and the sensational
life as such cannot relate itself together. Sensation in itself, Green wrote, is fleeting, momen-

tary, unnameable (because, while we name it,
it has become another), and for the same reason unknowable, the very negation of know-
ability. Were there no permanent objects of
conception for our sensations to be 'referred
to,' there would be no significant names, but
only noises, and a consistent sensationalism
must be speechless.[2] Green's intellectualism
was so earnest that it produced a natural and
an inevitable effect. But the atomistic and
unrelated sensations which he had in mind
were purely fictitious products of his rationalist
fancy. The psychology of our own day dis-
avows them utterly,[3] and Green's laborious
belaboring of poor old Locke for not having
first seen that his ideas of sensation were just
that impracticable sort of thing, and then fled
to transcendental idealism as a remedy, — his
belaboring of poor old Locke for this, I say, is
pathetic. Every examiner of the sensible life
in concreto must see that relations of every sort,
of time, space, difference, likeness, change,
rate, cause, or what not, are just as integral
members of the sensational flux as terms are,

and that conjunctive relations are just as true members of the flux as disjunctive relations are.[4] This is what in some recent writings of mine I have called the 'radically empiricist' doctrine (in distinction from the doctrine of mental atoms which the name empiricism so often suggests). Intellectualistic critics of sensation insist that sensations are *dis*-joined only. Radical empiricism insists that conjunctions between them are just as immediately given as disjunctions are, and that relations, whether disjunctive or conjunctive, are in their original sensible givenness just as fleeting and momentary (in Green's words), and just as 'particular,' as terms are. Later, both terms and relations get universalized by being conceptualized and named.[5] But all the thickness, concreteness, and individuality of experience exists in the immediate and relatively unnamed stages of it, to the richness of which, and to the standing inadequacy of our conceptions to match it, Professor Bergson so emphatically calls our attention.

And now I am happy to say that we can begin

to gather together some of the separate threads of our argument, and see a little better the general kind of conclusion toward which we are tending. Pray go back with me to the lecture before the last, and recall what I said about the difficulty of seeing how states of consciousness can compound themselves. The difficulty seemed to be the same, you remember, whether we took it in psychology as the composition of finite states of mind out of simpler finite states, or in metaphysics as the composition of the absolute mind out of finite minds in general. It is the general conceptualist difficulty of any one thing being the same with many things, either at once or in succession, for the abstract concepts of oneness and manyness must needs exclude each other. In the particular instance that we have dwelt on so long, the one thing is the all-form of experience, the many things are the each-forms of experience in you and me. To call them the same we must treat them as if each were simultaneously its own other, a feat on conceptualist principles impossible of performance.

On the principle of going behind the conceptual function altogether, however, and looking to the more primitive flux of the sensational life for reality's true shape, a way is open to us, as I tried in my last lecture to show. Not only the absolute is its own other, but the simplest bits of immediate experience are their own others, if that hegelian phrase be once for all allowed. The concrete pulses of experience appear pent in by no such definite limits as our conceptual substitutes for them are confined by. They run into one another continuously and seem to interpenetrate. What in them is relation and what is matter related is hard to discern. You feel no one of them as inwardly simple, and no two as wholly without confluence where they touch. There is no datum so small as not to show this mystery, if mystery it be. The tiniest feeling that we can possibly have comes with an earlier and a later part and with a sense of their continuous procession. Mr. Shadworth Hodgson showed long ago that there is literally no such object as the present moment except as an unreal postulate of abstract thought.[6] The 'passing' moment is, as I already have reminded you, the minimal fact, with the 'apparition of difference' inside of it as well as outside. If we do not feel both past and present in one field of feeling, we feel them not at all. We have the same many-in-one in the matter that fills the passing time. The rush of our thought forward through its fringes is the everlasting peculiarity of its life. We realize this life as something always off its balance, something in transition, something that shoots out of a darkness through a dawn into a brightness that we feel to be the dawn fulfilled. In the very midst of the continuity our experience comes as an alteration. 'Yes,' we say at the full brightness, '*this* is what I just meant.' 'No,' we feel at the dawning, 'this is not yet the full meaning, there is more to come.' In every crescendo of sensation, in every effort to recall, in every progress towards the satisfaction of desire, this succession of an emptiness and fulness that have reference to each other and are one flesh is the essence of the phenomenon. In every hindrance of desire the sense of an ideal presence which is absent in fact, of an absent, in a word, which the only function of the present is to *mean*, is even more notoriously there. And in the movement of pure thought we have the same phenomenon. When I say *Socrates is mortal*, the moment *Socrates* is incomplete; it falls forward through the *is* which is pure movement, into the *mortal* which is indeed bare mortal on the tongue, but for the mind is *that mortal*, the *mortal Socrates*, at last satisfactorily disposed of and told off.[7]

Here, then, inside of the minimal pulses of experience, is realized that very inner complexity which the transcendentalists say only the absolute can genuinely possess. The gist of the matter is always the same — something ever goes indissolubly with something else. You cannot separate the same from its other, except by abandoning the real altogether and taking to the conceptual system. What is immediately given in the single and particular instance is always something pooled and mutual, something with no dark spot, no point of ignorance. No one elementary bit of reality is eclipsed from the next bit's point of view, if only we take reality sensibly and in small enough pulses — and by us it has to be taken pulse-wise, for our span of consciousness is too short to grasp the larger collectivity of things except nominally and abstractly. No more of reality collected together at once is extant anywhere, perhaps, than in my experience of reading this page, or in yours of listening; yet within those bits of experience as they come to pass we get a fulness of content that no conceptual description can equal. Sensational experiences *are* their 'own others,' then, both internally and externally. Inwardly they are one with their parts, and outwardly they pass continuously into their next neighbors, so that events separated by years of time in a man's life hang together unbrokenly by the intermediary events. Their *names*, to be sure, cut them into separate conceptual entities, but no cuts existed in the continuum in which they originally came.

If, with all this in our mind, we turn to our

285

own particular predicament, we see that our old objection to the self-compounding of states of consciousness, our accusation that it was impossible for purely logical reasons, is unfounded in principle. Every smallest state of consciousness, concretely taken, overflows its own definition. Only concepts are self-identical; only 'reason' deals with closed equations; nature is but a name for excess; every point in her opens out and runs into the more; and the only question, with reference to any point we may be considering, is how far into the rest of nature we may have to go in order to get entirely beyond its overflow. In the pulse of inner life immediately present now in each of us is a little past, a little future, a little awareness of our own body, of each other's persons, of these sublimities we are trying to talk about, of the earth's geography and the direction of history, of truth and error, of good and bad, and of who knows how much more? Feeling, however dimly and subconsciously, all these things, your pulse of inner life is continuous with them, belongs to them and they to it. You can't identify it with either one of them rather than with the others, for if you let it develop into no matter which of those directions, what it develops into will look back on it and say, 'That was the original germ of me.'

In *principle*, then, the real units of our immediately-felt life are unlike the units that intellectualist logic holds to and makes its calculations with. They are not separate from their own others, and you have to take them at widely separated dates to find any two of them that seem unblent. Then indeed they do appear separate even as their concepts are separate; a chasm yawns between them; but the chasm itself is but an intellectualist fiction, got by abstracting from the continuous sheet of experiences with which the intermediary time was filled. It is like the log carried first by William and Henry, then by William, Henry, and John, then by Henry and John, then by John and Peter, and so on. All real units of experience *overlap*. Let a row of equidistant dots on a sheet of paper symbolize the concepts by which we intellectualize the world. Let a ruler long enough to cover at least three dots stand for our sensible experience. Then the conceived changes of the sensible experience can be symbolized by sliding the ruler along the line of dots. One concept after another will apply to it, one after another drop away, but it will always cover at least two of them, and no dots less than three will ever adequately cover *it*. You falsify it if you treat it conceptually, or by the law of dots.

What is true here of successive states must also be true of simultaneous characters. They also overlap each other with their being. My present field of consciousness is a centre surrounded by a fringe that shades insensibly into a subconscious more. I use three separate terms here to describe this fact; but I might as well use three hundred, for the fact is all shades and no boundaries. Which part of it properly is in my consciousness, which out? If I name what is out, it already has come in. The centre works in one way while the margins work in another, and presently overpower the centre

and are central themselves. What we conceptually identify ourselves with and say we
are thinking of at any time is the centre; but
our *full* self is the whole field, with all those
indefinitely radiating subconscious possibilities
of increase that we can only feel without conceiving, and can hardly begin to analyze. The
collective and the distributive ways of being
coexist here, for each part functions distinctly,
makes connexion with its own peculiar region
in the still wider rest of experience and tends
to draw us into that line, and yet the whole is
somehow felt as one pulse of our life, — not
conceived so, but felt so.

In principle, then, as I said, intellectualism's edge is broken; it can only approximate
to reality, and its logic is inapplicable to our
inner life, which spurns its vetoes and mocks
at its impossibilities. Every bit of us at every
moment is part and parcel of a wider self, it
quivers along various radii like the wind-rose
on a compass, and the actual in it is continuously one with possibles not yet in our present
sight.[8] And just as we are co-conscious with

our own momentary margin, may not we ourselves form the margin of some more really
central self in things which is co-conscious
with the whole of us? May not you and I be
confluent in a higher consciousness, and con-
fluently active there, tho we now know it not?

I am tiring myself and you, I know, by
vainly seeking to describe by concepts and
words what I say at the same time exceeds
either conceptualization or verbalization. As
long as one continues *talking*, intellectualism
remains in undisturbed possession of the field.
The return to life can't come about by talking.
It is an *act;* to make you return to life, I must
set an example for your imitation, I must
deafen you to talk, or to the importance of
talk, by showing you, as Bergson does, that the
concepts we talk with are made for purposes of
practice and not for purposes of insight. Or I
must *point*, point to the mere *that* of life, and
you by inner sympathy must fill out the *what*
for yourselves. The minds of some of you, I
know, will absolutely refuse to do so, refuse to
think in non-conceptualized terms. I myself

absolutely refused to do so for years together, even after I knew that the denial of manyness-in-oneness by intellectualism must be false, for the same reality does perform the most various functions at once. But I hoped ever for a revised intellectualist way round the difficulty, and it was only after reading Bergson that I saw that to continue using the intellectualist method was itself the fault. I saw that philosophy had been on a false scent ever since the days of Socrates and Plato, that an *intellectual* answer to the intellectualist's difficulties will never come, and that the real way out of them, far from consisting in the discovery of such an answer, consists in simply closing one's ears to the question. When conceptualism summons life to justify itself in conceptual terms, it is like a challenge addressed in a foreign language to some one who is absorbed in his own business; it is irrelevant to him altogether — he may let it lie unnoticed. I went thus through the 'inner catastrophe' of which I spoke in the last lecture; I had literally come to the end of my conceptual stock-in-trade, I was bankrupt intellectualistically, and had to change my base. No words of mine will probably convert you, for words can be the names only of concepts. But if any of you try sincerely and pertinaciously on your own separate accounts to intellectualize reality, you may be similarly driven to a change of front. I say no more: I must leave life to teach the lesson.

We have now reached a point of view from which the self-compounding of mind in its smaller and more accessible portions seems a certain fact, and in which the speculative assumption of a similar but wider compounding in remoter regions must be reckoned with as a legitimate hypothesis. The absolute is not the impossible being I once thought it. Mental facts do function both singly and together, at once, and we finite minds may simultaneously be co-conscious with one another in a superhuman intelligence. It is only the extravagant claims of coercive necessity on the absolute's part that have to be denied by *a priori* logic. As an hypothesis trying to make itself probable on analogical and inductive grounds, the absolute is entitled to a patient hearing. Which is as much as to say that our serious business from now onward lies with Fechner and his method, rather than with Hegel, Royce, or Bradley. Fechner treats the superhuman consciousness he so fervently believes in as an hypothesis only, which he then recommends by all the resources of induction and persuasion.

It is true that Fechner himself is an absolutist in his books, not actively but passively, if I may say so. He talks not only of the earth-soul and of the star-souls, but of an integrated soul of all things in the cosmos without exception, and this he calls God just as others call it the absolute. Nevertheless he *thinks* only of the subordinate superhuman souls, and content with having made his obeisance once for all to the august total soul of the cosmos, he leaves it in its lonely sublimity with no attempt to define its nature. Like the absolute, it is 'out of range,' and not an object for distincter vision. Psychologically, it seems to me that Fechner's God is a lazy postulate of his, rather than a part of his system positively thought out. As we envelop our sight and hearing, so the earth-soul envelops us, and the star-soul the earth-soul, until — what? Envelopment can't go on forever; it must have an *abschluss*, a total envelope must terminate the series, so God is the name that Fechner gives to this last all-enveloper. But if nothing escapes this all-enveloper, he is responsible for everything, including evil, and all the paradoxes and difficulties which I found in the absolute at the end of our third lecture recur undiminished. Fechner tries sincerely to grapple with the problem of evil, but he always solves it in the leibnitzian fashion by making his God non-absolute, placing him under conditions of 'metaphysical necessity' which even his omnipotence cannot violate. His will has to struggle with conditions not imposed on that will by itself. He tolerates provisionally what he has not created, and then with endless patience tries to overcome it and live it down. He has, in short, a history. Whenever Fechner tries to represent him clearly, his God becomes the ordinary God of theism, and ceases to be the absolutely totalized all-enveloper.[9] In this shape, he represents the ideal element in things solely, and is our champion and our helper and we his helpers, against the bad parts of the universe.

Fechner was in fact too little of a metaphysician to care for perfect formal consistency in these abstract regions. He believed in God in the pluralistic manner, but partly from convention and partly from what I should call intellectual laziness, if laziness of any kind could be imputed to a Fechner, he let the usual monistic talk about him pass unchallenged. I propose to you that we should discuss the question of God without entangling ourselves in advance in the monistic assumption. Is it probable that there is any superhuman consciousness at all, in the first place? When that is settled, the further question whether its form be monistic or pluralistic is in order.

Before advancing to either question, however, and I shall have to deal with both but very briefly after what has been said already, let me finish our retrospective survey by one more

remark about the curious logical situation of
the absolutists. For what have they invoked
the absolute except as a being the peculiar
inner form of which shall enable it to overcome the contradictions with which intellectualism has found the finite many as such to be
infected? The many-in-one character that, as
we have seen, every smallest tract of finite
experience offers, is considered by intellectualism to be fatal to the reality of finite experience. What can be distinguished, it tells us, is
separate; and what is separate is unrelated, for
a relation, being a 'between,' would bring only
a twofold separation. Hegel, Royce, Bradley,
and the Oxford absolutists in general seem to
agree about this logical absurdity of manyness-
in-oneness in the only places where it is empirically found. But see the curious tactics! Is the
absurdity *reduced* in the absolute being whom
they call in to relieve it? Quite otherwise,
for that being shows it on an infinitely greater
scale, and flaunts it in its very definition. The
fact of its not being related to any outward environment, the fact that all relations are inside

of itself, does n't save it, for Mr. Bradley's great argument against the finite is that *in* any given bit of it (a bit of sugar, for instance) the presence of a plurality of characters (whiteness and sweetness, for example) is self-contradictory; so that in the final end all that the absolute's name appears to stand for is the persistent claim of outraged human nature that reality *shall* not be called absurd. *Somewhere* there must be an aspect of it guiltless of self-contradiction. All we can see of the absolute, meanwhile, is guilty in the same way in which the finite is. Intellectualism sees what it calls the guilt, when comminuted in the finite object; but is too near-sighted to see it in the more enormous object. Yet the absolute's constitution, if imagined at all, has to be imagined after the analogy of some bit of finite experience. Take any *real* bit, suppress its environment and then magnify it to monstrosity, and you get identically the type of structure of the absolute. It is obvious that all your difficulties here remain and go with you. If the relative experience was inwardly absurd, the absolute experience is infinitely more so. Intellectualism, in short, strains off the gnat, but swallows the whole camel. But this polemic against the absolute is as odious to me as it is to you, so I will say no more about that being. It is only one of those wills of the wisp, those lights that do mislead the morn, that have so often impeded the clear progress of philosophy, so I will turn to the more general positive question of whether superhuman unities of consciousness should be considered as more probable or more improbable.

In a former lecture I went over some of the fechnerian reasons for their plausibility, or reasons that at least replied to our more obvious grounds of doubt concerning them. The numerous facts of divided or split human personality which the genius of certain medical men, as Janet, Freud, Prince, Sidis, and others, have unearthed were unknown in Fechner's time, and neither the phenomena of automatic writing and speech, nor of mediumship and 'possession' generally, had been recognized or studied as we now study them, so Fechner's stock of analogies is scant compared with our present one. He did the best with what he had, however. For my own part I find in some of these abnormal or supernormal facts the strongest suggestions in favor of a superior co-consciousness being possible. I doubt whether we shall ever understand some of them without using the very letter of Fechner's conception of a great reservoir in which the memories of earth's inhabitants are pooled and preserved, and from which, when the threshold lowers or the valve opens, information ordinarily shut out leaks into the mind of exceptional individuals among us. But those regions of inquiry are perhaps too spook-haunted to interest an academic audience, and the only evidence I feel it now decorous to bring to the support of Fechner is drawn from ordinary religious experience. I think it may be asserted that there *are* religious experiences of a specific nature, not deducible by analogy or psychological reasoning from our other sorts of experience. I think that they point with reasonable probability to the continuity of our consciousness with a wider spiritual environment from which the ordinary prudential man (who is the only man that scientific psychology, so called, takes cognizance of) is shut off. I shall begin my final lecture by referring to them again briefly.

VIII
CONCLUSIONS

LECTURE VIII

CONCLUSIONS

At the close of my last lecture I referred to the existence of religious experiences of a specific nature. I must now explain just what I mean by such a claim. Briefly, the facts I have in mind may all be described as experiences of an unexpected life succeeding upon death. By this I don't mean immortality, or the death of the body. I mean the deathlike termination of certain mental processes within the individual's experience, processes that run to failure, and in some individuals, at least, eventuate in despair. Just as romantic love seems a comparatively recent literary invention, so these experiences of a life that supervenes upon despair seem to have played no great part in official theology till Luther's time; and possibly the best way to indicate their character will be to point to a certain contrast between the inner life of ourselves and of the ancient Greeks and Romans.

Mr. Chesterton, I think, says somewhere,

303

A PLURALISTIC UNIVERSE

that the Greeks and Romans, in all that concerned their moral life, were an extraordinarily solemn set of folks. The Athenians thought that the very gods must admire the rectitude of Phocion and Aristides; and those gentlemen themselves were apparently of much the same opinion. Cato's veracity was so impeccable that the extremest incredulity a Roman could express of anything was to say, 'I would not believe it even if Cato had told me.' Good was good, and bad was bad, for these people. Hypocrisy, which church-Christianity brought in, hardly existed; the naturalistic system held firm; its values showed no hollowness and brooked no irony. The individual, if virtuous enough, could meet all possible requirements. The pagan pride had never crumbled. Luther was the first moralist who broke with any effectiveness through the crust of all this naturalistic self-sufficiency, thinking (and possibly he was right) that Saint Paul had done it already. Religious experience of the lutheran type brings all our naturalistic standards to bankruptcy. You are strong only by being

VIII. CONCLUSIONS

weak, it shows. You cannot live on pride or
self-sufficingness. There is a light in which
all the naturally founded and currently accepted distinctions, excellences, and safeguards
of our characters appear as utter childishness.
Sincerely to give up one's conceit or hope of
being good in one's own right is the only door
to the universe's deeper reaches.

These deeper reaches are familiar to evangelical Christianity and to what is nowadays
becoming known as 'mind-cure' religion or
'new thought.' The phenomenon is that of
new ranges of life succeeding on our most de-
spairing moments. There are resources in us
that naturalism with its literal and legal vir-
tues never recks of, possibilities that take our
breath away, of another kind of happiness and
power, based on giving up our own will and
letting something higher work for us, and these
seem to show a world wider than either physics
or philistine ethics can imagine. Here is a
world in which all is well, in *spite* of certain
forms of death, indeed *because* of certain forms
of death — death of hope, death of strength,

death of responsibility, of fear and worry, competency and desert, death of everything that paganism, naturalism, and legalism pin their faith on and tie their trust to.

Reason, operating on our other experiences, even our psychological experiences, would never have inferred these specifically religious experiences in advance of their actual coming. She could not suspect their existence, for they are discontinuous with the 'natural' experiences they succeed upon and invert their values. But as they actually come and are given, creation widens to the view of their recipients. They suggest that our natural experience, our strictly moralistic and prudential experience, may be only a fragment of real human experience. They soften nature's outlines and open out the strangest possibilities and perspectives.

This is why it seems to me that the logical understanding, working in abstraction from such specifically religious experiences, will always omit something, and fail to reach completely adequate conclusions. Death and failure, it will always say, *are* death and failure simply, and can nevermore be one with life; so religious experience, peculiarly so called, needs, in my opinion, to be carefully considered and interpreted by every one who aspires to reason out a more complete philosophy.

The sort of belief that religious experience of this type naturally engenders in those who have it is fully in accord with Fechner's theories. To quote words which I have used elsewhere, the believer finds that the tenderer parts of his personal life are continuous with a *more* of the same quality which is operative in the universe outside of him and which he can keep in working touch with, and in a fashion get on board of and save himself, when all his lower being has gone to pieces in the wreck. In a word, the believer is continuous, to his own consciousness, at any rate, with a wider self from which saving experiences flow in. Those who have such experiences distinctly enough and often enough to live in the light of them remain quite unmoved by criticism, from whatever quarter it may come, be it academic or scientific, or be it merely the voice of logical

common sense. They have had their vision
and they *know*—that is enough—that we inhabit an invisible spiritual environment from
which help comes, our soul being mysteriously
one with a larger soul whose instruments we
are.

One may therefore plead, I think, that Fechner's ideas are not without direct empirical
verification. There is at any rate one side of
life which would be easily explicable if those
ideas were true, but of which there appears no
clear explanation so long as we assume either
with naturalism that human consciousness is
the highest consciousness there is, or with
dualistic theism that there is a higher mind in
the cosmos, but that it is discontinuous with
our own. It has always been a matter of surprise with me that philosophers of the absolute
should have shown so little interest in this de-
partment of life, and so seldom put its phenomena in evidence, even when it seemed obvious
that personal experience of some kind must
have made their confidence in their own vision
so strong. The logician's bias has always been

too much with them. They have preferred the thinner to the thicker method, dialectical abstraction being so much more dignified and academic than the confused and unwholesome facts of personal biography.

In spite of rationalism's disdain for the particular, the personal, and the unwholesome, the drift of all the evidence we have seems to me to sweep us very strongly towards the belief in some form of superhuman life with which we may, unknown to ourselves, be co-conscious. We may be in the universe as dogs and cats are in our libraries, seeing the books and hearing the conversation, but having no inkling of the meaning of it all. The intellectualist objections to this fall away when the authority of intellectualist logic is undermined by criticism, and then the positive empirical evidence remains. The analogies with ordinary psychology and with the facts of pathology, with those of psychical research, so called, and with those of religious experience, establish, when taken together, a decidedly *formidable* probability in favor of a general view of the world almost identical with Fechner's. The outlines of the superhuman consciousness thus made probable must remain, however, very vague, and the number of functionally distinct 'selves' it comports and carries has to be left entirely problematic. It may be polytheistically or it may be monotheistically conceived of. Fechner, with his distinct earth-soul functioning as our guardian angel, seems to me clearly polytheistic; but the word 'polytheism' usually gives offence, so perhaps it is better not to use it. Only one thing is certain, and that is the result of our criticism of the absolute: the only way to escape from the paradoxes and perplexities that a consistently thought-out monistic universe suffers from as from a species of auto-intoxication — the mystery of the 'fall' namely, of reality lapsing into appearance, truth into error, perfection into imperfection; of evil, in short; the mystery of universal determinism, of the block-universe eternal and without a history, etc.; — the only way of escape, I say, from all this is to be frankly pluralistic and assume that the superhuman consciousness, how-

Spinozistic —

ever vast it may be, has itself an external environment, and consequently is finite. Present
day monism carefully repudiates complicity
with spinozistic monism. In that, it explains,
the many get dissolved in the one and lost,
whereas in the improved idealistic form they
get preserved in all their manyness as the one's
eternal object. The absolute itself is thus represented by absolutists as having a pluralistic
object. But if even the absolute has to have a
pluralistic vision, why should we ourselves hes-
itate to be pluralists on our own sole account?
Why should we envelop our many with the
'one' that brings so much poison in its train?

The line of least resistance, then, as it seems
to me, both in theology and in philosophy, is to
accept, along with the superhuman consciousness, the notion that it is not all-embracing, the
notion, in other words, that there is a God, but
that he is finite, either in power or in knowledge, or in both at once. These, I need hardly
tell you, are the terms in which common men
have usually carried on their active commerce
with God; and the monistic perfections that

311

to solve all problems: God
exist, but is not omnipotent or/and
infinate

a priori

make the notion of him so paradoxical practically and morally are the colder addition of remote professorial minds operating *in distans* upon conceptual substitutes for him alone.

Why cannot 'experience' and 'reason' meet on this common ground? Why cannot they compromise? May not the godlessness usually but needlessly associated with the philosophy of immediate experience give way to a theism now seen to follow directly from that experience more widely taken? and may not rationalism, satisfied with seeing her *a priori* proofs of God so effectively replaced by em-

empirical evidence

pirical evidence, abate something of her absolutist claims? Let God but have the least infinitesimal *other* of any kind beside him, and empiricism and rationalism might strike hands in a lasting treaty of peace. Both might then leave abstract thinness behind them, and seek together, as scientific men seek, by using all the analogies and data within reach, to build up the most probable approximate idea of what the divine consciousness concretely may be like. I venture to beg the younger

△ *use "science" (method) to find god*

VIII. CONCLUSIONS

Oxford idealists to consider seriously this alternative. Few men are as qualified by their intellectual gifts to reap the harvests that seem certain to any one who, like Fechner and Bergson, will leave the thinner for the thicker path.

Compromise and mediation are inseparable from the pluralistic philosophy. Only monistic dogmatism can say of any of its hypotheses, 'It is either that or nothing; take it or leave it just as it stands.' The type of monism prevalent at Oxford has kept this steep and brittle attitude, partly through the proverbial academic preference for thin and elegant logical solutions, partly from a mistaken notion that the only solidly grounded basis for religion was along those lines. If Oxford men could be ignorant of anything, it might almost seem that they had remained ignorant of the great empirical movement towards a pluralistic panpsychic view of the universe, into which our own generation has been drawn, and which threatens to short-circuit their methods entirely and become their religious rival unless they are willing to make themselves its

313

allies. Yet, wedded as they seem to be to the logical machinery and technical apparatus of absolutism, I cannot but believe that their fidelity to the religious ideal in general is deeper still. Especially do I find it hard to believe that the more clerical adherents of the school would hold so fast to its particular machinery if only they could be made to think that religion could be secured in some other way. Let empiricism once become associated with religion, as hitherto, through some strange misunderstanding, it has been associated with irreligion, and I believe that a new era of religion as well as of philosophy will be ready to begin. That great awakening of a new popular interest in philosophy, which is so striking a phenomenon at the present day in all countries, is undoubtedly due in part to religious demands. As the authority of past tradition tends more and more to crumble, men naturally turn a wistful ear to the authority of reason or to the evidence of present fact. They will assuredly not be disappointed if they open their minds to what the thicker and more radical empiricism has to say. I fully believe that such an empiricism is a more natural ally than dialectics ever were, or can be, of the religious life. It is true that superstitions and wild-growing over-beliefs of all sorts will undoubtedly begin to abound if the notion of higher consciousnesses enveloping ours, of fechnerian earth-souls and the like, grows orthodox and fashionable; still more will they superabound if science ever puts her approving stamp on the phenomena of which Frederic Myers so earnestly advocated the scientific recognition, the phenomena of psychic research so-called — and I myself firmly believe that most of these phenomena are rooted in reality. But ought one seriously to allow such a timid consideration as that to deter one from following the evident path of greatest religious promise? Since when, in this mixed world, was any good thing given us in purest outline and isolation? One of the chief characteristics of life is life's redundancy. The sole condition of our having anything, no matter what, is that we should have so much of it, that we are fortunate if we do not grow sick of the

It is only through
bad/average that we
find good

A PLURALISTIC UNIVERSE

sight and sound of it altogether. Everything
is smothered in the litter that is fated to accompany it. Without too much you cannot
have enough, of anything. Lots of inferior
books, lots of bad statues, lots of dull speeches,
of tenth-rate men and women, as a condition
of the few precious specimens in either kind
being realized! The gold-dust comes to birth
with the quartz-sand all around it, and this
is as much a condition of religion as of any
other excellent possession. There must be
extrication; there must be competition for
survival; but the clay matrix and the noble gem
must first come into being unsifted. Once
extricated, the gem can be examined separately,
conceptualized, defined, and insulated. But
this process of extrication cannot be short-
circuited — or if it is, you get the thin inferior
abstractions which we have seen, either the
hollow unreal god of scholastic theology, or
the unintelligible pantheistic monster, instead
of the more living divine reality with which
it appears certain that empirical methods tend
to connect men in imagination.

VIII. CONCLUSIONS

Arrived at this point, I ask you to go back to my first lecture and remember, if you can, what I quoted there from your own Professor Jacks — what he said about the philosopher himself being taken up into the universe which he is accounting for. This is the fechnerian as well as the hegelian view, and thus our end rejoins harmoniously our beginning. Philosophies are intimate parts of the universe, they express something of its own thought of itself. A philosophy may indeed be a most momentous reaction of the universe upon itself. It may, as I said, possess and handle itself differently in consequence of us philosophers, with our theories, being here; it may trust itself or mistrust itself the more, and, by doing the one or the other, deserve more the trust or the mistrust. What mistrusts itself deserves mistrust.

This is the philosophy of humanism in the widest sense. Our philosophies swell the current of being, add their character to it. They are part of all that we have met, of all that makes us be. As a French philosopher says, 'Nous sommes du réel dans le réel.' Our

thoughts determine our acts, and our acts rede-
termine the previous nature of the world.

Thus does foreignness get banished from
our world, and far more so when we take the
system of it pluralistically than when we take
it monistically. We are indeed internal parts
of God and not external creations, on any
possible reading of the panpsychic system.
Yet because God is not the absolute, but is
himself a part when the system is conceived
pluralistically, his functions can be taken as
not wholly dissimilar to those of the other
smaller parts,—as similar to our functions
consequently.

Having an environment, being in time, and
working out a history just like ourselves, he
escapes from the foreignness from all that is
human, of the static timeless perfect absolute.

Remember that one of our troubles with that
was its essential foreignness and monstrosity —
there really is no other word for it than that.
Its having the all-inclusive form gave to it an
essentially heterogeneous *nature* from our-

selves. And this great difference between absolutism and pluralism demands no difference
in the universe's material content — it follows
from a difference in the form alone. The all-
form or monistic form makes the foreignness
result, the each-form or pluralistic form leaves
the intimacy undisturbed.

No matter what the content of the universe
may be, if you only allow that it is *many* everywhere and always, that *nothing* real escapes
from having an environment; so far from
defeating its rationality, as the absolutists so
unanimously pretend, you leave it in possession of the maximum amount of rationality
practically attainable by our minds. Your relations with it, intellectual, emotional, and active,
remain fluent and congruous with your own
nature's chief demands.

It would be a pity if the word 'rationality'
were allowed to give us trouble here. It is one
of those eulogistic words that both sides claim
— for almost no one is willing to advertise his
philosophy as a system of irrationality. But
like most of the words which people used eulo-

eulogistic

gistically, the word 'rational' carries too many meanings. The most objective one is that of the older logic — the connexion between two things is rational when you can infer one from the other, mortal from Socrates, *e. g.;* and you can do that only when they have a quality in common. But this kind of rationality is just that logic of identity which all disciples of Hegel find insufficient. They supersede it by the higher rationality of negation and contradiction and make the notion vague again. Then you get the æsthetic or teleologic kinds of rationality, saying that whatever fits in any way, whatever is beautiful or good, whatever is purposive or gratifies desire, is rational in so far forth. Then again, according to Hegel, whatever is 'real' is rational. I myself said awhile ago that whatever lets loose any action which we are fond of exerting seems rational. It would be better to give up the word 'rational' altogether than to get into a merely verbal fight about who has the best right to keep it.

Perhaps the words 'foreignness' and 'intimacy,' which I put forward in my first lecture, express the contrast I insist on better than the words 'rationality' and 'irrationality'—let us stick to them, then. I now say that the notion of the 'one' breeds foreignness and that of the 'many' intimacy, for reasons which I have urged at only too great length, and with which, whether they convince you or not, I may suppose that you are now well acquainted. But what at bottom is meant by calling the universe many or by calling it one?

Pragmatically interpreted, pluralism or the doctrine that it is many means only that the sundry parts of reality *may be externally related.* Everything you can think of, however vast or inclusive, has on the pluralistic view a genuinely 'external' environment of some sort or amount. Things are 'with' one another in many ways, but nothing includes everything, or dominates over everything. The word 'and' trails along after every sentence. Something always escapes. 'Ever not quite' has to be said of the best attempts made anywhere in the universe at attaining all-inclusiveness. The pluralistic world is thus more like a federal republic than like an empire or a kingdom. However much may be collected, however much may report itself as present at any effective centre of consciousness or action, something else is self-governed and absent and unreduced to unity.

Monism, on the other hand, insists that when you come down to reality as such, to the reality of realities, everything is present to *everything* else in one vast instantaneous co-implicated completeness—nothing can in *any* sense, functional or substantial, be really absent from anything else, all things interpenetrate and telescope together in the great total conflux.

For pluralism, all that we are required to admit as the constitution of reality is what we ourselves find empirically realized in every minimum of finite life. Briefly it is this, that nothing real is absolutely simple, that every smallest bit of experience is a *multum in parvo* plurally related, that each relation is one aspect, character, or function, way of its being taken, or way of its taking something else; and that a bit of reality when actively engaged in one of these relations is not *by that very fact* engaged in all the other relations simultaneously. The relations are not *all* what the French call *solidaires* with one another. Without losing its identity a thing can either take up or drop another thing, like the log I spoke of, which by taking up new carriers and dropping old ones can travel anywhere with a light escort.

For monism, on the contrary, everything, whether we realize it or not, drags the whole universe along with itself and drops nothing. The log starts and arrives with all its carriers supporting it. If a thing were once disconnected, it could never be connected again, according to monism. The pragmatic difference between the two systems is thus a definite one. It is just thus, that if *a* is once out of sight of *b* or out of touch with it, or, more briefly, 'out' of it at all, then, according to monism, it must always remain so, they can never get together; whereas pluralism admits that on another occasion they may work together, or in some way be connected again. Monism allows for no

such things as 'other occasions' in reality —
in *real* or absolute reality, that is.

The difference I try to describe amounts,
you see, to nothing more than the difference
between what I formerly called the each-form
and the all-form of reality. Pluralism lets
things really exist in the each-form or distributively. Monism thinks that the all-form or col-
lective-unit form is the only form that is rational. The all-form allows of no taking up
and dropping of connexions, for in the all the
parts are essentially and eternally co-implicated.
In the each-form, on the contrary, a thing may
be connected by intermediary things, with a
thing with which it has no immediate or essential connexion. It is thus at all times in many
possible connexions which are not necessarily
actualized at the moment. They depend on
which actual path of intermediation it may
functionally strike into: the word 'or' names
a genuine reality. Thus, as I speak here, I may
look ahead *or* to the right *or* to the left, and in
either case the intervening space and air and
ether enable me to see the faces of a different

portion of this audience. My being here is independent of any one set of these faces.

If the each-form be the eternal form of reality no less than it is the form of temporal appearance, we still have a coherent world, and not an incarnate incoherence, as is charged by so many absolutists. Our 'multiverse' still makes a 'universe'; for every part, tho it may not be in actual or immediate connexion, is nevertheless in some possible or mediated connexion, with every other part however remote, through the fact that each part hangs together with its very next neighbors in inextricable interfusion. The type of union, it is true, is different here from the monistic type of *all-einheit*. It is not a universal co-implication, or integration of all things *durcheinander*. It is what I call the strung-along type, the type of continuity, contiguity, or concatenation. If you prefer greek words, you may call it the synechistic type. At all events, you see that it forms a definitely conceivable alternative to the through-and-through unity of all things at once, which is the type opposed to it by monism. You see also that it stands or falls with the notion I have taken such pains to defend, of the through-and-through union of adjacent minima of experience, of the confluence of every passing moment of concretely felt experience with its immediately next neighbors. The recognition of this fact of coalescence of next with next in concrete experience, so that all the insulating cuts we make there are artificial products of the conceptualizing faculty, is what distinguishes the empiricism which I call 'radical,' from the bugaboo empiricism of the traditional rationalist critics, which (rightly or wrongly) is accused of chopping up experience into atomistic sensations, incapable of union with one another until a purely intellectual principle has swooped down upon them from on high and folded them in its own conjunctive categories.

Here, then, you have the plain alternative, and the full mystery of the difference between pluralism and monism, as clearly as I can set it forth on this occasion. It packs up into a nutshell: — Is the manyness in oneness that indubitably characterizes the world we inhabit, a property only of the absolute whole of things, so that you must postulate that one-enormous-whole indivisibly as the *prius* of there being any many at all — in other words, start with the rationalistic block-universe, entire, unmitigated, and complete? — or can the finite elements have their own aboriginal forms of manyness in oneness, and where they have no immediate oneness still be continued into one another by intermediary terms — each one of these terms being one with its next neighbors, and yet the total 'oneness' never getting absolutely complete?

The alternative is definite. It seems to me, moreover, that the two horns of it make pragmatically different ethical appeals — at least they *may* do so, to certain individuals. But if you consider the pluralistic horn to be intrinsically irrational, self-contradictory, and absurd, I can now say no more in its defence. Having done what I could in my earlier lectures to break the edge of the intellectualistic *reductiones ad absurdum*, I must leave the issue in

your hands. Whatever I may say, each of you
will be sure to take pluralism or leave it, just
as your own sense of rationality moves and
inclines. The only thing I emphatically insist
upon is that it is a fully co-ordinate hypothesis with monism. This world *may*, in the last
resort, be a block-universe; but on the other
hand it *may* be a universe only strung-along,
not rounded in and closed. Reality *may* exist
distributively just as it sensibly seems to, after
all. On that possibility I do insist.

One's general vision of the probable usually
decides such alternatives. They illustrate
what I once wrote of as the 'will to believe.'
In some of my lectures at Harvard I have
spoken of what I call the 'faith-ladder,' as
something quite different from the *sorites* of the
logic-books, yet seeming to have an analogous
form. I think you will quickly recognize in
yourselves, as I describe it, the mental process
to which I give this name.

A conception of the world arises in you
somehow, no matter how. Is it true or not?
you ask.

VIII. CONCLUSIONS

It *might* be true somewhere, you say, for it is not self-contradictory.

It *may* be true, you continue, even here and now.

It is *fit* to be true, it would be *well if it were true*, it *ought* to be true, you presently feel.

It *must* be true, something persuasive in you whispers next; and then — as a final result —

It shall be *held for true*, you decide; it *shall be* as if true, for *you*.

And your acting thus may in certain special cases be a means of making it securely true in the end.

Not one step in this process is logical, yet it is the way in which monists and pluralists alike espouse and hold fast to their visions. It is life exceeding logic, it is the practical reason for which the theoretic reason finds arguments after the conclusion is once there. In just this way do some of us hold to the unfinished pluralistic universe; in just this way do others hold to the timeless universe eternally complete.

Meanwhile the incompleteness of the pluralistic universe, thus assumed and held to as the most probable hypothesis, is also represented by the pluralistic philosophy as being self-reparative through us, as getting its disconnections remedied in part by our behavior. 'We use what we are and have, to know; and what we know, to be and have still more.' [1] Thus do philosophy and reality, theory and action, work in the same circle indefinitely.

I have now finished these poor lectures, and as you look back on them, they doubtless seem rambling and inconclusive enough. My only hope is that they may possibly have proved suggestive; and if indeed they have been suggestive of one point of method, I am almost willing to let all other suggestions go. That point is that *it is high time for the basis of discussion in these questions to be broadened and thickened up.* It is for that that I have brought in Fechner and Bergson, and descriptive psychology and religious experiences, and have ventured even to hint at psychical research and other wild beasts of the philosophic desert. Owing possibly to the fact that Plato and

VIII. CONCLUSIONS

Aristotle, with their intellectualism, are the basis of philosophic study here, the Oxford brand of transcendentalism seems to me to have confined itself too exclusively to thin logical considerations, that would hold good in all conceivable worlds, worlds of an empirical constitution entirely different from ours. It is as if the actual peculiarities of the world that is were entirely irrelevant to the content of truth. But they cannot be irrelevant; and the philosophy of the future must imitate the sciences in taking them more and more elaborately into account. I urge some of the younger members of this learned audience to lay this hint to heart. If you can do so effectively, making still more concrete advances upon the path which Fechner and Bergson have so enticingly opened up, if you can gather philosophic conclusions of any kind, monistic or pluralistic, from the *particulars of life*, I will say, as I now do say, with the cheerfullest of hearts, 'Ring out, ring out my mournful rhymes, but ring the fuller minstrel in.'

NOTES

NOTES

LECTURE I

Note 1, page 5. — Bailey: *op. cit.*, First Series, p. 52.

Note 2, page 11. — *Smaller Logic*, § 194.

Note 3, page 16. — *Exploratio philosophica*, Part I, 1865, pp. xxxviii, 130.

Note 4, page 20. — Hinneberg: *Die Kultur der Gegenwart : Systematische Philosophie.* Leipzig: Teubner, 1907.

LECTURE II

Note 1, page 50. — The difference is that the bad parts of this finite are eternal and essential for absolutists, whereas pluralists may hope that they will eventually get sloughed off and become as if they had not been.

Note 2, page 51. — Quoted by W. Wallace: *Lectures and Essays*, Oxford, 1898, p. 560.

Note 3, page 51. — *Logic*, tr. Wallace, 1874, p. 181.

Note 4, page 52. — *Ibid.*, p. 304.

Note 5, page 53. — *Contemporary Review*, December, 1907, vol. 92, p. 618.

Note 6, page 57. — *Metaphysic*, sec. 69 ff.

Note 7, page 62. — *The World and the Individual*, vol. i, pp. 131–132.

Note 8, page 67. — A good illustration of this is to be found in a controversy between Mr. Bradley and the present writer, in *Mind* for 1893, Mr. Bradley contending (if I understood him rightly) that 'resemblance' is an illegitimate category, because it admits of degrees, and that the only real relations in comparison are absolute identity and absolute non-comparability.

NOTES

Note 9, page 75. — *Studies in the Hegelian Dialectic*, p. 184.

Note 10, page 75. — *Appearance and Reality*, 1893, pp. 141–142.

Note 11, page 76. — Cf. *Elements of Metaphysics*, p. 88.

Note 12, page 77. — *Some Dogmas of Religion*, p. 184.

Note 13, page 80. — For a more detailed criticism of Mr. Bradley's intellectualism, see Appendix A.

LECTURE III

Note 1, page 94. — Hegel, *Smaller Logic*, pp. 184–185.

Note 2, page 95. — Cf. Hegel's fine vindication of this function of contradiction in his *Wissenschaft der Logik*, Bk. ii, sec. 1, chap. ii, C, Anmerkung 3.

Note 3, page 95. — *Hegel*, in *Blackwood's Philosophical Classics*, p. 162.

Note 4, page 95. — *Wissenschaft der Logik*, Bk. i, sec. 1, chap. ii, B, a.

Note 5, page 96. — Wallace's translation of the *Smaller Logic*, p. 128.

Note 6, page 101. — Joachim, *The Nature of Truth*, Oxford, 1906, pp. 22, 178. The argument in case the belief should be doubted would be the higher synthetic idea: if two truths were possible, the duality of that possibility would itself be the one truth that would unite them.

Note 7, page 115. — *The World and the Individual*, vol. ii, pp. 385, 386, 409.

Note 8, page 116. — The best *un*inspired argument (again not ironical!) which I know is that in Miss M. W. Calkins's excellent book, *The Persistent Problems of Philosophy*, Macmillan, 1902.

Note 9, page 117. — Cf. Dr. Fuller's excellent article, ' Ethical monism and the problem of evil,' in the *Harvard Journal of Theology*, vol. i, No. 2, April, 1908.

Note 10, page 120. — *Metaphysic*, sec. 79.

Note 11, page 121. — *Studies in the Hegelian Dialectic*, secs. 150, 153.

Note 12, page 121. — *The Nature of Truth*, 1906, pp. 170–171.

Note 13, page 121. — *Ibid.*, p. 179.

Note 14, page 123. — The psychological analogy that certain finite tracts of consciousness are composed of isolable parts added together, cannot be used by absolutists as proof that such parts are essential elements of all consciousness. Other finite fields of consciousness seem in point of fact not to be similarly resolvable into isolable parts.

Note 15, page 128. — Judging by the analogy of the relation which our central consciousness seems to bear to that of our spinal cord, lower ganglia, etc., it would seem natural to suppose that in whatever superhuman mental synthesis there may be, the neglect and elimination of certain contents of which we are conscious on the human level might be as characteristic a feature as is the combination and interweaving of other human contents.

LECTURE IV

Note 1, page 143. — *The Spirit of Modern Philosophy*, p. 227.

Note 2, page 165. — Fechner: *Über die Seelenfrage*, 1861, p. 170.

Note 3, page 168. — Fechner's latest summarizing of his views, *Die Tagesansicht gegenüber der Nachtansicht*, Leipzig, 1879, is now, I understand, in process of translation. His

NOTES

Little Book of Life after Death exists already in two American versions, one published by Little, Brown & Co., Boston, the other by the Open Court Co., Chicago.

Note 4, page 176. — Mr. Bradley ought to be to some degree exempted from my attack in these last pages. Compare especially what he says of non-human consciousness in his *Appearance and Reality*, pp. 269–272.

LECTURE V

Note 1, page 182. — Royce: *The Spirit of Modern Philosophy*, p. 379.

Note 2, page 184. — *The World and the Individual*, vol. ii, pp. 58–62.

Note 3, page 190. — I hold to it still as the best description of an enormous number of our higher fields of consciousness. They demonstrably do not *contain* the lower states that know the same objects. Of other fields, however this is not so true; so, 'n the *Psychological Review* for 1895, vol. ii, p. 105 (see especially pp. 119–120), I frankly withdrew, in principle, my former objection to talking of fields of consciousness being made of simpler 'parts,' leaving the facts to decide the question in each special case.

Note 4, page 194. — I abstract from the consciousness attached to the whole itself, if such consciousness be there.

LECTURE VI

Note 1, page 250. — For a more explicit vindication of the notion of activity, see Appendix B, where I try to defend its recognition as a definite form of immediate experience against its rationalistic critics.

NOTES

I subjoin here a few remarks destined to disarm some possible critics of Professor Bergson, who, to defend himself against misunderstandings of his meaning, ought to amplify and more fully explain his statement that concepts have a practical but not a theoretical use. Understood in one way, the thesis sounds indefensible, for by concepts we certainly increase our knowledge about things, and that seems a theoretical achievement, whatever practical achievements may follow in its train. Indeed, M. Bergson might seem to be easily refutable out of his own mouth. His philosophy pretends, if anything, to give a better insight into truth than rationalistic philosophies give: yet what is it in itself if not a conceptual system? Does its author not reason by concepts exclusively in his very attempt to show that they can give no insight?

To this particular objection, at any rate, it is easy to reply. In using concepts of his own to discredit the theoretic claims of concepts generally, Bergson does not contradict, but on the contrary emphatically illustrates his own view of their practical rôle, for they serve in his hands only to 'orient' us, to show us to what quarter we must *practically turn* if we wish to gain that completer insight into reality which he denies that they can give. He directs our hopes away from them and towards the despised sensible flux. *What he reaches by their means is thus only a new practical attitude.* He but restores, against the vetoes of intellectualist philosophy, our naturally cordial relations with sensible experience and common sense. This service is surely only practical; but it is a service for which we may be almost immeasurably grateful. To trust our senses again with a good philosophic conscience! — who ever conferred on us so valuable a freedom before?

By making certain distinctions and additions it seems easy to meet the other counts of the indictment. Concepts are realities of a new order, with particular relations between them. These relations are just as much directly perceived, when we compare our various concepts, as the distance between two sense-objects is perceived when we look at it. Conception is an operation which gives us material for new acts of perception, then; and when the results of these are written down, we get those bodies of 'mental truth' (as Locke called it) known as mathematics, logic, and *a priori* metaphysics. To know all this truth is a theoretic achievement, indeed, but it is a narrow one; for the relations between conceptual objects as such are only the static ones of bare comparison, as difference or sameness, congruity or contradiction, inclusion or exclusion. Nothing *happens* in the realm of concepts ; relations there are 'eternal' only. The theoretic gain fails so far, therefore, to touch even the outer hem of the real world, the world of causal and dynamic relations, of activity and history. To gain insight into all that moving life, Bergson is right in turning us away from conception and towards perception.

By combining concepts with percepts, *we can draw maps of the distribution* of other percepts in distant space and time. To know this distribution is of course a theoretic achievement, but the achievement is extremely limited, it cannot be effected without percepts, and even then what it yields is only static relations. From maps we learn positions only, and the position of a thing is but the slightest kind of truth about it; but, being indispensable for forming our plans of action, the conceptual map-making has the enormous practical importance on which Bergson so rightly insists.

But concepts, it will be said, do not only give us eternal truths of comparison and maps of the positions of things, they bring new *values* into life. In their mapping function they

340

stand to perception in general in the same relation in which sight and hearing stand to touch — Spencer calls these higher senses only organs of anticipatory touch. But our eyes and ears also open to us worlds of independent glory: music and decorative art result, and an incredible enhancement of life's value follows. Even so does the conceptual world bring new ranges of value and of motivation to our life. Its maps not only serve us practically, but the mere mental possession of such vast pictures is of itself an inspiring good. New interests and incitements, and feelings of power, sublimity, and admiration are aroused.

Abstractness *per se* seems to have a touch of ideality. Royce's 'loyalty to loyalty' is an excellent example. 'Causes,' as anti-slavery, democracy, liberty, etc., dwindle when realized in their sordid particulars. The veritable ' cash-value' of the idea seems to cleave to it only in the abstract status. Truth at large, as Royce contends, in his *Philosophy of Loyalty*, appears another thing altogether from the true particulars in which it is best to believe. It transcends in value all those 'expediencies,' and is something to live for, whether expedient or inexpedient. Truth with a big T is a 'momentous issue'; truths in detail are 'poor scraps,' mere 'crumbling successes.' (*Op. cit.*, Lecture VII, especially § v.)

Is, now, such bringing into existence of a new *value* to be regarded as a theoretic achievement? The question is a nice one, for altho a value is in one sense an objective quality perceived, the essence of that quality is its relation to the will, and consists in its being a dynamogenic spur that makes our action different. So far as their value-creating function goes, it would thus appear that concepts connect themselves more with our active than with our theoretic life, so here again Bergson's formulation seems unobjectionable. Persons who have certain concepts are animated otherwise, pursue their own vital careers differently. It does n't necessarily follow that they understand other vital careers more intimately.

Again it may be said that we combine old concepts into new ones, conceiving thus such realities as the ether, God, souls, or what not, of which our sensible life alone would leave us altogether ignorant. This surely is an increase of our knowledge, and may well be called a theoretical achievement. Yet here again Bergson's criticisms hold good. Much as conception may tell us *about* such invisible objects, it sheds no ray of light into their interior. The completer, indeed, our definitions of ether-waves, atoms, Gods, or souls become, the less instead of the more intelligible do they appear to us. The learned in such things are consequently beginning more and more to ascribe a solely instrumental value to our concepts of them. Ether and molecules may be like co-ordinates and averages, only so many crutches by the help of which we practically perform the operation of getting about among our sensible experiences.

We see from these considerations how easily the question of whether the function of concepts is theoretical or practical may grow into a logomachy. It may be better from this point of view to refuse to recognize the alternative as a sharp one. The sole thing that is certain in the midst of it all is that Bergson is absolutely right in contending that the whole life of activity and change is inwardly impenetrable to conceptual treatment, and that it opens itself only to sympathetic apprehension at the hands of immediate feeling. All the *whats* as well as the *thats* of reality, relational as well as terminal, are in the end contents of immediate concrete perception. Yet the remoter unperceived *arrangements*, temporal, spatial, and logical, of these contents, are also something that we need to know as

NOTES

well for the pleasure of the knowing as for the practical help. We may call this need of arrangement a theoretic need or a practical need, according as we choose to lay the emphasis; but Bergson is accurately right when he limits conceptual knowledge to arrangement, and when he insists that arrangement is the mere skirt and skin of the whole of what we ought to know.

Note 2, page 266. — Gaston Rageot, *Revue Philosophique*, vol. lxiv, p. 85 (July, 1907).

Note 3, page 268. — I have myself talked in other ways as plausibly as I could, in my *Psychology*, and talked truly (as I believe) in certain selected cases; but for other cases the natural way invincibly comes back.

LECTURE VII

Note 1, page 278. — *Introduction to Hume*, 1874, p. 151.

Note 2, page 279. — *Ibid.*, pp. 16, 21, 36, *et passim*.

Note 3, page 279. — See, *inter alia*, the chapter on the 'Stream of Thought' in my own Psychologies; H. Cornelius, *Psychologie*, 1897, chaps. i and iii; G. H. Luquet, *Idées Générales de Psychologie*, 1906, *passim*.

Note 4, page 280. — Compare, as to all this, an article by the present writer, entitled 'A world of pure experience,' in the *Journal of Philosophy*, New York, vol. i, pp. 533, 561 (1905).

Note 5, page 280. — Green's attempt to discredit sensations by reminding us of their 'dumbness,' in that they do not come already *named*, as concepts may be said to do, only shows how intellectualism is dominated by verbality. The unnamed appears in Green as synonymous with the unreal.

Note 6, page 283. — *Philosophy of Reflection*, i, 248 ff.

NOTES

Note 7, page 284. — Most of this paragraph is extracted from an address of mine before the American Psychological Association, printed in the *Psychological Review*, vol. ii, p. 105. I take pleasure in the fact that already in 1895 I was so far advanced towards my present bergsonian position.

Note 8, page 289. — The conscious self of the moment, the central self, is probably determined to this privileged position by its functional connexion with the body's imminent or present acts. It is the present *acting* self. Tho the more that surrounds it may be 'subconscious' to us, yet if in its 'collective capacity' it also exerts an active function, it may be conscious in a wider way, conscious, as it were, over our heads.

On the relations of consciousness to action see Bergson's *Matière et Mémoire*, *passim*, especially chap. i. Compare also the hints in Münsterberg's *Grundzüge der Psychologie*, chap. xv; those in my own *Principles of Psychology*, vol. ii, pp. 581–592; and those in W. McDougall's *Physiological Psychology*, chap. vii.

Note 9, page 295. — Compare *Zend-Avesta*, 2d edition, vol. i, pp. 165 ff., 181, 206, 244 ff., etc.; *Die Tagesansicht*, etc., chap. v, § 6; and chap. xv.

LECTURE VIII

Note 1, page 330. — Blondel: *Annales de Philosophie Chrétienne*, June, 1906, p. 241.

APPENDICES

APPENDICES

APPENDIX A

THE THING AND ITS RELATIONS[1]

EXPERIENCE in its immediacy seems perfectly fluent. The active sense of living which we all enjoy, before reflection shatters our instinctive world for us, is self-luminous and suggests no paradoxes. Its difficulties are disappointments and uncertainties. They are not intellectual contradictions.

When the reflective intellect gets at work, however, it discovers incomprehensibilities in the flowing process. Distinguishing its elements and parts, it gives them separate names, and what it thus disjoins it cannot easily put together. Pyrrhonism accepts the irrationality and revels in its dialectic elaboration. Other philosophies try, some by ignoring, some by resisting, and some by turning the dialectic procedure against itself, negating its first negations, to restore the fluent sense of life again, and let redemption take the place of innocence. The perfection with which any philosophy may do this is the measure of its human success and of its importance in philosophic history. In an article entitled 'A world of pure experience,'[2] I tried my own hand sketchily at

[1] Reprinted from the *Journal of Philosophy, Psychology, and Scientific Methods*, vol. ii, New York, 1905, with slight verbal revision.

[2] *Journal of Philosophy, Psychology, and Scientific Methods*, vol. i, No. 20, p. 566.

the problem, resisting certain first steps of dialectics by insisting in a general way that the immediately experienced conjunctive relations are as real as anything else. If my sketch is not to appear too *näif*, I must come closer to details, and in the present essay I propose to do so.

I

'Pure experience' is the name which I gave to the immediate flux of life which furnishes the material to our later reflection with its conceptual categories. Only new-born babes, or men in semi-coma from sleep, drugs, illnesses, or blows, may be assumed to have an experience pure in the literal sense of a *that* which is not yet any definite *what*, tho ready to be all sorts of whats; full both of oneness and of manyness, but in respects that don't appear; changing throughout, yet so confusedly that its phases interpenetrate and no points, either of distinction or of identity, can be caught. Pure experience in this state is but another name for feeling or sensation. But the flux of it no sooner comes than it tends to fill itself with emphases, and these salient parts become identified and fixed and abstracted; so that experience now flows as if shot through with adjectives and nouns and prepositions and conjunctions. Its purity is only a relative term, meaning the proportional amount of unverbalized sensation which it still embodies.

THE THING AND ITS RELATIONS

Far back as we go, the flux, both as a whole and in its parts, is that of things conjunct and separated. The great continua of time, space, and the self envelop everything, betwixt them, and flow together without interfering. The things that they envelop come as separate in some ways and as continuous in others. Some sensations coalesce with some ideas, and others are irreconcilable. Qualities compenetrate one space, or exclude each other from it. They cling together persistently in groups that move as units, or else they separate. Their changes are abrupt or discontinuous; and their kinds resemble or differ; and, as they do so, they fall into either even or irregular series.

In all this the continuities and the discontinuities are absolutely co-ordinate matters of immediate feeling. The conjunctions are as primordial elements of 'fact' as are the distinctions and disjunctions. In the same act by which I feel that this passing minute is a new pulse of my life, I feel that the old life continues into it, and the feeling of continuance in no wise jars upon the simultaneous feeling of a novelty. They, too, compenetrate harmoniously. Prepositions, copulas, and conjunctions, 'is,' 'is n't,' 'then,' 'before,' 'in,' 'on,' 'beside,' 'between,' 'next,' 'like,' 'unlike,' 'as,' 'but,' flower out of the stream of pure experience, the stream of concretes or the sensational stream, as naturally as nouns and adjectives do, and they melt into it again as fluidly when we apply them to a new portion of the stream.

II

If now we ask why we must translate experience from a more concrete or pure into a more intellectualized form, filling it with ever more abounding conceptual distinctions, rationalism and naturalism give different replies.

The rationalistic answer is that the theoretic life is absolute and its interests imperative; that to understand is simply the duty of man; and that who questions this need not be argued with, for by the fact of arguing he gives away his case.

The naturalist answer is that the environment kills as well as sustains us, and that the tendency of raw experience to extinguish the experient himself is lessened just in the degree in which the elements in it that have a practical bearing upon life are analyzed out of the continuum and verbally fixed and coupled together, so that we may know what is in the wind for us and get ready to react in time. Had pure experience, the naturalist says, been always perfectly healthy, there would never have arisen the necessity of isolating or verbalizing any of its terms. We should just have experienced inarticulately and unintellectually enjoyed. This leaning on 'reaction' in the naturalist account implies that, whenever we intellectualize a relatively pure experience, we ought to do so for the sake of redescending to the purer or more concrete level again; and that if an intellect stays aloft among its abstract terms and generalized relations, and does not reinsert itself with its conclusions into some particular point of the immediate stream of life, it fails to finish out its function and leaves its normal race unrun.

Most rationalists nowadays will agree that naturalism gives a true enough account of the way in which our intellect arose at first, but they will deny these latter implications. The case, they will say, resembles that of sexual love. Originating in the animal need of getting another generation born, this passion has developed secondarily such imperious spiritual needs that, if you ask why another generation ought to be born at all, the answer is: 'Chiefly that love may go on.' Just so with our intellect: it originated as a practical means of serving life; but it has developed incidentally the function of understanding absolute truth; and life itself now seems to be given chiefly as a means by which that function may be prosecuted. But truth and the understanding of it lie among the abstracts and universals, so the intellect now carries on its higher business wholly in this region, without any need of redescending into pure experience again.

If the contrasted tendencies which I thus designate as naturalistic and rationalistic are not recognized by the reader, perhaps an example will make them more concrete. Mr. Bradley, for instance, is an ultra-rationalist. He admits that our intellect is primarily practical, but says that, for philosophers, the practical need is simply Truth.[1] Truth, moreover, must be assumed 'consistent.' Immediate experience has to be broken into subjects and qualities, terms and relations, to be understood as truth at all. Yet when so broken it is less consistent than ever. Taken raw, it is all undistinguished. Intellectualized, it is all distinction without oneness. 'Such an arrangement may *work*, but the theoretic problem is not solved' (p. 23). The question is, ' *How* the diversity can exist in harmony with the oneness' (p. 118). To go back to pure experience is unavailing. 'Mere feeling gives no answer to our riddle' (p. 104). Even if your intuition is a fact, it is not an *understanding*. 'It is a mere experience, and furnishes no consistent view' (pp. 108–109). The experiences offered as facts or truths 'I find that my intellect rejects because they contradict themselves. They offer a complex of diversities conjoined in a way which it feels is not its way and which it cannot repeat as its own. . . . For to be satisfied, my intellect must understand, and it cannot understand by taking a congeries in the lump' (p. 570). So Mr. Bradley, in the sole interests of 'understanding' (as he conceives that function), turns his back on finite

[1] *Appearance and Reality*, pp. 152–153.

experience forever. Truth must lie in the opposite direction, the direction of the absolute; and this kind of rationalism and naturalism, or (as I will now call it) pragmatism, walk thenceforward upon opposite paths. For the one, those intellectual products are most true which, turning their face towards the absolute, come nearest to symbolizing its ways of uniting the many and the one. For the other, those are most true which most successfully dip back into the finite stream of feeling and grow most easily confluent with some particular wave or wavelet. Such confluence not only proves the intellectual operation to have been true (as an addition may 'prove' that a subtraction is already rightly performed), but it constitutes, according to pragmatism, all that we mean by calling it true. Only in so far as they lead us, successfully or unsuccessfully, into sensible experience again, are our abstracts and universals true or false at all.

III

In Section the 6th of my article, 'A world of pure experience,' I adopted in a general way the common-sense belief that one and the same world is cognized by our different minds; but I left undiscussed the dialectical arguments which maintain that this is logically absurd. The usual reason given for its being absurd is that it assumes one object (to wit, the world) to stand in two relations at once; to my mind, namely, and again to yours; whereas a term taken in a second relation cannot logically be the same term which it was at first.

I have heard this reason urged so often in discussing with absolutists, and it would destroy my radical empiricism so utterly, if it were valid, that I am bound to give it an attentive ear, and seriously to search its strength.

For instance, let the matter in dispute be a term M, asserted to be on the one hand related to L, and on the other to N; and let the two cases of relation be symbolized by $L - M$ and $M - N$ respectively. When, now, I assume that the experience may immediately come and be given in the shape $L - M - N$, with no trace of doubling or internal fission in the M, I am told that this is all a popular delusion; that $L - M - N$ logically means two different experiences, $L - M$ and $M - N$, namely; and that although the absolute may, and indeed must, from its superior point of view, read its own kind of unity into M's two editions, yet as elements in finite experience the two M's lie irretrievably asunder, and the world between them is broken and unbridged.

In arguing this dialectic thesis, one must avoid slipping from the logical into the physical point of view. It would be easy, in taking a concrete example to fix one's ideas by, to choose one in which the letter M should stand for a collective noun of some sort, which noun, being related to L by one of its parts and to N by another, would inwardly be two things when it stood outwardly in both relations. Thus, one might say: 'David Hume, who weighed so many stone by his body, influences posterity by his doctrine.' The body and the doctrine are two things, between which our finite minds can discover no real sameness, though the same name covers both of them. And then, one might continue: 'Only an absolute is capable of uniting such a non-identity.' We must, I say, avoid this sort of example; for the dialectic insight, if true at all, must apply to terms and relations universally. It must be true of abstract units as well as of nouns collective; and if we prove it by concrete examples, we must take the simplest, so as to avoid irrelevant material suggestions.

Taken thus in all its generality, the absolutist contention seems to use as its major premise Hume's notion 'that all our distinct perceptions are distinct existences, and that the mind never perceives any real connexion among distinct existences.' Undoubtedly, since we use two phrases in talking first about 'M's relation to L' and then again about 'M's relation to N,' we must be having, or must have had, two distinct perceptions; — and the rest would then seem to follow duly. But the starting-point of the reasoning here seems to be the fact of the two *phrases;* and this suggests that the argument may be merely verbal. Can it be that the whole dialectic achievement consists in attributing to the experience talked-about a constitution similar to that of the language in which we describe it? Must we assert the objective doubleness of the M merely because we have to name it twice over when we name its two relations?

Candidly, I can think of no other reason than this for the dialectic conclusion![1] for, if we think, not of our words, but of any simple concrete matter which they may be held to signify, the experience itself belies the paradox asserted. We use indeed two separate concepts in analyzing our object, but we know them all the while to be but substitutional, and that the M in $L-M$ and the M in $M-N$ *mean* (*i. e.*, are capable of leading to and terminating in) one self-same piece, M, of sensible experience. This persistent identity of certain units, or emphases, or points, or objects, or members — call them what you will — of the experience-continuum, is just one of those conjunctive features of it, on which I am obliged to insist so emphatically. For samenesses are parts of experience's indefeasible structure. When I hear a bell-stroke and, as life flows on, its after-image dies away, I still hark back to it as 'that same

[1] Technically, it seems classable as a 'fallacy of composition.' A duality, predicable of the two wholes, $L-M$ and $M-N$, is forthwith predicated of one of their parts, M.

THE THING AND ITS RELATIONS

bell-stroke.' When I see a thing M, with L to the left of it and N to the right of it, I see it *as* one M; and if you tell me I have had to 'take' it twice, I reply that if I 'took' it a thousand times, I should still *see* it as a unit.[1] Its unity is aboriginal, just as the multiplicity of my successive takings is aboriginal. It comes unbroken as *that M*, as a singular which I encounter; they come broken, as *those* takings, as my plurality of operations. The unity and the separateness are strictly co-ordinate. I do not easily fathom why my opponents should find the separateness so much more easily understandable that they must needs infect the whole of finite experience with it, and relegate the unity (now taken as a bare postulate and no longer as a thing positively perceivable) to the region of the absolute's mysteries. I do not easily fathom this, I say, for the said opponents are above mere verbal quibbling; yet all that I can catch in their talk is the substitution of what is true of certain words for what is true of what they signify. They stay with the words, — not returning to the stream of life whence all the meaning of them came, and which is always ready to reabsorb them.

[1] I may perhaps refer here to my *Principles of Psychology*, vol. i, pp. 459 ff. It really seems 'weird' to have to argue (as I am forced now to do) for the notion that it is one sheet of paper (with its two surfaces and all that lies between) which is both under my pen and on the table while I write — the 'claim' that it is two sheets seems so brazen. Yet I sometimes suspect the absolutists of sincerity!

APPENDIX A

For aught this argument proves, then, we may continue to believe that one thing can be known by many knowers. But the denial of one thing in many relations is but one application of a still profounder dialectic difficulty. Man can't be good, said the sophists, for man is *man* and *good* is good; and Hegel and Herbart in their day, more recently H. Spir, and most recently and elaborately of all, Mr. Bradley, inform us that a term can logically only be a punctiform unit, and that not one of the conjunctive relations between things, which experience seems to yield, is rationally possible.

Of course, if true, this cuts off radical empiricism without even a shilling. Radical empiricism takes conjunctive relations at their face-value, holding them to be as real as the terms united by them. The world it represents as a collection, some parts of which are conjunctively and others disjunctively related. Two parts, themselves disjoined, may nevertheless hang together by intermediaries with which they are severally connected, and the whole world eventually may hang together similarly, inasmuch as *some* path of conjunctive transition by which to pass from one of its parts to another may always be discernible. Such determinately various hanging-together may be called *concatenated* union, to distinguish it from the 'through-and-through' type of union, 'each in all and all in each' (union of *total conflux,* as one might call it), which monistic systems hold to obtain when things are taken in their absolute reality. In a concatenated world a partial conflux often is experienced. Our concepts and our sensations are confluent; successive states of the same ego, and feelings of the same body are confluent. Where the experience is not of conflux, it may be of conterminousness (things with but one thing between); or of contiguousness (nothing between); or of likeness; or of nearness; or of simultaneousness; or of in-ness; or of on-ness; or of for-ness; or of simple with-ness; or even of mere and-ness, which last relation would make of however disjointed a world otherwise, at any rate for that occasion a universe 'of discourse.' Now Mr. Bradley tells us that none of these relations, as we actually experience them, can possibly be real.[1] My next duty, accordingly, must be to rescue radical empiricism from Mr. Bradley. Fortunately, as it seems to me, his general contention, that the very notion of relation is

[1] Here again the reader must beware of slipping from logical into phenomenal considerations. It may well be that we *attribute* a certain relation falsely, because the circumstances of the case, being complex, have deceived us. At a railway station we may take our own train, and not the one that fills our window, to be moving. We here put motion in the wrong place in the world, but in its original place the motion is a part of reality. What Mr. Bradley means is nothing like this, but rather that such things as motion are nowhere real, and that, even in their aboriginal and empirically incorrigible seats, relations are impossible of comprehension.

APPENDIX A

unthinkable clearly, has been successfully met by many critics.[1]

It is a burden to the flesh, and an injustice both to readers and to the previous writers, to repeat good arguments already printed. So, in noticing Mr. Bradley, I will confine myself to the interests of radical empiricism solely.

V

The first duty of radical empiricism, taking given conjunctions at their face-value, is to class some of them as more intimate and some as more external. When two terms are *similar*, their very natures enter into the relation. Being *what* they are, no matter where or when, the likeness never can be denied, if asserted. It continues predicable as long as the terms continue. Other relations, the *where* and the *when*, for example, seem adventitious. The sheet of paper may be 'off' or 'on' the table, for example; and in either case the relation involves only the outside of its terms. Having an outside, both of them, they contribute by it to the relation. It is external: the term's inner nature is irrelevant to it. Any

[1] Particularly so by Andrew Seth Pringle-Pattison, in his *Man and the Cosmos;* by L. T. Hobhouse, in chapter xii (the Validity of Judgment) of his *Theory of Knowledge;* and by F. C. S. Schiller, in his *Humanism*, Essay XI. Other fatal reviews (in my opinion) are Hodder's, in the *Psychological Review*, vol. i, 307; Stout's, in the *Proceedings of the Aristotelian Society*, 1901–02, p. 1; and MacLennan's, in the *Journal of Philosophy*, etc., vol. i, 403.

book, any table, may fall into the relation, which is created *pro hac vice*, not by their existence, but by their casual situation. It is just because so many of the conjunctions of experience seem so external that a philosophy of pure experience must tend to pluralism in its ontology. So far as things have space-relations, for example, we are free to imagine them with different origins even. If they could get to *be*, and get into space at all, then they may have done so separately. Once there, however, they are *additives* to one another, and, with no prejudice to their natures, all sorts of space-relations may supervene between them. The question of how things could come to be, anyhow, is wholly different from the question what their relations, once the being accomplished, may consist in.

Mr. Bradley now affirms that such external relations as the space-relations which we here talk of must hold of entirely different subjects from those of which the absence of such relations might a moment previously have been plausibly asserted. Not only is the *situation* different when the book is on the table, but the *book itself* is different as a book, from what it was when it was off the table.[1] He admits that 'such external relations

---

[1] Once more, don't slip from logical into physical situations. Of course, if the table be wet, it will moisten the book, or if it be slight enough and the book heavy enough, the book will break it down. But such collateral phenomena are not the point at issue. The point is whether the successive relations 'on' and 'not-on' can rationally (not

seem possible and even existing. . . . That you do not alter what you compare or rearrange in space seems to common sense quite obvious, and that on the other side there are as obvious difficulties does not occur to common sense at all. And I will begin by pointing out these difficulties. . . . There is a relation in the result, and this relation, we hear, is to make no difference in its terms. But, if so, to what does it make a difference? [*does n't it make a difference to us onlookers, at least?*] and what is the meaning and sense of qualifying the terms by it? [*Surely the meaning is to tell the truth about their relative position.*[1]] If, in short, it is external to the terms, how can it possibly be true *of* them? [*Is it the 'intimacy' suggested by the little word 'of,' here, which I have underscored, that is the root of Mr. Bradley's trouble?*] . . . If the terms from their inner nature do not enter into the relation, then, so far as they are concerned, they seem related for no reason at all. . . . Things are spatially related, first in one way, and then become related in another way, and yet in no way them-

physically) hold of the same constant terms, abstractly taken. Professor A. E. Taylor drops from logical into material considerations when he instances color-contrast as a proof that *A*, 'as contra-distinguished from *B*, is not the same thing as mere *A* not in any way affected' (*Elements of Metaphysics*, 1903, p. 145). Note the substitution, for 'related,' of the word 'affected,' which begs the whole question.

[1] But 'is there any sense,' asks Mr. Bradley, peevishly, on p. 579, 'and if so, what sense, in truth that is only outside and "about" things?' Surely such a question may be left unanswered.

selves are altered; for the relations, it is said, are but external. But I reply that, if so, I cannot *understand* the leaving by the terms of one set of relations and their adoption of another fresh set. The process and its result to the terms, if they contribute nothing to it [*surely they contribute to it all there is 'of' it!*] seem irrational throughout. [*If 'irrational' here means simply 'non-rational,' or non-deducible from the essence of either term singly, it is no reproach; if it means 'contradicting' such essence, Mr. Bradley should show wherein and how.*] But, if they contribute anything, they must surely be affected internally. [*Why so, if they contribute only their surface? In such relations as 'on,' 'a foot away,' 'between,' 'next,' etc., only surfaces are in question.*] . . . If the terms contribute anything whatever, then the terms are affected [*inwardly altered?*] by the arrangement. . . . That for working purposes we treat, and do well to treat, some relations as external merely, I do not deny, and that of course is not the question at issue here. That question is . . . whether in the end and in principle a mere external relation [*i. e., a relation which can change without forcing its terms to change their nature simultaneously*] is possible and forced on us by the facts.' [1]

Mr. Bradley next reverts to the antinomies of space, which, according to him, prove it to be unreal, although it appears as so prolific a medium of external relations;

[1] *Appearance and Reality*, 2d edition, pp. 575–576.

and he then concludes that 'Irrationality and externality cannot be the last truth about things. Somewhere there must be a reason why this and that appear together. And this reason and reality must reside in the whole from which terms and relations are abstractions, a whole in which their internal connexion must lie, and out of which from the background appear those fresh results which never could have come from the premises' (p. 577). And he adds that 'Where the whole is different, the terms that qualify and contribute to it must so far be different. . . . They are altered so far only [*how far? farther than externally, yet not through and through?*], but still they are altered. . . . I must insist that in each case the terms are qualified by their whole [*qualified how? — do their external relations, situations, dates, etc., changed as these are in the new whole, fail to qualify them 'far' enough?*], and that in the second case there is a whole which differs both logically and psychologically from the first whole; and I urge that in contributing to the change the terms so far are altered' (p. 579).

Not merely the relations, then, but the terms are altered: *und zwar* 'so far.' But just *how* far is the whole problem; and 'through-and-through' would seem (in spite of Mr. Bradley's somewhat undecided utterances [1])

[1] I say 'undecided,' because, apart from the 'so far,' which sounds terribly half-hearted, there are passages in these very pages in which Mr. Bradley admits the pluralistic thesis. Read, for example, what he says, on p. 578, of a billiard ball keeping its 'character' unchanged,

to be the full bradleyan answer. The 'whole' which he here treats as primary and determinative of each part's manner of 'contributing,' simply *must*, when it alters, alter in its entirety. There *must* be total conflux of its parts, each into and through each other. The 'must' appears here as a *Machtspruch*, as an *ipse dixit* of Mr. Bradley's absolutistically tempered 'understanding,' for he candidly confesses that how the parts *do* differ as they contribute to different wholes, is unknown to him (p. 578).

Although I have every wish to comprehend the authority by which Mr. Bradley's understanding speaks, his words leave me wholly unconverted. 'External relations' stand with their withers all unwrung, and

though, in its change of place, its 'existence' gets altered; or what he says, on p. 579, of the possibility that an abstract quality A, B, or C, in a thing, 'may throughout remain unchanged' although the thing be altered; or his admission that in red-hairedness, both as analyzed out of a man and when given with the rest of him, there may be 'no change' (p. 580). Why does he immediately add that for the pluralist to plead the non-mutation of such abstractions would be an *ignoratio elenchi* ? It is impossible to admit it to be such. The entire *elenchus* and inquest is just as to whether parts which you can abstract from existing wholes can also contribute to other wholes without changing their inner nature. If they can thus mould various wholes into new *gestalt-qualitäten*, then it follows that the same elements are logically able to exist in different wholes [whether physically able would depend on additional hypotheses]; that partial changes are thinkable, and through-and-through change not a dialectic necessity; that monism is only an hypothesis; and that an additively constituted universe is a rationally respectable hypothesis also. All the theses of radical empiricism, in short, follow.

remain, for aught he proves to the contrary, not only practically workable, but also perfectly intelligible factors of reality

VI

Mr. Bradley's understanding shows the most extraordinary power of perceiving separations and the most extraordinary impotence in comprehending conjunctions. One would naturally say 'neither or both,' but not so Mr. Bradley. When a common man analyzes certain *whats* from out the stream of experience, he understands their distinctness *as thus isolated.* But this does not prevent him from equally well understanding their combination with each other *as originally experienced in the concrete,* or their confluence with new sensible experiences in which they recur as 'the same.' Returning into the stream of sensible presentation, nouns and adjectives, and *thats* and abstract *whats,* grow confluent again, and the word 'is' names all these experiences of conjunction. Mr. Bradley understands the isolation of the abstracts, but to understand the combination is to him impossible.[1] 'To understand a complex *AB,*' he

---

[1] So far as I catch his state of mind, it is somewhat like this: 'Book,' 'table,' 'on' — how does the existence of these three abstract elements result in *this* book being livingly on *this* table? Why is n't the table on the book? Or why does n't the 'on' connect itself with another book, or something that is not a table? Must n't something *in* each of the three elements already determine the two others to *it*, so that they do not settle elsewhere or float vaguely? Must n't the *whole fact be*

THE THING AND ITS RELATIONS

says, 'I must begin with *A* or *B*. And beginning, say
with *A*, if I then merely find *B*, I have either lost *A*,
or I have got beside *A*, [*the word 'beside' seems here
vital, as meaning a conjunction 'external' and therefore
unintelligible*] something else, and in neither case have
I understood.[1] For my intellect cannot simply unite a
diversity, nor has it in itself any form or way of togetherness, and you gain nothing if, beside *A* and *B*, you offer
me their conjunction in fact. For to my intellect that
is no more than another external element. And "facts,"
once for all, are for my intellect not true unless they
satisfy it. . . . The intellect has in its nature no
principle of mere togetherness' (pp. 570, 572).

Of course Mr. Bradley has a right to define 'intellect'
as the power by which we perceive separations but not
unions — provided he give due notice to the reader.
But why then claim that such a maimed and amputated
power must reign supreme in philosophy, and accuse on
its behoof the whole empirical world of irrationality?
It is true that he elsewhere (p. 568) attributes to the
intellect a *proprius motus* of transition, but says that

prefigured in each part, and exist *de jure* before it can exist *de facto*?
But, if so, in what can the jural existence consist, if not in a spiritual
miniature of the whole fact's constitution actuating every partial factor
as its purpose? But is this anything but the old metaphysical fallacy
of looking behind a fact *in esse* for the ground of the fact, and finding
it in the shape of the very same fact *in posse*? Somewhere we must
leave off with a *constitution* behind which there is nothing.

[1] Apply this to the case of 'book-on-table'! W. J.

when he looks for *these* transitions in the detail of living experience, he 'is unable to verify such a solution' (p. 569).

Yet he never explains what the intellectual transitions would be like in case we had them. He only defines them negatively — they are not spatial, temporal, predicative, or causal; or qualitatively or otherwise serial; or in any way relational as we naïvely trace relations, for relations *separate* terms, and need themselves to be hooked on *ad infinitum*. The nearest approach he makes to describing a truly intellectual transition is where he speaks of A and B as being 'united, each from its own nature, in a whole which is the nature of both alike' (p. 570). But this (which, *pace* Mr. Bradley, seems exquisitely analogous to 'taking a congeries in a lump,' if not to 'swamping') suggests nothing but that *conflux* which pure experience so abundantly offers, as when 'space,' 'white,' and 'sweet' are confluent in a 'lump of sugar,' or kinesthetic, dermal, and optical sensations confluent in 'my hand.' [1] All that I can verify in the transitions which Mr. Bradley's intellect desiderates as its *proprius motus* is a reminiscence of these and other sensible conjunctions (especially space-conjunc-

[1] How meaningless is the contention that in such wholes (or in 'book-on-table,' 'watch-in-pocket,' etc.) the relation is an additional entity *between* the terms, needing itself to be related again to each! Both Bradley (*Appearance and Reality*, pp. 32-33) and Royce (*The World and the Individual*, i, 128) lovingly repeat this piece of profundity.

tions), but a reminiscence so vague that its originals are not recognized. Bradley, in short, repeats the fable of the dog, the bone, and its image in the water. With a world of particulars, given in loveliest union, in conjunction definitely various, and variously definite, the 'how' of which you 'understand' as soon as you see the fact of them,[1] for there is no how except the constitution of the fact as given; with all this given him, I say, in pure experience, he asks for some ineffable union in the abstract instead, which, if he gained it, would only be a duplicate of what he has already in his full possession. Surely he abuses the privilege which society grants to all of us philosophers, of being puzzle-headed.

Polemic writing like this is odious; but with absolutism in possession in so many quarters, omission to defend my radical empiricism against its best known champion would count as either superficiality or inability. I have to conclude that its dialectic has not invalidated in the least degree the usual conjunctions by which the world, as experienced, hangs so variously together. In particular it leaves an empirical theory of knowledge intact, and lets us continue to believe with common sense that one object *may* be known, if we have any ground for thinking that it *is* known, to many knowers.

---

[1] The 'why' and the 'whence' are entirely other questions, not under discussion, as I understand Mr. Bradley. Not how experience gets itself born, but how it can be what it is after it is born, is the puzzle.

APPENDIX B

THE EXPERIENCE OF ACTIVITY[1]

. . . MR. BRADLEY calls the question of activity a scandal to philosophy, and if one turns to the current literature of the subject — his own writings included — one easily gathers what he means. The opponents cannot even understand one another. Mr. Bradley says to Mr. Ward: 'I do not care what your oracle is, and your preposterous psychology may here be gospel if you please; . . . but if the revelation does contain a meaning, I will commit myself to this: either the oracle is so confused that its signification is not discoverable, or, upon the other hand, if it can be pinned down to any definite statement, then that statement will be false.' [2] Mr. Ward in turn says of Mr. Bradley: 'I cannot even imagine the state of mind to which his description applies. . . . It reads like an unintentional travesty of Herbartian Psychology by one who has tried to improve upon it without being at the pains to master it.' Münsterberg excludes a view opposed to his own by saying that with any one who holds it a *verständigung* with him is '*grundsätzlich ausgeschlossen*'; and Royce,

[1] President's Address before the American Psychological Association, December, 1904. Reprinted from the *Psychological Review*, vol. xii, 1905, with slight verbal revision.

[2] *Appearance and Reality*, p. 117. Obviously written *at* Ward, though Ward's name is not mentioned.

370

in a review of Stout,[1] hauls him over the coals at great length for defending 'efficacy' in a way which I, for one, never gathered from reading him, and which I have heard Stout himself say was quite foreign to the intention of his text.

In these discussions distinct questions are habitually jumbled and different points of view are talked of *durcheinander*.

(1) There is a psychological question: Have we perceptions of activity? and if so, what are they like, and when and where do we have them?

(2) There is a metaphysical question: Is there a *fact* of activity? and if so, what idea must we frame of it? What is it like? and what does it do, if it does anything? And finally there is a logical question:

(3) Whence do we *know* activity? By our own feelings of it solely? or by some other source of information? Throughout page after page of the literature one knows not which of these questions is before one; and mere description of the surface-show of experience is proffered as if it implicitly answered every one of them. No one of the disputants, moreover, tries to show what pragmatic consequences his own view would carry, or what assignable particular differences in any one's experience it would make if his adversary's were triumphant.

[1] *Mind*, N. S., VI, 379.

APPENDIX B

It seems to me that if radical empiricism be good for anything, it ought, with its pragmatic method and its principle of pure experience, to be able to avoid such tangles, or at least to simplify them somewhat. The pragmatic method starts from the postulate that there is no difference of truth that does n't make a difference of fact somewhere; and it seeks to determine the meaning of all differences of opinion by making the discussion hinge as soon as possible upon some practical or particular issue. The principle of pure experience is also a methodical postulate. Nothing shall be admitted as fact, it says, except what can be experienced at some definite time by some experient; and for every feature of fact ever so experienced, a definite place must be found somewhere in the final system of reality. In other words: Everything real must be experienceable somewhere, and every kind of thing experienced must somewhere be real.

Armed with these rules of method, let us see what face the problems of activity present to us.

By the principle of pure experience, either the word 'activity' must have no meaning at all, or else the original type and model of what it means must lie in some concrete kind of experience that can be definitely pointed out. Whatever ulterior judgments we may eventually come to make regarding activity, *that sort* of thing will be what the judgments are about. The first step to take, then, is to ask where in the stream of experience we seem to find what we speak of as activity. What we are to think of the activity thus found will be a later question.

Now it is obvious that we are tempted to affirm activity wherever we find anything *going on.* Taken in the broadest sense, any apprehension of something *doing,* is an experience of activity. Were our world describable only by the words 'nothing happening,' 'nothing changing,' 'nothing doing,' we should unquestionably call it an 'inactive' world. Bare activity, then, as we may call it, means the bare fact of event or change. 'Change taking place' is a unique content of experience, one of those 'conjunctive' objects which radical empiricism seeks so earnestly to rehabilitate and preserve. The sense of activity is thus in the broadest and vaguest way synonymous with the sense of 'life.' We should feel our own subjective life at least, even in noticing and proclaiming an otherwise inactive world. Our own reaction on its monotony would be the one thing experienced there in the form of something coming to pass.

This seems to be what certain writers have in mind when they insist that for an experient to be at all is to be active. It seems to justify, or at any rate to explain, Mr. Ward's expression that we *are* only as we are active,[1]

---

[1] *Naturalism and Agnosticism*, vol. ii, p. 245. One thinks naturally of the peripatetic *actus primus* and *actus secundus* here.

for we *are* only as experients; and it rules out Mr. Bradley's contention that 'there is no original experience of anything like activity.' What we ought to say about activities thus simply given, whose they are, what they effect, or whether indeed they effect anything at all — these are later questions, to be answered only when the field of experience is enlarged.

Bare activity would thus be predicable, though there were no definite direction, no actor, and no aim. Mere restless zigzag movement, or a wild *ideenflucht*, or *rhapsodie der wahrnehmungen*, as Kant would say, would constitute an active as distinguished from an inactive world.

But in this actual world of ours, as it is given, a part at least of the activity comes with definite direction; it comes with desire and sense of goal; it comes complicated with resistances which it overcomes or succumbs to, and with the efforts which the feeling of resistance so often provokes; and it is in complex experiences like these that the notions of distinct agents, and of passivity as opposed to activity arise. Here also the notion of causal efficacy comes to birth. Perhaps the most elaborate work ever done in descriptive psychology has been the analysis by various recent writers of the more complex activity-situations. In their descriptions, exquisitely subtle some of them,[1] the activity appears as the *gestalt-*

---

[1] Their existence forms a curious commentary on Professor

qualität or the *fundirte inhalt* (or as whatever else you may please to call the conjunctive form) which the content falls into when we experience it in the ways which the describers set forth. Those factors in those relations are what we *mean* by activity-situations; and to the possible enumeration and accumulation of their circumstances and ingredients there would seem to be no natural bound. Every hour of human life could contribute to the picture gallery; and this is the only fault that one can find with such descriptive industry — where is it going to stop? Ought we to listen forever to verbal pictures of what we have already in concrete form in our own breasts? [1] They never take us off the superficial plane. We knew the facts already — less spread out and separated, to be sure — but we knew them still. We always felt our own activity, for example, as 'the expansion of an idea with which our Self is identified, against an obstacle'; and the following out of such a definition through a multitude of cases elaborates the obvious so as to be little more than an exercise in synonymic speech.

All the descriptions have to trace familiar outlines, and to use familiar terms. The activity is, for example,

Münsterberg's dogma that will-attitudes are not describable. He himself has contributed in a superior way to their description, both in his *Willenshandlung*, and in his *Grundzüge*, Part II, chap. ix, § 7.

[1] I ought myself to cry *peccavi*, having been a voluminous sinner in my own chapter on the will.

APPENDIX B

attributed either to a physical or to a mental agent, and is either aimless or directed. If directed, it shows tendency. The tendency may or may not be resisted. If not, we call the activity immanent, as when a body moves in empty space by its momentum, or our thoughts wander at their own sweet will. If resistance is met, *its* agent complicates the situation. If now, in spite of resistance, the original tendency continues, effort makes its appearance, and along with effort, strain or squeeze. Will, in the narrower sense of the word, then comes upon the scene, whenever, along with the tendency, the strain and squeeze are sustained. But the resistance may be great enough to check the tendency, or even to reverse its path. In that case, we (if 'we' were the original agents or subjects of the tendency) are overpowered. The phenomenon turns into one of tension simply, or of necessity succumbed-to, according as the opposing power is only equal, or is superior to ourselves.

Whosoever describes an experience in such terms as these, describes an experience *of* activity. If the word have any meaning, it must denote what there is found. *There* is complete activity in its original and first intention. What it is 'known-as' is what there appears. The experiencer of such a situation possesses all that the idea contains. He feels the tendency, the obstacle, the will, the strain, the triumph, or the passive giving up, just as he feels the time, the space, the swiftness or

376

intensity, the movement, the weight and color, the pain and pleasure, the complexity, or whatever remaining characters the situation may involve. He goes through all that ever can be imagined where activity is supposed. If we suppose activities to go on outside of our experience, it is in forms like these that we must suppose them, or else give them some other name; for the word 'activity' has no imaginable content whatever save these experiences of process, obstruction, striving, strain, or release, ultimate *qualia* as they are of the life given us to be known.

Were this the end of the matter, one might think that whenever we had successfully lived through an activity-situation we should have to be permitted, without provoking contradiction, to say that we had been really active, that we had met real resistance and had really prevailed. Lotze somewhere says that to be an entity all that is necessary is to *gelten* as an entity, to operate, or be felt, experienced, recognized, or in any way realized, as such. In our activity-experiences the activity assuredly fulfils Lotze's demand. It makes itself *gelten*. It is witnessed at its work. No matter what activities there may really be in this extraordinary universe of ours, it is impossible for us to conceive of any one of them being either lived through or authentically known otherwise than in this dramatic shape of something sustaining a felt purpose against felt obstacles and over-

APPENDIX B

coming or being overcome. What 'sustaining' means
here is clear to any one who has lived through the
experience, but to no one else; just as 'loud,' 'red,'
'sweet,' mean something only to beings with ears, eyes,
and tongues. The *percipi* in these originals of experience is the *esse;* the curtain is the picture. If there is
anything hiding in the background, it ought not to be
called activity, but should get itself another name.

This seems so obviously true that one might well
experience astonishment at finding so many of the ablest
writers on the subject flatly denying that the activity
we live through in these situations is real. Merely to
feel active is not to be active, in their sight. The agents
that appear in the experience are not real agents, the
resistances do not really resist, the effects that appear are
not really effects at all.[1] It is evident from this that

[1] *Verborum gratiâ :* 'The feeling of activity is not able, quâ feeling,
to tell us anything about activity ' (Loveday: *Mind*, N. s., X., 463);
'A sensation or feeling or sense of activity . . . is not, looked at in
another way, a feeling of activity at all. It is a mere sensation shut up
within which you could by no reflection get the idea of activity. . . .
Whether this experience is or is not later on a character essential to
our perception and our idea of activity, it, as it comes first, is not in
itself an experience of activity at all. It, as it comes first, is only so
for extraneous reasons and only so for an outside observer' (Bradley,
Appearance and Reality, 2d edition, p. 605); 'In dem tätigkeitsge-
fühle leigt an sich nicht der geringste beweis für das vorhandensein
einer psychischen tätigkeit' (Münsterberg: *Grundzüge*, etc., p. 67).
I could multiply similar quotations, and would have introduced some
of them into my text to make it more concrete, save that the mingling

mere descriptive analysis of any one of our activity-experiences is not the whole story, that there is some-

of different points of view in most of these author's discussions (not in Münsterberg's) make it impossible to disentangle exactly what they mean. I am sure in any case to be accused of misrepresenting them totally, even in this note, by omission of the context, so the less I name names and the more I stick to abstract characterization of a merely possible style of opinion, the safer it will be. And apropos of misunderstandings, I may add to this note a complaint on my own account. Professor Stout, in the excellent chapter on 'Mental Activity,' in vol. i of his *Analytic Psychology*, takes me to task for identifying spiritual activity with certain muscular feelings, and gives quotations to bear him out. They are from certain paragraphs on 'the Self,' in which my attempt was to show what the central nucleus of the activities that we call 'ours' is. I found it in certain intracephalic movements which we habitually oppose, as 'subjective,' to the activities of the transcorporeal world. I sought to show that there is no direct evidence that we feel the activity of an inner spiritual agent as such (I should now say the activity of 'consciousness' as such, see my paper 'Does consciousness exist?' in the *Journal of Philosophy*, vol. i, p. 477). There are, in fact, three distinguishable 'activities' in the field of discussion: the elementary activity involved in the mere *that* of experience, in the fact that *something* is going on, and the farther specification of this *something* into two *whats*, an activity felt as 'ours,' and an activity ascribed to objects. Stout, as I apprehend him, identifies 'our' activity with that of the total experience-process, and when I circumscribe it as a part thereof, accuses me of treating it as a sort of external appendage to itself (pp. 162–163), as if I 'separated the activity from the process which is active.' But all the processes in question are active, and their activity is inseparable from their being. My book raised only the question of *which* activity deserved the name of 'ours.' So far as we are 'persons,' and contrasted and opposed to an 'environment,' movements in our body figure as our activities; and I am unable to find any other activities that are ours in this strictly personal sense. There is a wider sense in which the whole 'choir of heaven and furniture of the earth,' thing still to tell *about* them that has led such able writers to conceive of a *Simon-pure* activity, of an activity *an sich*, that does, and does n't merely appear to

and their activities, are ours, for they are our 'objects.' But 'we' are here only another name for the total process of experience, another name for all that is, in fact; and I was dealing with the personal and individualized self exclusively in the passages with which Professor Stout finds fault.

The individualized self, which I believe to be the only thing properly called self, is a part of the content of the world experienced. The world experienced (otherwise called the 'field of consciousness') comes at all times with our body as its centre, centre of vision, centre of action, centre of interest. Where the body is is 'here'; when the body acts is 'now'; what the body touches is 'this'; all other things are 'there' and 'then' and 'that.' These words of emphasized position imply a systematization of things with reference to a focus of action and interest which lies in the body; and the systematization is now so instinctive (was it ever not so?) that no developed or active experience exists for us at all except in that ordered form. So far as 'thoughts' and 'feelings' can be active, their activity terminates in the activity of the body, and only through first arousing its activities can they begin to change those of the rest of the world. The body is the storm centre, the origin of co-ordinates, the constant place of stress in all that experience-train. Everything circles round it, and is felt from its point of view. The word 'I,' then, is primarily a noun of position, just like 'this' and 'here.' Activities attached to 'this' position have prerogative emphasis, and, if activities have feelings, must be felt in a peculiar way. The word 'my' designates the kind of emphasis. I see no inconsistency whatever in defending, on the one hand, 'my' activities as unique and opposed to those of outer nature, and, on the other hand, in affirming, after introspection, that they consist in movements in the head. The 'my' of them is the emphasis, the feeling of perspective-interest in which they are dyed.

us to do, and compared with whose real doing all this phenomenal activity is but a specious sham.

The metaphysical question opens here; and I think that the state of mind of one possessed by it is often something like this: 'It is all very well,' we may imagine him saying, 'to talk about certain experience-series taking on the form of feelings of activity, just as they might take on musical or geometric forms. Suppose that they do so; suppose that what we feel is a will to stand a strain. Does our feeling do more than *record* the fact that the strain is sustained? The *real* activity, meanwhile, is the *doing* of the fact; and what is the doing made of before the record is made? What in the will *enables* it to act thus? And these trains of experience themselves, in which activities appear, what makes them *go* at all? Does the activity in one bit of experience bring the next bit into being? As an empiricist you cannot say so, for you have just declared activity to be only a kind of synthetic object, or conjunctive relation experienced between bits of experience already made. But what made them at all? What propels experience *überhaupt* into being? *There* is the activity that *operates*; the activity *felt* is only its superficial sign.'

To the metaphysical question, popped upon us in this way, I must pay serious attention ere I end my remarks, but, before doing so, let me show that without leaving the immediate reticulations of experience, or asking what makes activity itself act, we still find the distinction between less real and more real activities forced upon us, and are driven to much soul-searching on the purely phenomenal plane.

We must not forget, namely, in talking of the ultimate character of our activity-experiences, that each of them is but a portion of a wider world, one link in the vast chain of processes of experience out of which history is made. Each partial process, to him who lives through it, defines itself by its origin and its goal; but to an observer with a wider mind-span who should live outside of it, that goal would appear but as a provisional halting-place, and the subjectively felt activity would be seen to continue into objective activities that led far beyond. We thus acquire a habit, in discussing activity-experiences, of defining them by their relation to something more. If an experience be one of narrow span, it will be mistaken as to what activity it is and whose. You think that *you* are acting while you are only obeying some one's push. You think you are doing *this*, but you are doing something of which you do not dream. For instance, you think you are but drinking this glass; but you are really creating the liver-cirrhosis that will end your days. You think you are just driving this bargain, but, as Stevenson says somewhere, you are laying down a link in the policy of mankind.

THE EXPERIENCE OF ACTIVITY

Generally speaking, the onlooker, with his wider field of vision, regards the *ultimate outcome* of an activity as what it is more really doing; and *the most previous agent* ascertainable, being the first source of action, he regards as the most real agent in the field. The others but transmit that agent's impulse; on him we put responsibility; we name him when one asks us, 'Who's to blame?'

But the most previous agents ascertainable, instead of being of longer span, are often of much shorter span than the activity in view. Brain-cells are our best example. My brain-cells are believed to excite each other from next to next (by contiguous transmission of katabolic alteration, let us say), and to have been doing so long before this present stretch of lecturing-activity on my part began. If any one cell-group stops its activity, the lecturing will cease or show disorder of form. *Cessante causa, cessat et effectus* — does not this look as if the short-span brain activities were the more real activities, and the lecturing activities on my part only their effects? Moreover, as Hume so clearly pointed out, in my mental activity-situation the words physically to be uttered are represented as the activity's immediate goal. These words, however, cannot be uttered without intermediate physical processes in the bulb and vagi nerves, which processes nevertheless fail to figure in the mental activity-series at all. That series, therefore, since it leaves out vitally real steps of action, cannot represent the real activities. It is something purely subjective; the *facts* of activity are elsewhere. They are something far more interstitial, so to speak, than what my feelings record.

The *real* facts of activity that have in point of fact been systematically pleaded for by philosophers have, so far as my information goes, been of three principal types.

The first type takes a consciousness of wider time-span than ours to be the vehicle of the more real activity. Its will is the agent, and its purpose is the action done.

The second type assumes that 'ideas' struggling with one another are the agents, and that the prevalence of one set of them is the action.

The third type believes that nerve-cells are the agents, and that resultant motor discharges are the acts achieved.

Now if we must de-realize our immediately felt activity-situations for the benefit of either of these types of substitute, we ought to know what the substitution practically involves. *What practical difference ought it to make if,* instead of saying naïvely that 'I' am active now in delivering this address, I say that *a wider thinker is active*, or that *certain ideas are active*, or that *certain nerve-cells are active*, in producing the result?

This would be the pragmatic meaning of the three hypotheses. Let us take them in succession in seeking a reply.

THE EXPERIENCE OF ACTIVITY

If we assume a wider thinker, it is evident that his purposes envelop mine. I am really lecturing *for* him; and altho I cannot surely know to what end, yet if I take him religiously, I can trust it to be a good end, and willingly connive. I can be happy in thinking that my activity transmits his impulse, and that his ends prolong my own. So long as I take him religiously, in short, he does not de-realize my activities. He tends rather to corroborate the reality of them, so long as I believe both them and him to be good.

When now we turn to ideas, the case is different, inasmuch as ideas are supposed by the association psychology to influence each other only from next to next. The 'span' of an idea, or pair of ideas, is assumed to be much smaller instead of being larger than that of my total conscious field. The same results may get worked out in both cases, for this address is being given anyhow. But the ideas supposed to 'really' work it out had no prevision of the whole of it; and if I was lecturing for an absolute thinker in the former case, so, by similar reasoning, are my ideas now lecturing for me, that is, accomplishing unwittingly a result which I approve and adopt. But, when this passing lecture is over, there is nothing in the bare notion that ideas have been its agents that would seem to guarantee that my present purposes in lecturing will be prolonged. *I* may have ulterior developments in view; but there is no certainty that my ideas as such will wish to, or be able to, work them out.

The like is true if nerve-cells be the agents. The activity of a nerve-cell must be conceived of as a tendency of exceedingly short reach, an 'impulse' barely spanning the way to the next cell — for surely that amount of actual 'process' must be 'experienced' by the cells if what happens between them is to deserve the name of activity at all. But here again the gross resultant, as *I* perceive it, is indifferent to the agents, and neither wished or willed or foreseen. Their being agents now congruous with my will gives me no guarantee that like results will recur again from their activity. In point of fact, all sorts of other results do occur. My mistakes, impotencies, perversions, mental obstructions, and frustrations generally, are also results of the activity of cells. Altho these are letting me lecture now, on other occasions they make me do things that I would willingly not do.

The question *Whose is the real activity ?* is thus tantamount to the question *What will be the actual results ?* Its interest is dramatic; how will things work out ? If the agents are of one sort, one way; if of another sort, they may work out very differently. The pragmatic meaning of the various alternatives, in short, is great. It makes more than a merely verbal difference which opinion we take up.

THE EXPERIENCE OF ACTIVITY

You see it is the old dispute come back! Materialism and teleology; elementary short-span actions summing themselves 'blindly,' or far foreseen ideals coming with effort into act.

Naïvely we believe, and humanly and dramatically we like to believe, that activities both of wider and of narrower span are at work in life together, that both are real, and that the long-span tendencies yoke the others in their service, encouraging them in the right direction, and damping them when they tend in other ways. But how to represent clearly the *modus operandi* of such steering of small tendencies by large ones is a problem which metaphysical thinkers will have to ruminate upon for many years to come. Even if such control should eventually grow clearly picturable, the question how far it is successfully exerted in this actual world can be answered only by investigating the details of fact. No philosophic knowledge of the general nature and constitution of tendencies, or of the relation of larger to smaller ones, can help us to predict which of all the various competing tendencies that interest us in this universe are likeliest to prevail. We know as an empirical fact that far-seeing tendencies often carry out their purpose, but we know also that they are often defeated by the failure of some contemptibly small process on which success depends. A little thrombus in a statesman's meningeal artery will throw an empire out of gear.

APPENDIX B

Therefore I cannot even hint at any solution of the pragmatic issue. I have only wished to show you that that issue is what gives the real interest to all inquiries into what kinds of activity may be real. Are the forces that really act in the world more foreseeing or more blind? As between 'our' activities as 'we' experience them, and those of our ideas, or of our brain-cells, the issue is well defined.

I said awhile back (p. 381) that I should return to the 'metaphysical' question before ending; so, with a few words about that, I will now close my remarks.

In whatever form we hear this question propounded, I think that it always arises from two things, a belief that *causality* must be exerted in activity, and a wonder as to how causality is made. If we take an activity-situation at its face-value, it seems as if we caught *in flagrante delicto* the very power that makes facts come and be. I now am eagerly striving, for example, to get this truth which I seem half to perceive, into words which shall make it show more clearly. If the words come, it will seem as if the striving itself had drawn or pulled them into actuality out from the state of merely possible being in which they were. How is this feat performed? How does the pulling *pull*? How do I get my hold on words not yet existent, and when they come, by what means have I *made* them come? Really it is the problem

388

of creation; for in the end the question is: How do I make them *be*? Real activities are those that really make things be, without which the things are not, and with which they are there. Activity, so far as we merely feel it, on the other hand, is only an impression of ours, it may be maintained; and an impression is, for all this way of thinking, only a shadow of another fact.

Arrived at this point, I can do little more than indicate the principles on which, as it seems to me, a radically empirical philosophy is obliged to rely in handling such a dispute.

If there *be* real creative activities in being, radical empiricism must say, somewhere they must be immediately lived. Somewhere the *that* of efficacious causing and the *what* of it must be experienced in one, just as the what and the that of 'cold' are experienced in one whenever a man has the sensation of cold here and now. It boots not to say that our sensations are fallible. They are indeed; but to see the thermometer contradict us when we say 'it is cold' does not abolish cold as a specific nature from the universe. Cold is in the arctic circle if not here. Even so, to feel that our train is moving when the train beside our window moves, to see the moon through a telescope come twice as near, or to see two pictures as one solid when we look through a stereoscope at them, leaves motion, nearness, and solidity still in being — if not here, yet each in its proper seat elsewhere. And wherever the seat of real causality *is*, as ultimately known 'for true' (in nerve-processes, if you will, that cause our feelings of activity as well as the movements which these seem to prompt), a philosophy of pure experience can consider the real causation as no other *nature* of thing than that which even in our most erroneous experiences appears to be at work. Exactly what appears there is what we *mean* by working, tho we may later come to learn that working was not exactly *there*. Sustaining, persevering, striving, paying with effort as we go, hanging on, and finally achieving our intention — this *is* action, this *is* effectuation in the only shape in which, by a pure experience-philosophy, the whereabouts of it anywhere can be discussed. Here is creation in its first intention, here is causality at work.[1] To treat this offhand as the bare illusory

---

[1] Let me not be told that this contradicts a former article of mine, 'Does consciousness exist?' in the *Journal of Philosophy* for September 1, 1904 (see especially page 489), in which it was said that while 'thoughts' and 'things' have the same natures, the natures work 'energetically' on each other in the things (fire burns, water wets, etc.), but not in the thoughts. Mental activity-trains are composed of thoughts, yet their members do work on each other: they check, sustain, and introduce. They do so when the activity is merely associational as well as when effort is there. But, and this is my reply, they do so by other parts of their nature than those that energize physically. One thought in every developed activity-series is a desire or thought of purpose, and all the other thoughts acquire a feeling tone from their relation of harmony or oppugnancy to this. The interplay of these secondary tones (among which 'interest,' 'difficulty,' and 'effort' fig-

surface of a world whose real causality is an unimaginable ontological principle hidden in the cubic deeps, is, for the more empirical way of thinking, only animism in another shape. You explain your given fact by your 'principle,' but the principle itself, when you look clearly at it, turns out to be nothing but a previous little spiritual copy of the fact. Away from that one and only kind of fact your mind, considering causality, can never get.[1]

ure) runs the drama in the mental series. In what we term the physical drama these qualities play absolutely no part. The subject needs careful working out; but I can see no inconsistency.

[1] I have found myself more than once accused in print of being the assertor of a metaphysical principle of activity. Since literary misunderstandings retard the settlement of problems, I should like to say that such an interpretation of the pages I have published on effort and on will is absolutely foreign to what I meant to express. I owe all my doctrines on this subject to Renouvier; and Renouvier, as I understand him, is (or at any rate then was) an out and out phenomenist, a denier of 'forces' in the most strenuous sense. Single clauses in my writing, or sentences read out of their connexion, may possibly have been compatible with a transphenomenal principle of energy; but I defy any one to show a single sentence which, taken with its context, should be naturally held to advocate that view. The misinterpretation probably arose at first from my having defended (after Renouvier) the indeterminism of our efforts. 'Free will' was supposed by my critics to involve a supernatural agent. As a matter of plain history, the only 'free will' I have ever thought of defending is the character of novelty in fresh activity-situations. If an activity-process is the form of a whole 'field of consciousness,' and if each field of consciousness is not only in its totality unique (as is now commonly admitted), but has its elements unique (since in that situation they are all dyed in the total), then novelty is perpetually entering the world and what happens there is

APPENDIX B

I conclude, then, that real effectual causation as an ultimate nature, as a 'category,' if you like, of reality, is *just what we feel it to be*, just that kind of conjunction which our own activity-series reveal. We have the whole butt and being of it in our hands; and the healthy thing for philosophy is to leave off grubbing underground for what effects effectuation, or what makes action act, and to try to solve the concrete questions of where effectuation in this world is located, of which things are the true causal agents there, and of what the more remote effects consist.

From this point of view the greater sublimity traditionally attributed to the metaphysical inquiry, the grubbing inquiry, entirely disappears. If we could know what causation really and transcendentally is in itself, the only *use* of the knowledge would be to help us to recognize an actual cause when we had one, and so to track the future course of operations more intelligently out. The mere abstract inquiry into causation's hidden nature is not more sublime than any other inquiry equally abstract. Causation inhabits no more sublime level than anything else. It lives, apparently,

not pure *repetition*, as the dogma of the literal uniformity of nature requires. Activity-situations come, in short, each with an original touch. A 'principle' of free will, if there were one, would doubtless manifest itself in such phenomena, but I never saw, nor do I now see, what the principle could do except rehearse the phenomenon beforehand, or why it ever should be invoked.

in the dirt of the world as well as in the absolute, or in man's unconquerable mind. The worth and interest of the world consists not in its elements, be these elements things, or be they the conjunctions of things; it exists rather in the dramatic outcome of the whole process, and in the meaning of the succession stages which the elements work out.

My colleague and master, Josiah Royce, in a page of his review of Stout's *Analytic Psychology*, in *Mind* for 1897, has some fine words on this point with which I cordially agree. I cannot agree with his separating the notion of efficacy from that of activity altogether (this I understand to be one contention of his), for activities are efficacious whenever they are real activities at all. But the inner nature both of efficacy and of activity are superficial problems, I understand Royce to say; and the only point for us in solving them would be their possible use in helping us to solve the far deeper problem of the course and meaning of the world of life. Life, says our colleague, is full of significance, of meaning, of success and of defeat, of hoping and of striving, of longing, of desire, and of inner value. It is a total presence that embodies worth. To live our own lives better in this presence is the true reason why we wish to know the elements of things; so even we psychologists must end on this pragmatic note.

The urgent problems of activity are thus more con-

APPENDIX B

crete. They all are problems of the true relation of longer-span to shorter-span activities. When, for example, a number of 'ideas' (to use the name traditional in psychology) grow confluent in a larger field of consciousness, do the smaller activities still coexist with the wider activities then experienced by the conscious subject? And, if so, do the wide activities accompany the narrow ones inertly, or do they exert control? Or do they perhaps utterly supplant and replace them and short-circuit their effects? Again, when a mental activity-process and a brain-cell series of activities both terminate in the same muscular movement, does the mental process steer the neural processes or not? Or, on the other hand, does it independently short-circuit their effects? Such are the questions that we must begin with. But so far am I from suggesting any definitive answer to such questions, that I hardly yet can put them clearly. They lead, however, into that region of pan-psychic and ontologic speculation of which Professors Bergson and Strong have lately enlarged the literature in so able and interesting a way. The results of these authors seem in many respects dissimilar, and I understand them as yet but imperfectly; but I cannot help suspecting that the direction of their work is very promising, and that they have the hunter's instinct for the fruitful trails.

394

APPENDIX C

ON THE NOTION OF REALITY AS CHANGING

In my *Principles of Psychology* (vol. ii, p. 646) I gave
the name of the 'axiom of skipped intermediaries and
transferred relations' to a serial principle of which the
foundation of logic, the *dictum de omni et nullo* (or, as I
expressed it, the rule that what is of a kind is of that
kind's kind), is the most familiar instance. More than
the more is more than the less, equals of equals are equal,
sames of the same are the same, the cause of a cause is
the cause of its effects, are other examples of this serial
law. Altho it applies infallibly and without restriction
throughout certain abstract series, where the 'sames,'
'causes,' etc., spoken of, are 'pure,' and have no properties save their sameness, causality, etc., it cannot be applied offhand to concrete objects with numerous properties and relations, for it is hard to trace a straight line
of sameness, causation, or whatever it may be, through
a series of such objects without swerving into some
'respect' where the relation, as pursued originally, no
longer holds: the objects have so many 'aspects' that
we are constantly deflected from our original direction,
and find, we know not why, that we are following something different from what we started with. Thus a cat
is in a sense the same as a mouse-trap, and a mouse-
trap the same as a bird-cage; but in no valuable or

easily intelligible sense is a cat the same as a bird-cage. Commodore Perry was in a sense the cause of the new régime in Japan, and the new régime was the cause of the russian Douma; but it would hardly profit us to insist on holding to Perry as the cause of the Douma: the terms have grown too remote to have any real or practical relation to each other. In every series of real terms, not only do the terms themselves and their associates and environments change, but we change, and their *meaning* for us changes, so that new kinds of sameness and types of causation continually come into view and appeal to our interest. Our earlier lines, having grown irrelevant, are then dropped. The old terms can no longer be substituted nor the relations 'transferred,' because of so many new dimensions into which experience has opened. Instead of a straight line, it now follows a zigzag; and to keep it straight, one must do violence to its spontaneous development. Not that one might not possibly, by careful seeking (tho I doubt it), *find* some line in nature along which terms literally the same, or causes causal in the same way, might be serially strung without limit, if one's interest lay in such finding. Within such lines our axioms might hold, causes might cause their effect's effects, etc.; but such lines themselves would, if found, only be partial members of a vast natural network, within the other lines of which you could not say, in any sense that a wise man or a sane man would ever think of, in any sense that would not be concretely *silly*, that the principle of skipt intermediaries still held good. In the *practical* world, the world whose significances we follow, sames of the same are certainly not sames of one another; and things constantly cause other things without being held responsible for everything of which those other things are causes.

Professor Bergson, believing as he does in a heraclitean 'devenir réel,' ought, if I rightly understand him, positively to deny that in the actual world the logical axioms hold good without qualification. Not only, according to him, do terms change, so that after a certain time the very elements of things are no longer what they were, but relations also change, so as no longer to obtain in the same identical way between the new things that have succeeded upon the old ones. If this were really so, then however indefinitely sames might still be substituted for sames in the logical world of nothing but pure sameness, in the world of real operations every line of sameness actually started and followed up would eventually give out, and cease to be traceable any farther. Sames of the same, in such a world, will not always (or rather, in a strict sense will never) be the same as one another, for in such a world there *is* no literal or ideal sameness among numerical differents. Nor in such a world will it be true that the cause of the cause is

APPENDIX C

unreservedly the cause of the effect; for if we follow lines of real causation, instead of contenting ourselves with Hume's and Kant's eviscerated schematism, we find that remoter effects are seldom aimed at by causal intentions,[1] that no one kind of causal activity continues indefinitely, and that the principle of skipt intermediaries can be talked of only *in abstracto*.[2]

Volumes i, ii, and iii of the *Monist* (1890–1893) contain a number of articles by Mr. Charles S. Peirce, articles the originality of which has apparently prevented their making an immediate impression, but which, if I mistake not, will prove a gold-mine of ideas for thinkers of the coming generation. Mr. Peirce's views, tho reached so differently, are altogether congruous with Bergson's. Both philosophers believe that the appearance of novelty in things is genuine. To an observer standing outside of its generating causes, novelty can appear only as so much 'chance'; to one who stands inside it is the expression of 'free creative activity.' Peirce's 'tychism' is thus practically synonymous with Bergson's 'devenir réel.' The common objection to admitting novelties is that by jumping abruptly in, *ex nihilo*, they shatter the world's rational continuity. Peirce meets this objection by combining his tychism

---

[1] Compare the douma with what Perry aimed at.

[2] Compare Appendix B, as to what I mean here by 'real' casual activity.

with an express doctrine of 'synechism' or continuity, the two doctrines merging into the higher synthesis on which he bestows the name of 'agapasticism (*loc. cit.*, iii, 188), which means exactly the same thing as Bergson's 'évolution créatrice.' Novelty, as empirically found, does n't arrive by jumps and jolts, it leaks in insensibly, for adjacents in experience are always interfused, the smallest real datum being both a coming and a going, and even numerical distinctness being realized effectively only after a concrete interval has passed. The intervals also deflect us from the original paths of direction, and all the old identities at last give out, for the fatally continuous infiltration of otherness warps things out of every original rut. Just so, in a curve, the same direction is *never* followed, and the conception of it as a myriad-sided polygon falsifies it by supposing it to do so for however short a time. Peirce speaks of an ' infinitesimal' tendency to diversification. The mathematical notion of an infinitesimal contains, in truth, the whole paradox of the same and yet the nascent other, of an identity that won't *keep* except so far as it keeps *failing*, that won't *transfer*, any more than the serial relations in question transfer, when you apply them to reality instead of applying them to concepts alone.

A friend of mine has an idea, which illustrates on such a magnified scale the impossibility of tracing the same line through reality, that I will mention it here. He thinks that nothing more is needed to make history 'scientific' than to get the content of any two epochs (say the end of the thirteenth and the end of the nineteenth century) accurately defined, then accurately to define the direction of the change that led from the one epoch into the other, and finally to prolong the line of that direction into the future. So prolonging the line, he thinks, we ought to be able to define the actual state of things at any future date we please. We all feel the essential unreality of such a conception of 'history' as this; but if such a synechistic pluralism as Peirce, Bergson, and I believe in, be what really exists, every phenomenon of development, even the simplest, would prove equally rebellious to our science should the latter pretend to give us literally accurate instead of approximate, or statistically generalized, pictures of the development of reality.

I can give no further account of Mr. Peirce's ideas in this note, but I earnestly advise all students of Bergson to compare them with those of the french philosopher.

INDEX

INDEX TO THE LECTURES

INDEX

his God; and religious experience, 308.

FERRIER, Jas., 13.

Finite experience, 39, 48, 182, 192-193.

Finiteness, of God, 111, 124, 294.

Foreignness, 31.

German manner of philosophizing, 17.

GOD, 24 f., 111, 124, 193, 240, 294.

GREEN, T. H., 6, 24, 137, 278.

HALDANE, R. B., 138.

HEGEL, Lecture III, *passim*, 11, 85, 207, 211, 219, 296. His vision, 88, 98 f., 104; his use of double negation, 102; his vicious intellectualism 106; Haldane on, 138; McTaggart on, 140; Royce on, 143.

HODGSON, S. H., 282.

Horse, 265.

HUME, 19, 267.

Idealism, 36. See Absolutism.

Identity, 93.

Immortality, Fechner's view of, 171.

' Independent' beings, 55, 58.

Indeterminism, 77.

Infinity, 229.

Influence, 258, 561.

Intellect, its function is practical, 247 f., 252.

Intellectualism, vicious, 60, 218.

Intellectualist logic, 216, 259, 261.

Intellectualist method, 291.

Interaction, 56.

Intimacy, 31.

Irrationality, 81; of the absolute, 117-129.

JACKS, L, P., 35.

JOACHIM, H., 121, 141.

JONES, H., 52.

KANT, 19, 199, 238, 240.

LEIBNITZ, 119.

Life, 523.

Log, 323.

Logic, 92, 211; intellectualist, 217, 242.

LOTZE, 55, 120.

LUTHER, 304.

McTAGGART, 51, 74 f., 120, 140 f., 183.

Manyness in oneness, 322. See Compounding.

Mental chemistry, 185.

MILL, J. S., 242, 260.

Mind, dust theory, 189.

Mind, the eternal, 137. See Absolute.

Monism, 36, 117, 125, 201, 313, 321 f.; Fechner's, 153. See Absolutism.

Monomaniacs, 78.

Motion, 233, 238, 254; Zeno on, 228.

MYERS, F. W. H., 315.

Nature, 21, 286.

Negation, 93 f.; double, 102.

Newton, 260.

404

INDEX

Other, 95, 312; 'its own other,' 108 f., 282.

Oxford, 3, 313, 331.

Pantheism, 24, 28.

PAULSEN, 18, 22.

Personality, divided, 298.

Philosophers, their method, 9; their common desire, 11 f.; they must reason, 13.

Philosophies, their types, 23, 31.

PHOCION, 304.

Plant-soul, 165 f.

Pluralism, 45, 76, 79, 311, 319, 321 f.

Polytheism, 310.

Practical reason, 329.

Psychic synthesis, 185. See Compounding.

Psychical research, 299.

'Quâ,' 39, 47, 267, 270.

'Quatenus,' 47, 267.

Rationalism defined, 7, 98; its thinness, 144, 237.

Rationality, 81, 112 f., 319 f.

Reality, 262 f., 264, 283 f.

Reason, 286, 312.

Relating, 7.

Relations, 70, 278 ff.; 'external,' 80.

Religious experiences, 305 f.

RITCHIE, 72.

ROYCE, 61 f., 115, 173, 182 f., 197, 207, 212, 265, 296.

Same, 269, 281.

Savage philosophy, 21.

Science, 145.

Sensations, 279.

Socialism, 78.

SOCRATES, 284.

Soul, 199, 209.

'Some,' 79.

Sphinx, 22.

SPINOZA, 47.

Spiritualistic philosophy, 23.

Sugar, 220, 232.

Synthesis, psychic. See Compounding.

TAYLOR, A. E., 76, 139, 212.

Theism, 24.

Thick, the, 136.

'Thickness' of Fechner's philosophy, 144.

Thin, the, 136.

Thinness of the current transcendentalism, 144, 174 f.

Time, 232.

Units of reality, 287.

Vision, in philosophy, 20.

WELLS, H. G., 78.

Will to believe, 328.

Witnesses, as implied in experience, 200.

WUNDT, W., 185.

ZENO, 228.